VALUES, ENDS, AND SOCIETY

VALUES, ENDS, AND SOCIETY

IAN DAVISON

UNIVERSITY OF
QUEENSLAND PRESS

Typeset by Academy Press Pty. Ltd., Brisbane
Printed and bound by Times Printers Sdn. Bhd., Singapore

Distributed in the United Kingdom, Europe, the Middle East, Africa, and the Caribbean by Prentice-Hall International, International Book Distributors Ltd., 66 Wood Lane End, Hemel Hempstead, Herts., England

National Library of Australia
Cataloguing-in-Publication data

Davison, Ian, 1939–.
Values, ends and society.

Index.
Bibliography.
ISBN 0 7022 1483 3.

1. Worth. 2. Social values. I. Title.

301.21

CONTENTS

FOR

CRAIG
LIANE
and
GUY ROBERT

"Cheshire-Puss," she began, rather timidly, as she did not at all know whether it would like the name: however, it only grinned a little wider. "Come, it's pleased so far," thought Alice, and she went on. "Would you tell me, please, which way I ought to go from here?"

"That depends a good deal on where you want to get to," said the Cat.

Lewis Carroll

ACKNOWLEDGMENTS

Some of the material in this book first appeared in a different form in *The Australian Humanist* edited by Bruce Muirden. While a number of people asisted with the preparation of the final manuscript, I am particularly grateful to Patricia Clarkson and Ian Warfield who helped check the manuscript, to Robin Faux and Brenda Adams who very kindly volunteered for the thankless task of typing the manuscript, and to Terri McCormack without whose help, criticism and encouragement, this book would never have been written.
Cover design depicts a construction in Mylar and aluminium, "Earth Sea" by Jill Harvey.

INTRODUCTION

Western society has never possessed a critical philosophy of ends. Like all preceding societies it has evolved its particular doctrines as to what actions are morally right and wrong, what courses of action are desirable or undesirable, and of the ultimate purpose of human life. In Europe before the eighteenth century all such judgements of ends were associated with the Christian Church; subsequently they have become involved with economic criteria, individualism, and state institutions. Doctrines of ends have always been categorically asserted rather than developed on a rational basis by critical methods. Attempts have frequently been made to justify established systems of ends by an appeal to reason, but such attempts always serve to confirm existing moral codes and ideas of ends rather than to discover what they could, might, or should be.

The question of ends has three aspects. There is the problem of moral choice, of what is the right or good action in any particular set of circumstances, of what is the morally appropriate end of man. Most cultures show substantial agreement on actions held to be categorically wrong; murder, theft, offences against property, and acts that could endanger social stability are almost universally condemned. The issue is less clear when problems involving non-moral choice and morally neutral ends are involved. Agreed goals differ markedly from society to society and even within the one society at different stages of its history. Some approve the pursuit of material and financial ends, others accentuate the importance of particular intellectual, military, religious, and ideological goals, goals that generally reflect the social organization of that society. In most cases, a person is presented with choices between several courses of action and makes his own decision in the light of existing social attitudes. Moral and non-moral choices are ultimately aspects of a single problem: on what basis is a decision to be made? The difference lies in moral attitudes being more firmly held and of more immediate significance to the society, whereas non-moral choice is more a matter of personal preference and individual benefit.

The final question involves the point, purpose, and meaning of human existence. This is a psychological issue, but it is no less important than the need to decide between alternative courses of action and goals. The view of the purpose of life that people hold has a determining influence on the types of choices a person is inclined to make and on the values they espouse. Most philosophies, and all higher religions, have decreed a particular purpose in life, but few have attempted to understand what it means to have a purpose in life, or what the characteristics of such a purpose could or must be.

How to judge what the morally right or good action is in any situation? How to know what is the best choice to make in any situation? What is the purpose of life? These are the fundamental questions of ends.

These issues of ends are more important now than in any previous period in history. Technological progress has endowed the human race with greater control over its environment and over the forces at work in society—particularly economic forces—than enjoyed by any preceding society. This increase in power has made the need to choose ends wisely of corresponding importance. When the capacity of people to make effective changes was limited, the impact of the decisions they made was small; now that the effect decisions have can be very great, it is essential to develop a basis for making these choices. This is true not only of decisions affecting societies but also of decisions that individual people make in their own lives. The stable tradition-limited life of the village has been replaced by a way of life in which a greater variety of ends and a wider range of choice are available than ever before. This increase in potential freedom results in an increase in the decisions that a person must make, and also in the potential importance of those decisions. The possible gains are greater, but so too is the possible damage a wrong decision may cause.

As the possibilities open both to individuals and to societies have widened, the directions provided by the past have tended to disappear. Few people today accept the earlier Christian idea of absolute morality; even theologians are moving to a situationalist morality which judges the context as important as the moral quality of the choice made. The influence of tradition has declined as past values have grown increasingly irrelevant to technological society. The collapse of old traditions, the rejection of religious dogmas, the speed of social change, and the vastly increased technical capacity of mankind have all resulted in a complete confusion over ends. As people have grown able to do more, they have become less certain as to what to do. Past criteria have been rejected, and nothing has appeared to take their place. Worse, with this confusion over the problem of what to do has gone an increasing sense of the purposelessness of life, of its lack of meaning, significance, and relevance. There is a qualitative emptiness at the centre of many people's lives, a sense of futility, frustration, rootlessness, and despair that makes an irony of the new capacity endowed by technology. Not only do many people not know what to do with this capability, they have little interest in doing anything at all.

The need is not for new dogmas about the ends of life and the goals that people should seek. What is required is a critical method for evaluating competing doctrines of ends and for permitting choice to be made on a rational basis. This would comprise a method or calculus rather than a body of asserted beliefs, and would differ as greatly from these beliefs as the scientific method differs from creation myths. Indeed, the analogy is appropriate. Creation myths attempt to describe what has happened in the past, while the scientific method provides the means to evaluate such beliefs objectively and to replace them with more substantial beliefs. Doctrines of ends assert what should be done in the future, whereas a critical teleology could provide the means for evaluating actions and doctrines of ends and for replacing these doctrines with criteria. What is required in short is a set of techniques capable of comparing and evaluating ends, and of understanding the question of the purpose of life. This book attempts to show how such a study can be begun.

There is no way of knowing *a priori* how a critical teleology could be developed. One approach is to examine the various schemes of ends that have been advanced in the past, to investigate similarities and contrasts, and to determine the social effects that they have had. This would result in a comparative study of dogmas of ends, but not the techniques necessary for their evaluation. The latter can only be developed by intuition, by considering what type of framework could apply to assertions of ends and how they are to be made intelligible. This process is similar to the intuitive step that scientists make in moving from data to explanatory hypothesis.

A critical study of ends only becomes necessary once existing doctrines prove inadequate. Few people now accept in their entirety the ends implied in religion or philosophy, but there remains one dogma of ends still taken seriously in Western society. This is the utilitarian view that the purpose of life lies in the pursuit of individual happiness, a doctrine that provides both criteria for making choices and a psychological sense of purpose in life. Before any new framework of ends can be developed, it is necessary to show that the utilitarian approach cannot be valid. The first part of this book involves an investigation of the nature of human happiness, the sources of happiness, and its validity as an end in life.

Before the question of what to do is considered, it is important to understand why in fact people do the things that they do, why they make the choices that they actually make and pursue the ends that appear important to them. These reasons often prove to be quite different to the reasons people give. This issue involves the larger questions of why people do anything at all, of the sources of motivation, and of the nature of interactions between a society and its members. Doctrines of ends represent rationalizations of forces acting within a society. Unless these are understood it is impossible to guarantee that any theory of ends will not simply mirror the current values of society. These issues of motivation, of social interactions and values, are discussed in Part 2. They involve the nature of human emotions, social interactions, and motivational relationships, and necessitate replacing rational ideas of motivation with non-rational views. These emotional and motivational factors are closely allied to the problem of purpose in life, or, more accurately, of why modern life often seems pointless, meaningless, and empty in a way that primitive existence does not.

Once a rational scheme of ends has been developed there remains the problem of knowing how to achieve the particular ends that it indicates. In practice, the means that a society has to hand strongly influence its views of ends. Christianity was particularly suited to achieving purported spiritual ends but incapable of meeting technological needs; hence it viewed the end of life as spiritual. The capacity that comes with technology is similarly selective; it is capable of meeting material needs, but relatively useless where emotional or social needs are involved. The strengths and weaknesses of technology largely determine the ends that this society pursues, but these are not necessarily the only or even the best set of goals. To pursue ends independently of the influence of technology and economics requires a more general understanding of means and a greater power to move towards ends that are not associated with economic or technological factors. Means involve manipulation, either of material objects or, more generally, of symbols, ideas, and information. To attain a goal is to operate on the world in some way, and such an operation requires understanding some aspect of the world.

Part 3 is an analysis of knowledge and understanding as means to attain goals. The notion of understanding as an operative model, rather than as a particular quantity, is developed and contrasted with simple information. Knowing involves having data of some description, but understanding involves the creation of analogue models which can be applied to data, and which alone ensure that a person can operate in the world with some degree of confidence. Language is the most familiar and widely used form of analogue model, but suffers from severe limitations, a fact that has affected all philosophical discussion and in particular the philosophical discussion of ends.

The central issue of this book, of determining which ends to pursue and of judging between doctrines of ends, is developed in the fourth part. Most cultures have accepted that a clear distinction exists between means and ends, and that while most actions and objects constitute means, a few are always to be considered as ends. The shift from a static to a dynamic world-view and the adoption of an evolutionary frame of thought have together destroyed this distinction. It is possible to construct a criterion of ends that allows for development on the assumption that the means-ends dichotomy is artificial, and to use this criterion to evaluate other doctrines of ends. This is the *possibilities criterion*, which is applicable both to moral and non-moral issues and which, unlike other systems of ends, provides the criterion for its own extension.

Finally, the ideas developed in the first four parts are used to evaluate the ideas of ends current in Western society. The doctrine of the pursuit of happiness is essentially an economic doctrine; the means to achieve happiness are usually held to be economic factors, production, consumption, wealth, material assets, and an ever-growing supply of consumer goods. In order to go beyond the conventional economic goals it is essential to re-examine economics, both in its ideological or normative role and in its factual content. Economic theory, like Christianity, provides both techniques to choose between competing ends and a general doctrine as to the purpose of life. This purpose is the pursuit of happiness through the consumption of goods and services. Economic ideology is, however, inadequate in that it limits human activity to purely economic pursuits. Additionally, the formal economic theory associated with economic ideology is deficient both in its methodology and in its understanding of how people are motivated.

Determining the desired future shape of society is possibly the most important role that a sophisticated teleology could play. This does not involve projecting any particular Utopia but rather deciding what ends a society should contribute to, and what priorities should be involved in human affairs. Economic society is now going through a major transition stage, giving place to a completely new form of society. The opportunity exists to influence, at least to a degree, the type of society that emerges, but this requires criteria of choice which are independent of social values and, in particular, of the values of economic society. These new trends in society and the choices that need to be made are outlined in the concluding chapter on post-economic society.

PART ONE

HAPPINESS AND ENDS

1
THE CONVENTIONAL WISDOM

Familiar ideas make the best starting point. Most people, asked what is the purpose, aim, or meaning in their lives, to what end do they work, or for what reason do they pursue their various occupations, give one answer: to achieve happiness.

In order to attain happiness people take part in the considerable range of recreations available in a modern society—going to shows, the theatre, and musical performances, playing sport, engaging in hobbies, reading, writing, painting, and playing musical instruments, collecting stamps, working in a home workshop. In order to obtain happiness they improve their economic position, buy new and improved labour-saving devices and consumer goods, bigger and more powerful cars, new stereo sets, furniture, and holiday cottages; they go on world tours, seek acquaintances and lovers, improve their jobs and their education, or buy a business. Often the connection between happiness and the ends pursued is far from direct, but in almost every case the same final justification emerges. People follow their diverse and varied ends because they hope to find happiness in them.

This happiness may be associated with a higher living standard, with economic security, or with the particular goods and services that people desire. It may be the happiness associated with doing the things they enjoy doing; running a business, succeeding in a profession, or indulging their artistic ability. It may even be the happiness that comes from spending a day relaxing in natural scenery or driving a powerful car. In the final analysis, everything people do, every activity they engage in, every end they aspire to has this one justification—the attainment of personal happiness.

This preoccupation with happiness is by no means universal. It tends to emerge in highly individualistic societies where people are to a great extent free to pursue their own ends. A tradition-directed society or a totalitarian state embraces values largely indifferent to the happiness or well-being of the individual. Nietzsche once commented that man does not pursue happiness: only the Englishman does. It is interesting to speculate on his comments could he return to the consumer-directed society of the present. Preoccupation with the pursuit of happiness tends to emerge in societies that are economically developed, which provide a wide assortment of goods and services and which offer a wide range of activities, occupations, and recreations. A primitive society with virtually no variety of either occupations or goods would be unlikely to consider the pursuit of happiness the end in life. There is simply no alternative to the traditional way of life, nor any reason to pursue happiness.

In retrospect, it is hardly surprising that a pursuit of happiness ethic emerged at the same time as the developed consumer economy. The philosophical theory that justified this ethic was developed by economic thinkers in England in the nineteenth century—Jeremy Bentham, James Mill, John Stuart Mill, and their followers. This school, described as utilitarian—an economic concept in itself—held that all things were to be considered good or bad in so far as they contributed to one particular end. For Bentham that end was human happiness. Any action or object or condition that promoted human happiness was without further qualification good; anything which detracted from the sum of human happiness was an evil, no matter what other effects it may have had.

As a theory, hedonistic utilitarianism has the attraction of simplicity. But from a logical or philosophical point of view it is open to attack on a number of counts, a point not lost on generations of professional philosophers. Bentham argued that, since people do obviously seek their own happiness, everyone should seek personal happiness, and, moreover, that a value system can be constructed on this observation of fact. But as emphasized below, it is logically impermissible to base either injunctions or sets of values on statements of fact. The observation that people do pursue happiness, whether or not factually true, is no justification for arguing that people *should* pursue happiness. Indeed if they already do so, such injunctions are pointless. Equally, the fact that people do pursue happiness is no justificution for valuing things in terms of happiness. These are among the conventional arguments raised against hedonistic utilitarianism; yet, despite these objections, most people do implicitly accept the attitude, if not the logic, of hedonism. The value of anything depends on how far it is conducive to happiness or pleasure or satisfaction. To be happy is the universal aim; happiness is the one good requiring no justification beyond itself.

While most people feel quite sure of what they mean when discussing happiness, this is far from being the case. The term *happiness* is ambiguous, having at least two quite different meanings and a host of lesser connotations. Happiness, as the word is generally used in Western society, indicates a psychological condition. It is equivalent to euphoria and elation. Happiness is the Hollywood feeling of walking on air, the sense of delight and exhilaration on a beautiful spring day when one is young and in love and God is in his heaven. This use of the term *happiness* refers exclusively to a person's state of mind, and has nothing to do with his material condition, nor with the state of the world. It is possible for the poorest and most unfortunate of men to be happy, and for the most prosperous people to be depressed and miserable.

There is a second common usage of the term *happiness*. This refers not to a psychological state of elation, but to what is now referred to as well-being. The happy man of classical literature was one who had been favoured by fate, but not necessarily one who was in a state of euphoria. The ancient happinesses included such items as good health, long life, and prosperity; political guarantees of the right to pursue happiness refer to the pursuit of well-being rather than to psychological euphoria. Much of the confusion in discussing happiness hinges on this ambiguity. Typically, discussion begins by using happiness in the psychological sense, and then moves to the well-being sense. All people want to be psychologically happy, to avoid sadness and depression. People also believe they have a right to be well-off, to have a certain degree of good health and economic security. The result is a belief that they have a right to psychological happiness. If they are not enjoying feelings of elation, there is something seriously wrong with their world.

This confusion is compounded by a similar confusion in the use of the term *pleasure.* As normally used, *pleasure* indicates a physiological quantity associated with nerves and the senses. Pleasure is the opposite of pain. It is what a person experiences lying in the warm sun, eating a rich meal, or in sexual intercourse. But the term *pleasure* is also used with psychological connotations. When a person refers to the pleasure of someone's company, or the pleasure to be derived from literature or music, they are clearly referring to psychological happiness. If it is not accepted that happiness and pleasure are different quantities, one is committed to arguing that physical pain is the same thing as sadness and depression, a scarcely tenable proposition.

The result is that three quite separate concepts tend to be confused in any discussion of happiness. Physical pleasure, with its opposite pain, is associated with physical causes and physiological processes. Psychological happiness, the opposite of sadness and depression, is associated with psychological causes and processes taking place within an individual's mind. Well-being, good fortune, or welfare, by whatever name known, is a relatively objective observable quantity, associated with health, standard of living, satisfactory inter-personal relationships, and a good environment.

Tentatively, happiness is defined here as *a psychological reaction to, and awareness of, well-being*. Moreover, happiness, no matter what its source or intensity, is considered as one unique quantity. There are not innumerable varieties of happiness but only changes in intensity. Happiness always has the same character no matter what its source.

2
THE SOURCES OF HAPPINESS

There are as many potential sources of happiness as there are human activities and interests. Almost any material object, occupation, or physical condition is a potential source of happiness. Nevertheless, these innumerable sources of happiness tend to fall within three major areas of human life. These are creative activity, affectionate relationships, and sense usage.

Any activity that a person engages in and sees as creative or purposive is a potential source of happiness. These activities may be as complex as the founding and operation of a large business corporation, they may take the form of artistic, literary, or intellectual creativity, or they may be as simple as pottering around in a home workshop and building model boats. Any question of the objective importance of the activity is irrelevant. As long as a person is using his own skills, imagination, and energy in a manner that is purposive and directed towards some end, the activity is a potential source of happiness.

Affectionate relationships, the giving and taking of affection and the showing of emotional responses, are a second major source of happiness. These can range in intensity from a passionate sexual relationship to the casual camaraderie of an army barracks or a lonely old spinster's devotion to her cats. The intensity of emotional involvement bears no relationship to the intensity or duration of the happiness that may result. After a long period of loneliness, even casual friendship can provide intense delight, while often an intense affair will generate as much misery as happiness.

The third factor giving rise to happiness is the simple use of the senses. A beautiful view will often cause the most intense delight, as will pleasing music and sounds, the taste of fine food, and even physical pleasure. Indeed, because physical pleasure usually gives rise to happiness, just as pain gives rise to misery and despair, it is often impossible to tell where the effect of one begins and the other ends. The physical and the psychological are not clear-cut logical categories but inextricably interwoven elements of a person's make-up. This is, in part at least, a reason for the confusion between happiness and pleasure.

There are other minor sources of happiness that fall outside this scheme—for example, the happiness associated with a change of condition when a person wins a lottery or attains a promotion. Another source is involved with the imagination; people day-dreaming or fantasizing derive happiness by achieving in their imagination goals which they cannot obtain in real life. If neatness is desired, both of these sources of happiness can be included under activity.

The idea that happiness derives from these three sources—activity, affection, and sense usage—can be developed empirically by the most suspect of all psychological processes, introspection. In retrospect, however, it represents a polar view of the world. Those things closest to people are those with which their own skills, capacity, and ego are involved. The next circle comprises those things with which no ego involvement exists, but with which a strong emotional attachment has been formed. These are usually other people, but can also be pets and places with which one has fond associations. Last and most remote are those things with which a sensory relationship alone exists. There can be no question of ego involvement or emotional attachment to a beautiful mountain panorama, to sound, or to warmth. They are simply experienced.

In practice the sources of happiness rarely, if ever, fall neatly within such categories. Generally two, and often three, areas will be involved in any enjoyable experience. Artistic creation involves both the satisfaction of creativity and the delight of the senses. A sexual affair generates happiness both from affection and from physical pleasure. Community tasks or work in a theatre group provide both the satisfaction of activity and the delight derived from personal relationships.

From a Darwinian view of the world, every part of an organism, no matter how insignificant it may appear, has some function or role. Otherwise it could never have evolved, or, having evolved, would have atrophied because it conferred no survival advantage. This is as true of psychological entities as of physical appendages. No matter how insignificant they may seem, if they endure they have some survival advantage to offer. The capacity for pleasure and pain plays a clear role in the survival of animal life. Pain is an indicator that both warns a creature that something is wrong and motivates it to act. But because pain and pleasure are rough and ready indicators, lacking fine discrimination and adaptability, they are of diminishing use once intelligence and social life develop. At this stage the far more refined and more subtle psychological indicator of happiness comes into operation. Happiness performs the same functions at the psychological level that pleasure performs at the physiological level. It indicates whether a person is or is not living in accord with genuine needs and to some extent provides motivation, although this function is not as important as generally believed.

The three major sources of happiness—creative activity, affectionate relationships, and sense usage—represent the major psychological needs of human beings. For a hypothetical primitive it is obvious that in order to survive he must indulge in some directed activity, whether it is the making of tools or the pursuit of game. The development of emotional relationships is equally necessary, for without it there can be no family life, no protection of children, and no tribal society. And the use of the senses is of far more importance for survival in a primitive setting than in a civilized environment. While these three elements are essential to the physical survival of primitive man, they are also essential for emotional well-being and mental development. A person uses his creative activity as a nucleus around which he integrates his personality, much as an oyster forms a pearl around a particle of grit. What people do is determined by their personality, but their personality is also determined to a large degree by what they do. There is a continuing interaction between the two.

In much the same way people need affectionate relationships in order to develop their personalities and keep their emotional equipment operative. Without the sharing of emotional responses—the experience of love, hate, aggression, compassion, reverence, and disgust—a person never becomes capable of developing his own emotional repertoire. Emotional responses are learnt rather than innate. Finally, even the capacity to use the senses to their full extent is essential for development of the personality. This again is not an innate human capacity. People must be taught by the society how to employ their senses, and also to form the perceptions that make the data of the senses intelligible.

Just how important creative activity, the establishment of affectionate relationships, and the use of the senses are becomes evident when they are denied. Deprived of the means of self-expression through activity, an individual's personality rapidly atrophies. He becomes less capable of coping with problems, bored, apathetic, resentful, and psychologically unstable. The phenomenon of tunnel vision sets in and limits his range of activity. This deterioration of personality is illustrated by people who are suddenly unemployed. Their job, even if not particularly interesting, was the central activity in their lives; denied this, they are denied their self-image. They become indifferent to their appearance, shuffle in queues to obtain unemployment pay or look for work, and generally lose interest in life. Rendered redundant by economic changes over which they lack control, they come to see themselves as having no social value. A vicious circle is set up; without an interesting occupation the personality contracts, and as their personality changes, they become less capable of seeking creative activity.

In much the same way people who are emotionally isolated from others suffer a deterioration of their entire personality. They become generally introverted, emotionally atrophied, and unable to cope with life. And people who are denied sensory stimulation—as, for example, in laboratory experiments involving isolation in warm water—experience the same reaction. Disorientation, personality deterioration, and the beginnings of psychosis result.

Boredom, loneliness, and sense loss—psychologically, these are among the most destructive conditions that people can be exposed to. And to a considerable degree these conditions are the rule rather than the exception in industrial urban society.

Most people spend much of their lives doing work at a factory bench or an office desk that is dull, dreary, repetitive, and uncreative. For the majority, recreation means entertainment, either through films, television, or the evening press, leaving less time for creative pursuits.

A characteristic of suburbia and the large cities is their increasing loss of community. The impact of numbers, the competitiveness, and the pressures to achieve results tend to isolate a person from his fellows. It is increasingly true and increasingly commented on by social observers that people rarely know their neighbours, or even those they work with. Anomie and emotional isolation are the rule whether on the subway, in the street, at the factory bench, or at a sporting fixture. Additionally, the environment that has been allowed to develop in the cities must be among the most appalling that human beings have ever been subjected to. Air pollution, noise, dust, heat, visual dreariness, and noxious smells are the inevitable and expected accompaniment of urban life. In factories, noise, stench and visual ugliness predominate, while even in modern office buildings the senses are intentionally deadened. Air-conditioning prevents people experiencing heat or cold, acoustic insulation eliminates noise, and the general dreariness of acoustic tiles, vinyl floors, and plastic wood partitions eliminate any chance of visual stimulation.

In this urban and suburban environment the senses are, and must be, forever shut off. The only opportunity most people have to exercise them with joy is during infrequent visits to the countryside. But even this escape becomes less and less available as the natural environment is first exploited and finally polluted by industrial wastes resulting from its exploitation. What is true for people in urban settings is even truer for such social offenders and outcasts as prisoners and mental patients. Denied creative activity, isolated for the most part from affectionate relationships, and restricted to an environment that limits sense stimulation, such people must almost inevitably suffer a degeneration of personality.

Creative activity, affectionate relationships, and sense usage, as well as being the main sources of psychological happiness, are also the basic psychological goods required by human beings to develop a coherent personality. The first two are, as suggested below, essential for society to function properly. For without a developed emotional range there can be little effective motivation. Creative activity depends on the capacity for affectionate relationships, but at the same time it integrates the personality so that affectionate relationships and motivation are possible.

3
THE LIMITS OF HAPPINESS

Knowing the sources of happiness would appear to be a guarantee that one can achieve happiness—psychological happiness at least—most of the time. In practice this does not follow. If happiness is an indicator of how well people live in accord with their psychological needs, periods of unhappiness are inevitable. People cannot meet these needs all the time, and for the indicator to be effective it must provide for periods of considerable unhappiness as well as periods of happiness.

There is an even more compelling reason why people cannot expect to be happy all the time. It hinges on the fact that happiness is an entirely psychological quantity; happiness and unhappiness have no reference outside the human mind, so that the two come, in time, to a state of balance. Suppose for example that a person has won the lottery or been blessed with some comparable good fortune. In the normal course of events he will experience considerable delight, happiness, or euphoria from this sudden good luck. If he should have a second lottery win, he will still experience considerable delight, but less than on the first occasion. And if he should win a third, and fourth, and even fifth time, a stage will finally be reached when the win means nothing to him. A law of diminishing returns operates so that in time not even the most spectacular event will generate any happiness. Moreover, when a time comes that the person does not win the lottery, he will experience considerable unhappiness because his good fortune has deserted him.

Since happiness is a psychological quantity, the mind is forever resetting its datum, or its sensitivity, according to past events. This is inevitable because there is no objective external criterion of any kind to which it can refer. People can never know the intensity of other people's happiness or unhappiness, and there is no external social criterion against which feelings can be measured. The only way one can be aware of present happiness or unhappiness is by reference to previous conditions. After long periods of considerable happiness small setbacks have a disproportionate effect, because the psychological zero datum has been in effect moved up. To put it another way, the sensitivity to adverse conditions has increased because of a long period of happiness. The mind only knows its own immediately prior states, and uses the mean, quite unconsciously, as a datum. A long spell of slight depression may be followed by a burst of intense happiness, or a period of intense happiness may be followed by intense depression. Obviously, happiness in this view is associated with change of state rather than with the state itself, and uneventful periods will give rise in time to only slight elation or depression.

If a graph of a person's subjective happiness were plotted over a reasonable time—a period of several months—then the areas above the no-happiness datum will balance out the areas below that datum. This is the inevitable result of the mind setting its own datum on the basis of experience. Expressed mathematically, the time integral of subjective happiness equals zero, given a sufficient period of time. That is:

$$\int_{t_1}^{t_2} H\,dt = 0$$

Theoretical arguments are rarely persuasive, but in this case the theoretical argument is supported by observations from life. Every person subjective enough to note his own degree of happiness and depression will be aware of it. In some people the swings are not particularly large; they experience neither intense joy nor sorrow. In others, the swing is far greater in its amplitude; in the case of the manic-depressive the extremes of happiness and depression may be so great as to be incapacitating. But no matter how great a person's sensitivity or how wide the swing of feelings, this observation holds. The time-intensity of happiness balances the time-intensity of unhappiness.

Support for this idea is general in literature. Bernard Shaw not only agreed that people cannot be happy all the time, but felt that it was undesirable that they should be, declaring that a lifetime of complete happiness would be a hell on earth. Henry Miller has commented, not without a certain resentment, that his periods of creative elation were followed by profound depression. Albert Camus in his working notebooks observed the same thing with greater equanimity. At least a score of other leading writers and thinkers have made the same point in a way suggesting that for them it is self-evident. A person cannot be happy all the time.

Despite this, the pursuit of happiness continues as the main preoccupation, the dogma of ends and the criterion of values for Western society. To a considerable extent this is a consequence of the prevailing economic ethos and the mass merchandising it entails. It is astonishing just how many advertisements make direct or implicit reference to happiness, delight, and pleasure; almost every conceivable service and commodity, from cigarettes, drinks, food, clothing, cosmetics, motor vehicles, and employment agencies to airline travel are advertised at some stage as a means to happiness. This advertising is one of the most potent sources of discontent in this society, for the majority of people have come to expect, if unconsciously, that once they have the new house, the new car, the new television, the washing machine, the stereo set, and the home movie camera that they will thereby achieve happiness. What they achieve instead is resentment and frustration. The pursuit of happiness seems not so much a bore as a cheat and a delusion. People who play the consumer game according to the rules expect to be rewarded according to the rules, and the reward is not forthcoming.

It is not only the advertising world that holds out happiness as a bribe and incentive. The rewards-and-fairies mentality of many parents, schoolteachers, and religious societies gives rise to the same attitude. If a person is good, or obedient, or follows the tenets of the religion, he will find true happiness. If not, only misery and despair await him. This type of argument is far more common than might be supposed, particularly among middle-class families and religious organizations.

The main objection to hedonist utilitarianism, however, whether as formalized in philosophy or as displayed in the pages of *Playboy* and the *New Yorker*, is that most mature people do not pursue their many activities and goals as a means to abstract happiness, even though they use happiness as their justification. Most people play a sport because they like playing that sport, seek out particular forms of recreation because they want to partake of that recreation, and buy particular lines of goods because they want them, or have been convinced that they want them. It is true that members of the consumer society expect, unconsciously, to be happy when they have attained their particular ends, but they rarely take part in their diverse activities for the sake of immediate happiness. Bentham and Mill have in fact introduced a false monism into Western thought. While this made their economic-oriented philosophy a good deal tidier, it did violence to the facts. People do things because they want to do those things, not because of long cerebral calculations about happiness or pleasure or some similar abstraction. These only arise when people are asked to justify their behaviour. Moreover, many people are aware that if they did pursue these ends simply for the possible happiness to be derived from them, they would neither obtain happiness nor appreciate the activities. Anxious determination to be happy distracts from the activity itself.

The realization that a person can never accumulate a large balance of happiness over unhappiness appears at first sight sobering and pessimistic. In fact it liberates an individual from the belief that only by pursuing certain generally socially approved activities can happiness be attained. No matter what sort of life a person lives, within reason, his happiness and unhappiness will balance out. Even if the mechanism described does not result in an exact balance, the result will balance so closely as to make the pursuit of happiness irrelevant. Some criterion of ends other than happiness, some alternative basis for establishing aims and directions must be found.

One obvious alternative to happiness as an end in life is well-being, the classical sense of happiness. Even if people cannot hope to be in a constant state of euphoria and ecstasy, they can still hope to be well-off. Moreover, the pursuit of "well-offness" seems both more dignified and more far-sighted than the pursuit of euphoria. Personal ecstasy can be maintained for a long time by the use of drugs or electric stimulation of brain centres, but this is hardly an existence that would appeal to most people. Welfare is a more objective quantity reflecting the quality of a person's life and his social environment.

There is fairly wide agreement on the items that make up well-being. They include such things as physical and mental health, a degree of economic security, personal freedom, a reasonable standard of education, social acceptance, creative activity, affectionate relationships, and a tolerable physical environment. The last three represent the factors of psychological happiness described above.

In fact, all these elements of well-being, well-offness, or *euness* to coin a more convenient term, still fail to give any direction or end to life. All are means which allow people to function to the best of their ability. Once achieved, they provide no information as to how a person should use them or what direction to take. A motor vehicle requires fuel, oil, water, hydraulic fluid, and certain routine maintenance if it is to operate satisfactorily, but such information tells nothing about the use that the vehicle should be put to, nor the direction in which it should be driven. Information on basic human needs, whether these be physical, social, or psychological, provides no insight into the sort of life a person should live or the goals that he should, may, or can strive for. Welfare in the broad sense simply provides the individual with the widest potential range of action. Unfortunately, welfare, like psychological happiness, has now become entangled with material ends and economic thinking. To be well-off indicates that a person possesses in abundance the material goods of life and the capacity to obtain them. Such items as health, freedom, and education are subsumed under the economic label because it is generally possible to obtain them in return for money. Any element of welfare that cannot be bought is either ignored or detailed to the state as its responsibility.

PART TWO

EMOTIONS AND VALUES

4

REASON AND EMOTION

Western society tends to draw a sharp distinction between the intellectual and the emotional aspects of human nature. Associated with this view is the assumption that behaviour is either rationally or emotionally motivated, or more generally finds its source in some combination of the emotional and the intellectual.

The flaw in this approach is that, while both reason and emotions are involved in any course of action, emotions alone are capable of giving rise to behaviour. Questions such as Why do anything at all?, let alone Why do the right or moral thing?, result when pursued far enough in some statement with emotional content—some desire, hatred, or revulsion. There are both logical and psychological reasons for this.

Appeals to rationality alone, either to motivate a person or to justify a course of action, must logically end in a potential regress. To insist that a person should perform a particular action because of an anticipated result invites the question why, reasonably, should he strive for that result. A similar logical regress is encountered in explanations of why a specific action was performed.

From a psychological viewpoint, people almost never act in response to an extended process of reasoned steps, intermediate stages, and final satisfaction. The majority either take part in a particular activity they enjoy for the sake of that activity or seek intermediate satisfaction such as payment for work. Most activities have only short-term ends in view, and attempts to rationalize them reflect only the higher standing of rationality as against the more suspect emotions.

The idea that emotions are the initiating factor in all behaviour is far from new. The philosopher David Hume stated that reason was slave to the passions; Freud rephrased this somewhat more opaquely when he suggested that the ego derives its energy from the id. The consequence is that reason, logic, and indeed all rational processes simply serve as transfer functions between the particular emotions and the desired end. Abstract reasoning is historically a more recent development than the capacity for emotions, and permits a considerable flexibility of response to the emotional impetus. Civilized man is capable of approaching his goals with a subtlety, a circularity, and an indirectness quite impossible for wild animals or primitive man. The primitive chases and catches his food and clothing; the need and the response are immediately related. Modern man may indulge in any occupation from architectural design to organized crime in order to meet his needs.

Claims that emotional reactions alone are responsible for behaviour raise questions about the source of these reactions. The possibilities are that they are either innate in human nature, that they derive from the person's particular experience, or that they have their source in the society. Many strong emotions, for instance, fear of fire, hatred of particular people, and revulsion towards particular conditions, clearly have their source in particular, often intensely unpleasant, experiences, but the areas in which people display strong emotions are diverse and go far beyond their personal experience. Such emotional responses include hatred of Communists, contempt for homosexuals, reverence for the Virgin Mary, fear of the Chinese or of the Americans, the Jews, Negroes, or Socialists, and suspicion of big business. While such attitudes are allegedly based on experience, the attitudes usually precede first-hand experience, which in any case serves only to confirm an established prejudice. The fact that a person has never met a Communist, a Manichean heretic, or even a homosexual does not preclude his having the strongest feeling about such people.

It is often claimed in support of reason as a source of motivation that emotions reflect only an examination of evidence, as for example hatred of the Nazis. While this is plausible, particularly to those who hate fascism, it overlooks the fact that equally strong emotions justified with the same appeal to reason are often entertained in regard to Catholics, Communists, and capitalists. Even where the same information is available, men of presumed good will prove capable of embracing very different attidues. Moreover, history has a habit of reversing, or at least holding irrelevant, the most strongly justified verdicts of an age. The reasons that made the First World War seem so laudable or the Crusades so necessary appear, at this remove, more than a little suspect. The rationalizations of one era rarely prove acceptable to later ages.

If experience seems a less than satisfactory source of a person's emotional responses, it is even less plausible to claim that such responses are innate. While they may be as general as the desire for money and material possessions, or the hatred of suffering or servitude, it is simply not true that all men at all times have displayed such reactions. The one possibility remaining is that the bulk of a person's emotional responses derive from the social group. The springs of behaviour are emotional rather than rational, and social rather than individualistic.

This suggests that human beings have the capacity to link an emotional state—love, hate, fear, envy, and desire—with a particular field, resulting in an enduring emotional disposition. Such fields may be material objects, activities, or a particular condition. The resulting responses may be as general as the desire for possessions, or as specific as reverence for a particular patron saint. But in almost all cases the connection is acquired from the society, or the sub-society, of which the person is a member.

The term *emotive-mechanism* is used here to describe a particular conjunction of emotional response and the stimulus giving rise to it. Emotive-mechanisms are not to be identified with emotions themselves. The latter are transitory phenomena while the mechanisms are a persistent aspect of personality. They may or may not result in activity depending on the particular setting and on the individual, but they are always a potential source of activity. Where the response takes place in an area conventionally regarded as moral by the particular society, emotive-mechanisms are generally referred to as values. Where responses are non-moral, the mechanisms are more usually described as attitudes or predispositions. It may be noted in passing that even the term *values* implies that some evaluation has been made, and that people act from rational considerations. Wherever possible this society attempts to rationalize behaviour, and to support it by appeals to reason rather than the more suspect emotions.

This theory of emotive-mechanism formation is no more than a description of what happens; it does not pretend to be an explanation of how it happens. To picture the linking of emotions and stimulus is a simplification akin to picturing Dalton's atoms as provided with hooks by which they join together. It is probable that several mechanisms are involved: fields of tension, Pavlovian conditioning, and free-floating emotional patterns, to name but a few. Moreover, it is not intended to define emotions themselves; such definition is probably as impracticable as providing a definition of red. For the present it is more useful to simply instance examples of emotions, and leave the term *emotions* undefined.

A person may prove responsive to the emotive patterns of his society in one of two ways—by internalizing them or by reflecting them. A child internalizes the values, or emotive-mechanisms, of his parents during the process of early education, incorporating them into his personality, generally under conditions of strong emotional stress. Once internalization is complete the child is independent of his parents in this regard; he has made their values his values. He will go on hating Communists, or capitalists, Jews, or Negroes, loving his country, being ashamed of sex, revering holy relics, and desiring material possessions until a new set of emotive-mechanisms is established, or until experience breaks down the original set. In the case of reflection, a person responds to the emotional displays of a particular group or society as if they were his own, and acts upon them, but does not internalize them to any great extent. This type of reflective behaviour can be observed in any social setting. If one person shows acute embarrassment, others present tend to share this embarrassment. If a person shows intense anger, others in contact with him respond with anger, either directed towards him or towards some external agent. There is obviously a continuum between internalization and reflection, and emotions that are originally reflected may in time be internalized as emotive-mechanisms.

These two types of reaction correspond to the inner-directed and other-directed character types as described by David Riesman in his book *The Lonely Crowd*. Extreme inner-direction is typified by those nineteenth century Protestants with fixed values who travelled to the most distant colonies, taking their emotional equipment with them intact. An example of other-directed character type is the organization man who quite inadvertently adjusts his values to those of his social group. Inner-directed people are commonly regarded as having stronger character, or as displaying higher moral integrity, than other-directed people, who tend to be dismissed as morally weak or as opportunists. Such judgements are pointless. Every society, if it is to be successful, develops the character type most appropriate to its needs. The other-directed personality could never have founded the British Empire; the more inflexible inner-directed personality may prove an encumbrance to large business organizations.

That group interests and non-rational impulses may be more important than rational self-interest has been understood for a century at least. Marx, by pointing to the unsuspected working of a hypothetical dialectic, suggested only that historical change does not lead where people intend it to lead. It was still possible to view rational man as the victim of forces he was unable to control, while still having a clear idea of where his own interests lay. Claims that human behaviour itself is non-rational go far beyond this; on such a view human behaviour has become one of the unintelligible social forces. This approach was first outlined by the Italian sociologist and economist Vilfredo Pareto towards the end of the nineteenth century, anticipating Freud's ideas on individual non-rationalism by some thirty years. Pareto insisted that while people believed themselves to act in terms of reason, good sense, and enlightened self-interest, such beliefs served as little more than rationalizations. The real impulse was non-rational and emotional. In one example, the deep-seated horror of and desire to punish murder claimed its rational basis in the law. In fact, both the law itself and the punishment can be traced to deep-seated emotional attitudes to murder; the justifying link between law and punishment exists only in the imagination.

Historically, Pareto is the founder of emotive-mechanism theories of behaviour. But a disjointed and somewhat bizarre theory of personality prevented his providing a secure basis for the theory or from developing it further. In addition, the acerbity of his writing deterred many critics, for he insisted on classing among non-rational ideologies not only Communism and totalitarianism but liberalism and nationalism. This was hardly welcome in an age that considered itself liberal, rational, and rightly nationalistic.

5

THE ORIGINS OF BEHAVIOUR

Superimposed on the organic evolution of life has been a secondary evolution of animal behaviour. The simplest forms of life such as the amoeba respond automatically to physical and chemical stimuli, advancing towards food, retreating from danger, and reproducing by cellular division at regular intervals. Insects display tropistic patterns of behaviour following a sequence of built-in responses which on termination give rise to new sets of responses. As a classic example, certain wasps display elaborate egg-laying behaviour, digging a burrow, finding and paralysing a caterpillar, dragging it back to the nest, laying eggs in it, and finally sealing the burrow. If the sequence is disturbed at any stage, the wasp is unable to adjust to the change. Its behaviour is inflexible, the result of a short life-span that precludes learning.

Among more highly developed animal species behaviour is generally primary-drive stimulated, directed towards the satisfaction of hunger and thirst or of maternal and sexual feelings, and triggered by chemical signals. In contrast to the tropistic behaviour of insects, primary-drive behaviour exhibits considerable flexibility. In particular, it is possible for learning to modify the type of response made to a particular need. More sophisticated behavioural mechanisms appeared among the mammals, reaching their highest development in the primates and in man. An extensive repertoire of emotional responses, developing in conjunction with intelligent reasoning, provided a high degree of flexibility and adaptability. The primates were thus able to deal with a wider range of situations, and to deal with them in a more flexible manner than less developed species. At every stage, increasing flexibility, adaptability, and complexity characterized the evolution of behaviour.

These patterns of behaviour parallel the development of control modes in technology. The most elementary control mechanism is the interlocked system, used on simple process control. A fan starts a condenser, the condenser starts the pumps, the pumps start the compressor. This corresponds to the tropistic behaviour of insects. A higher degree of sophistication is represented by the feedback control system, often glorified by the term *cybernetic control*. An example is thermostatic control of room temperature; as the room becomes too hot, the heat is shut down, when the room grows cold, the heating is increased. Such feedback control systems are capable of considerable sophistication; heating can be either turned on and off, it can be varied in proportion to the temperature, in response to how fast the room is heating, and to the time it has been over-hot. Feedback control systems correspond to hunger- and thirst-satisfying behaviour and to many of the control functions within living organisms—for example, body temperature and heart-rate mechanisms.

The most complex and flexible control system is the on-line computer, which can respond in theory to any number of changing conditions and can control variables in the most complex manner. Instances are the computer controls of large steel mills, oil refineries, and chemical plants. These systems not only allow precise and continuous control but permit the type of control itself to be changed by varying the programme. This cannot be done with a simple interlocked or feedback control system, which, once installed, always provides the same type of control. The computer control mode parallels the behaviour of the mammals, where the programme is provided by the emotions, and to a lesser extent by the reasoning capacity. Variations in the programme are supplied by learning. Insects never learn by experience; mammals do, and in this lies one of their great evolutionary advantages.

Given this perspective it is readily seen how the capacity to develop emotive-mechanisms evolved. The higher animals learn by experience, but that experience can often be fatal. Even when not fatal, it is inevitably time consuming. An animal that can learn from the experience of others of its kind enjoys a substantial survival advantage.

The higher primates exhibit a wide range of emotional responses coupled with emotional displays: delight on discovering tasty fruit, fear of predators such as snakes, and horror at the sight of a mutilated body. In time the primates developed the capacity to act on the emotional cues provided by others of their kind. There was no need to try every fruit in the jungle; they simply sought out those fruit and titbits shown to be desirable by the tribe's reaction. There was no need for a near escape from a snake before the young avoided snakes; the terror shown by others was sufficient to spur them to flight. Eventually the capacity both to exhibit emotional cues and to respond to cues provided by the group gave the primates a substantial survival advantage. Natural selection furthered this capacity. As a result, each member of the species carried a complete socially developed programme with him, often going far beyond individual experience. Inevitably experience would reinforce the emotive-mechanisms formed, as when the succulent fruit was tasted or the snake barely avoided, but the imitative reaction usually preceded the experience.

These attitudes were conveyed by a wide range of facial expressions, bodily postures, and gestures. Ever since Darwin's discussion of emotions in animals, zoologists have debated exactly why animals developed the capacity to display emotions, as against simply experiencing them. There is no immediate advantage in emotional displays for the individual, but a considerable advantage to a species which is either tribal or spends time bringing up its young. Animals that do not rear their young never evolve this capacity; snakes, mercifully, do not display their emotions.

The parallel between the way human cultures pass on skills and information—for the most part verbally—and the way in which the higher animals pass on emotional responses is obvious. Human knowledge, however, consists largely of data, while the emotional responses common to the higher primates and mankind are effectively programmes, providing a pattern of responses. With verbalization, the range of emotive-mechanisms came to be extended almost indefinitely. It was no longer necessary to see a snake or desirable food to establish emotional connections. Words can be conveniently regarded as symbols, and it is possible to set up values and patterns of response in respect to things never seen and indeed with things that may not exist. In addition, connections can be set up with abstractions, processes, and conditions, something that is clearly impossible for non-verbal creatures. Because human beings are adept at using symbols—a flag for a country, a cross, trident, or crescent for a religious creed—strong values can be associated with the most abstract entities.

The advantage of emotive-mechanisms over homeostatic or tropistic behavioural mechanisms lies in their flexibility. In a primitive tribe or even in the sub-cultures of a highly developed society, values of good and bad, desirable and undesirable, are established imitatively, but the manner in which related goals are reached depends largely on the individual. While cultures generally define more or less accepted methods of reaching goals, often institutionalized and hallowed by tradition, these methods usually involve the use of reason as a transfer function. Reason provides a flexible link or buffered area between the impulse and the response. A person may, for example, have internalized the social connection between material possessions and desirability. But there are many ways in which he can gain the secular heaven of stereo sets, hand-made suits, European sports cars, and expensive movie cameras. He can join a corporation and work his way into a well-paid position; he may take a college course and sell his special skills and knowledge; he can set up his own business; or he can turn to a life of crime.

But this very flexibility between the impetus and the method of attaining an end, between the emotional side of human nature and the rational, has drawbacks as well as advantages. These drawbacks never become significant within the tribal setting, but in civilization they have become all-important. For outside the tribal setting there is no way that the interaction of reason and emotion can ever be guaranteed.

6
SPIRITUAL EQUIPMENT

Tribal societies possess a number of mechanisms for passing on the emotional patterns necessary for their existence. While it is natural to assume that farmers will inevitably farm and put aside grain for the succeeding year, that the trader will continue to trade, and the hunter to hunt, this is far from the case; some agency must exist to transmit the values supporting these activities. In the absence of such machinery, as when social breakdown follows the impact of a foreign culture, these activities go neglected. Enlightened self-interest as a motive is an invention of the eighteenth century.

Internalizing of values, or conditioning, usually involves the exhibition of a strong display of emotion towards a particular field, experienced under conditions of apprehension, fear, or guilt on the part of the person being socialized. This process may range in severity from the benign punishment of children, through tribal initiation rites and dramatic religious conversion, to the savage brainwashing of political prisoners. In all cases the principle is the same. The effectiveness of this internalizing process depends both on the degree of anxiety, apprehension, and emotional excitement exhibited by the person being conditioned and on the intensity of the emotional display of those doing the conditioning. Internalizing appears to take place most readily among people subject to emotional exhaustion or to strong feelings of guilt, although the subject's existing emotional make-up is important. Where a complete reversal of values is sought, as with political brainwashing and religious conversion, the breaking down of old values necessarily precedes the instillation of the new.

The archaeologist Gordon Childe used the term *spiritual equipment* to describe that body of myth, legend, ceremony, pageantry, and rite that characterizes primitive peoples and provides the means for instilling values. He likened this equipment to the technical equipment—metallurgy, tools, agricultural techniques—that provide the material means for the culture to endure. That even the most marginally surviving cultures, the African Bushmen and the Australian Aborigines, have such spiritual equipment testifies to its necessity. Were it a cultural luxury, societies living in more marginal conditions would have long ago dispensed with it.

By means of their spiritual equipment, particularly rites, ceremonies, and pageants, societies formalize the passing on of emotive-mechanisms. In fertility rites and ceremonies the sanctity of growth and agriculture is stressed. These emotional displays provide the continuing motivation for the farmer and the husbandman. Initiation rites, teeth-filing and puberty rites not only provide the initiate with the sacred information of his culture but also reinforce emotional moral values. In short, spiritual equipment provides a setting in which either anxiety or emotional excitement can be concentrated, isolated from the distractions of day-to-day life, and used to establish emotive-mechanisms. All cultures require institutions of this kind, for their survival depends on being able to pass on, in unaltered form, the values that sustain them.

Such ceremonies generally use symbols or representations to facilitate social conditioning. These provide a focus for the emotions; an idol, a holy grove, a sacred tree, or a ciborium all become intensely emotionally charged, hallowed, revered, and awe-inspiring, simply because intense emotions of a particular type are manifested towards them.

The use of spiritual equipment persists in developed societies in greatly diluted forms. A Catholic High Mass, for example, is an intensely moving emotional experience, confirming the emotive attachments that make the faith viable. On the secular side, military ceremonial, inspection parades, and the like reaffirm those values that make a military organization's existence possible; respect for rank and those in authority, discipline, order, and obedience. Parades, particularly funeral parades with their muffled drums and measured step, are as emotionally moving as any religious ceremony. The present trend doing away with square bashing, spit and polish, and "bull" generally, all in the name of reason, can only result in a failing of discipline and finally of effectiveness and motivation. In fact, the elimination of "meaningless" ceremony and ritual can only result in a generation of demotivated and unconditioned recruits.

7

THE EVOLUTION OF VALUES

The values that a society evolves reflect its needs and its way of life. An agricultural society exhibits reverence for the soil—often symbolized as an earth-mother—for generation and growth, and for agricultural pursuits in general. Such societies not only revere the natural forces of sun, rain, and fecundity necessary for their survival, they emotionally imbue the work of planting, cultivation, and harvest by elaborate ceremonies and ritual. In contrast with developed civilizations, motivation is built into the society's fabric; its members do not work because of emotional values involved with economics—money being emotionally charged, material goods being emotionally charged—they work because it is the ordained sacred duty of man. Since no reasoned steps intervene between activity and motivation, work in a stable primitive society is not resented in the way that it is in the West. Much the same applies in primitive societies that depend basically on trade, but in this case the sanctity of property and of material goods is stressed; a higher value is placed on the virtues of thrift, hard work, regularity, and saving. Among such societies there is less reverence for the natural forces that make the harvest possible, and more for the human attributes conducive to trade.

It appears that many of the higher religions contain in fossilized form the values general at the time of their foundation. Hinduism is principally an agrarian value religion, as is Pentateuch Judaism with its emphasis on "sweat of the brow" agrarianism. Islam and Protestantism appear more trading-value religions, emphasizing those emotive-mechanisms essential for a trading society to develop. If this is so, the balance between competing religions—Islam and Hinduism for example—can be expected to depend more on Marxist factors of economic organization than on missionary zeal, although the explanation is by no means as simple as this.

Emotive-mechanisms are capable of evolving to meet the needs of a changing society. No social group, with the possible exception of the most primitive tribe, is entirely homogeneous, either in behaviour or in the structure of its values. Specialization for such tasks as weapon maker, medicine man, smith, carpenter, and chief, for example, introduces the possibility of new values which would be disastrous if distributed through the whole society. Often these specialized values are transmitted from father to son at the same time that a particular skill is taught. Many of the most stable societies, for instance the Pacific Islanders, with their system of hereditary chieftains, display a specialization of rulership values within families. Indeed, there is probably more to be said for a hereditary aristocracy capable of passing on its values unadulterated than the democratic West is prepared to admit. These specialized values, with the addition of random and asocial values, perform the same function for a society as recessive and maladaptive genes do for a species. A species possessing only those hereditary characteristics that fit it for its present environment would be incapable of change; recessive and maladaptive genes provide the flexibility needed to meet new conditions.

This variety in a society's emotive-mechanisms permits natural selection to operate, favouring groups that have values appropriate to their mode of life and to a large extent eliminating those having values that are maladaptive. This selection can take place both within and without a social group. In the extreme case, a tribe or society with maladaptive values will be physically eliminated. More commonly, a particular body of values will simply lose its adherents to a more dynamic and adaptive value system. Such encroachment may take place either violently or by assimilation when the advantages of the new value system become apparent. Military conquests, for example, almost always result in the conquered taking over the conquerors' value system, in much the same way that a primitive people take over a conquerors' religious creed. Examples of such internalization of value systems could be quoted indefinitely: the Christianizing of the New World; the adoption by middle-class Indians of Edwardian English values; the Communization of Eastern Europe, and the adoption by the Japanese of American economic values. At times, when a religious creed is held with particular conviction, only parts of a new value system will be adopted. The ancient Jews, during the period of the captivity, retained their monotheistic religion but adopted many of the elements of Hammurabi's code. In addition they adopted the communal values of their urbanized captors, changing from an agricultural to a basically trading culture in the process. The Jewish people, incidentally, represent an instance of the power of adaptive values to hold a society together under the most adverse conditions. They evolved, under the challenge of nomadic desert life, spiritual equipment that has preserved their culture through three thousand years of adversity—a feat probably without any parallel. So strong are their values, and so effective the spiritual equipment for passing them on, that they remain one of the most highly motivated and creative of cultures on earth.

New value systems also arise from within a culture in response to social needs. Such new systems, however, only appear if they serve the psychological, social, or economic needs of the society more adequately than existing values. Christianity, and for a time Mithraism, emerged from the decay of the Roman Empire following the disintegration of its state-associated religion. Because the polytheistic state religion was no longer credited, it failed to give emotional support in times of increasing crisis. The new, individualistic and otherworldly religions were able to meet this emotional need, making their final victory inevitable. The values of medieval Catholicism were communalistic, agrarian, and largely inimical to commercial expansion; the Church, by setting its face against usury and by its doctrine of a just price, limited the economic opportunities of its adherents. In consequence those who did not recognize its rulings, as for example the Florentines and the Jews, acquired a disproportionate economic advantage. Their example was followed by others, but it was not until the Reformation, and the breaking away of national Churches, that this economic freedom could be used to the full, as exemplified by the success of the Protestant English and Dutch trading societies. Economic development, as characterized by eighteenth- and nineteenth- century England and northern Europe, requires a strong emphasis on individualism, hard work, and personal thrift to ensure capital accumulation; in short, it requires the Protestant virtues.

Values can thus be seen to develop according to Toynbee's theory of challenge and response. If a society can evolve or import, in adequate time, emotive connections appropriate to changing economic and social conditions, it may prove capable of meeting the challenge. If it fails to do so it will either perish or survive at a more primitive cultural level. But generally, once the challenge has been met, the new values that have proved successful tend to decay unless there is a continuing challenge. With this decay the quality of the civilization changes, and it becomes prey to internal or external attack.

Values can be adaptive, maladaptive, or neutral—that is, anadaptive—to the needs of a particular society. All developed societies contain, and can afford to contain, a number of maladaptive values; these not only keep alive the possibility of change but also provide a richness that the society would otherwise lack. In many cases such values can be traced back several thousand years, constituting a kind of Jungian racial memory—fossilized loves, petrified hates—passed on by the sheer intensity of attached emotions. The hatred and revulsion displayed towards homosexuals, common to Western societies, appear to have originated in Old Testament strictures against the worship of Baal. Homosexuality was involved in such worship; the Hebrews condemned these practices on grounds that were finally religious, with the result that highly charged emotional attachments, held with the greatest self-righteousness, passed from Judaism into Christianity, and thence into the legal codes of the West.

Anadaptive values, those that appear to have no social utility, are more common than might be expected. An example is the hostility towards cruelty to animals common in European cultures, but largely unknown and, indeed, unintelligible to Asians. It appears to have no survival value for the culture, but is nevertheless held with the greatest passion by a majority of Westerners. Among the more successful adaptive values of modern societies are patriotism, the respect for learning and knowledge, and the entire range of economic values. Patriotic values, the secular religion associated with territory, make the modern nation state possible. Without the emotional charging of the fatherland concept by means of flags, national anthems, state figureheads, and national celebrations, people could not be induced to work for and, indeed, to die for their country. Moreover, many societies owe their survival to a policy, intentional or unintentional, of provoking friction with neighbouring states, thereby generating a challenge and then responding to it. The resulting antagonism consolidates the nation in the name of national security and refurbishes patriotic values which would otherwise decay. As an instance, Rome in its early stages maintained a state of almost constant warfare with its neighbours, which strengthened its patriotic determination and made the establishment of its empire possible. The same response can be seen in the history of the British Empire, when patriotic fervour was continually refurbished by historically senseless campaigns in Afghanistan, in China, and by numerous gunboat expeditions to Africa. Similar behaviour characterizes a number of nations, minor and major, to the present day; a border clash or an ideological war not only distracts from such internal problems as student radicals and revisionists, it also re-establishes patriotic values. It is regrettable but true that strong patriotic emotions can only be sustained over a long term by provoking crises.

The high value placed on knowledge and information in this society reflects its basic needs. Hunting nomads worship gods of the chase and animal spirits. Agrarian cultures worship vegetation spirits and fertility gods. Trading and mercantile cultures develop values and religious beliefs that are economically useful to the society; Manus Islanders and the nineteenth-century British typify this type of value system. Highly industrialized societies are absolutely dependent on knowledge for their survival. While knowledge has always been important for group survival, it has in the past been secondary to its field; the knowledge of where game could be caught or how bread was made is only part of the hunting or food-preparation process. It seems doubtful whether primitive people even have a concept of information as such.

The importance of information has now produced a vast information ecology, along with the values needed to support it.

Nobody would now dream of questioning whether information or knowledge is good in itself, or whether education is desirable; they are simply known to be good, just as grace and faith were known to be good in medieval society. Processes in human societies develop a Newtonian inertia of their own. The pursuit of knowledge, no matter how useless and pointless, has no foreseeable termination and, as long as there are Ph.D.s to be written and Ph.D. scholars to write them, can be expected to continue indefinitely. Indeed, the collection of information parallels at an abstract level the acquisitiveness of the average suburbanite. The suburbanite collects cars, furniture, and china animals on the television set; the scholar and intellectual collect facts, information, and ideas—the more recondite and esoteric, the more impressive. The meet symbol of Western civilization is not the spear of the hunter, the plow of the husbandman, or even the scales of the merchant; it is the data bank of a digital computer.

It is reasonably easy to show how favourable emotive-mechanisms develop and spread through a culture, and how maladaptive mechanisms are largely eliminated. But the origin of completely new emotive connections, completely original reactions to a field, is more difficult to explain. Many obviously derive from experience, and persist within the culture even when the original need has long since vanished. Many evolve by slow shifts in emphasis and content. But quite often new values appear to emerge fully developed to meet a particular social need. The development of these emotive links can only be made by an intuitive leap of faith; there can be no reason for suddenly exhibiting a particular and quite novel emotional response to knowledge, productivity, non-violence, or monotheism. Just as it is the philosophers and thinkers who develop new ideas and concepts, or, more accurately, who crystallize them out of the intellectual ambience of the culture, so it is the seers, the prophets, the visionaries, and the mystics who develop new emotive-mechanisms.

Muhammad introduced strong emotive-mechanisms in regard to idolatry and monotheism. Buddha took the basic value system of Hinduism and added values relating to compassion and non-attachment. Gandhi held values relating to non-violence and passive resistance. Christ took the formal, rigid monotheism of Judaism and added values involved with love—agape—humility, and service. Indeed, by emphasizing the importance of love—emotional attachments—towards one's fellow man, to God, and to God's creation, Christ showed himself intuitively aware of the importance of the emotional side of human nature. In preaching emotional attachment, he was in effect developing emotive-mechanisms for emotive-mechanisms.

Values, attitudes, dispositions, indeed all emotive-mechanisms are essentially atomistic; there can be no general connection within a person's mind to any particular emotion. It is possible to revere Christ and be indifferent to the Virgin, to hate cruelty to people, but be indifferent to cruelty to animals, to value productivity highly and be indifferent to knowledge. Equally, it is possible for a person to be strongly moral in one area, for example in respect to business integrity, and still have the sexual morality of an alley cat. The only constraint is that the human mind responds with a certain degree of consistency to the world; it cannot operate with an excessive disparity in closely related values. Despite this atomism, there is a tendency to collect the values of a particular milieu into a package deal as it were, and impart them together. Such value constellations are typified by the higher religions, and by ideologies, such as communism, fascism, and liberalism. The term *ideology* is an attempt, again, to indicate that their content is basically ideas, and to relate them to rational intellectual processes. But ideologies are basically non-rational, and their content is emotional. They are, in short, constellations of emotive-mechanisms. The term *emotology* is convenient to emphasize their emotive-mechanism content, it being understood that *ideology* and *emotology* are interchangeable terms.

Every age tends to interpret history according to the prime object of consciousness at that time. When Gibbon wrote *The Decline and Fall of the Roman Empire*, religion was the main object of consciousness of his contemporaries, and probably the aspect of life that they took most seriously. Accordingly, Gibbon naturally tended to interpret the fall of Rome in terms that were religious, describing it as the triumph of barbarism and religion. By the time Marx came to write *Capital*, the prime object of consciousness had shifted from religion to economics. Religion was still very important to most people, but more of their mental energy was now directed towards economic ends.

As a result, Marx interpreted most of history in basically economic terms and made the economic organization of society fundamental to his philosophy. Everything else was unceremoniously relegated to the superstructure.

Following Darwin's publication of *The Origin of Species*, attempts were made by minor thinkers, in particular by the Social Darwinists, to explain history from the point of view of evolutionary forces. Currently, owing to the impetus of increasing information and the demands for entertainment, both available in vaster quantities than ever before, the prime object of consciousness has turned towards communication and the use of media. Most administrative and desk jobs are entirely concerned with the communication of information; most spare time is devoted to absorbing entertainment through the media. Inevitably, media analysts have attempted to interpret all history on the basis of the type of communication media used, whether it is linear or holistic, and whether received by eye or by ear.

But human history is a process of such complexity, involving so many different factors, such a variety of influences and determinants that it appears ludicrous to attempt interpretation according to any one factor. Religion, economics, and communication modes are all influences of greater or lesser importance in the history of a society. Moreover, their relative importance varies from society to society. Tibetan history, for example, can be more readily understood from a religious rather than an economic point of view, while the opposite would be true of a history of Singapore.

Among the current prime objects of consciousness are the social sciences—psychology, sociology, anthropology, and archaeology. And it could be objected that the value-evolution analysis, outlined above, is an attempt to interpret history again simply according to what most interests us—psychological and sociological factors as against religious or economic determinants. This is not so. The plurality and complexity of history is fully admitted. Rather it is an attempt to show that social and psychological forces and interests—mostly non-rational—must be admitted, along with a number of other factors, in any programme to interpret history. This is something that neither Marx the monist nor Gibbon the rationalist would be prepared to concede.

8
GROUP FORMATION

A favourite fiction of the eighteenth century was that, at some distant time, human beings had come together to formulate a social contract for mutual help and protection. Under the terms of this hypothetical contract men had agreed to give up much of their independence for the advantages to be gained from communal life, and to delegate power to a ruler. Hobbes used this theory not only to explain the origins of civil society but to justify absolute monarchy. Rousseau admitted that probably no such bargain was ever struck, but held it was necessary to see how it could have been in order to understand the origins of society and its operation.

The fault in such theorizing is that it assumes human beings are principally motivated by reason, and that only by reason could they be led to give up immediate independence for long-term advantages. In fact there never was a time when individual human beings, suffering a life that was nasty, brutish, and short, could have come together to ameliorate their lot. Higher primates lead a tribal existence, and it is reasonable to assume that the tree-dwelling ancestors of mankind lived in a tribal society. Moreover, among primitive tribes there is far greater conformity than in the most authoritarian developed society. Primitives think primarily in terms of the tribal community, the "we", and only marginally distinguish themselves from the group. The hypothetical independence that primitive man surrendered under the terms of a social contract never in fact existed. A theory involving emotive-mechanisms makes any hypothetical agreement on laws of conduct or morality redundant. It is not even necessary to appeal, as Hume did, to an awareness of social utility to explain the rise of legal codes and morality. If all members of a group have effectively the same emotive-mechanisms, all will display the same emotional responses. Since these values have presumably evolved to suit the conditions of the society, they will automatically have social utility.

The existence of emotive-mechanisms illuminates the origins of civil society, but it does not explain the strength of the bonds that exist within a group once it has been established. These bonds depend on the existence of bigotry-mechanism. The characteristic of other people to which we react most strongly is their value structure. It is hard not to feel well inclined towards a person who agrees with us in our most cherished likes and dislikes, tastes, attitudes, and moral values; it is hard to like a person who differs from us in values which we hold important. These differences are far more important than differences in clothing, skin colour, speech, and so on, except where these differences serve as signals for value systems; the beard of a hippie, the skull-cap of a Jew, the habit of a nun, or the blue shirt of the working-class militant. Indeed, similarity of values cuts across almost all other divisions of mankind. A middle-class Indian will relate to a middle-class European far more readily than to a lower-class Indian. An aristocrat from the West will find more sympathy with an Eastern ruler than with a Western democrat.

In the hypothetical primitive society, tribes clearly have a greater chance of survival if they can prevent diffusion or absorption into other tribes. The main difference between tribes lies in their value systems, associated with their religious worship, and signalled by their particular dress and manner. Hence there evolved bigotry-mechanism, the lamented sense of "them" and "us", the in-group and the out-group, the Aryans and the lesser breeds, the elect and the gentiles. It is not necessary to invoke elaborate theorizing to show how such a bigotry-mechanism evolved. Even among primitive tribes the ability to involve their ego with their emotive-mechanisms must have existed to some extent. Selection would favour those tribes with the strongest ability to egotize their values. Bigotry, a means of accomplishing this, allows a person to extend his self feelings towards others with the same values. The familiar sense of "us" and "them" is thus established, and can be found among such diverse associations as rival groups of football fans, each with their own totemic devices, and opposing sides in a religious war. The dynamics of group formation are provided by the capacity to absorb emotive-mechanisms from the society, and to identify with those holding similar values. All social life, and indeed civilization itself, depends on the operation of these two mechanisms. Civilization is the implication of mimicry.

Any selection of people with roughly similar backgrounds, brought together regularly in a face-to-face situation, will tend to form a group. All that is needed is a situation in which they can signal and receive emotional responses. Such an opportunity may be provided in a university setting, a work group, or a sporting club. The particular values developed and intensified may be those common to type, as with a businessmen's group or an extremist political club; they may simply be associated with a particular sporting club and its symbol. But at times quite new ideologies may be formulated to support groups that have formed almost incidentally. An instance is provided by the new generation of adult students, and in particular Japanese students. Previously such people had been influenced by strict and conservative family environments, but with long periods spent at university, in tutorials, coffee bars, and dormitories, the vertical emotional relationship with parents weakens and the horizontal relationship with peers predominates. The geometry of a social situation is far more important than beliefs or interests, and, in the circumstances, any ideology that proves capable of cementing the group together is apt to be adopted.

In general, the content of a group's ideology will bear little relevance to the real interests of the individuals in the group. But to assert this is to misunderstand what is happening. Groups evolve emotive-mechanisms that ensure the survival of the group rather than those that promote the individual well-being of members, or even the rational best ends of that group. This is true of political extremist organizations, true of vested interest groups in government and industry, and true of a military platoon. The rule that nature sacrifices individuals for the species applies in society; the dynamics of group formation are such that evolved values will generally result in sacrifice of the individual in the interest of group survival.

Since it is face-to-face contact that makes group formation, and hence motivation, possible, motivation can be reduced or even eliminated by isolating members of potential groups. Effectively, this is done to pensioners and those on relief who cannot afford to meet together constantly, and hence never form a group consciousness, an ideology, or the values that could motivate them to determined action. If pensioners could be forced into one another's company to the extent that students are, their political impact could be considerable. As a corollary, if it is really desired to end all political activity by students, it is necessary only to educate them in the isolation of their homes by television and printed literature. In isolation, no motivation is possible.

Just as the sub-groups of a society are specialized for knowledge and skills, so too are they specialized for values and attitudes. Trades groups have specialized values of respect for skill; the military possess emotive-mechanisms associated with discipline and respect for rank; businessmen have the particular twentieth century version of the Protestant ethic. These values are not only specialized within the group; they become intensified by interaction with the group. Business "brain storming" meetings, as one instance, exist ostensibly to produce new ideas and policies. In fact, they function as a motivating group, and intensify emotional attachments relating to the corporation, the new product, the new sales target. Usually the emotional display is provided by the leader, is picked up and magnified by the group in the course of free-floating discussion. The popularity of T-groups in business, applauded by management eager to adopt the latest and most fashionable departures, and condemned by a number of psychiatrists, is a classic example of the use of groups for motivation.

A similar process occurs in some closed religious sects. Wesley originally organized the Methodist Church as closed worship groups anticipating the closed therapy group of the twentieth century and Alcoholics Anonymous. Intuitively he realized that social structure as well as ideological content was fundamental to the survival of a religion. But once Methodism became an established religion it abandoned the structure that had been its strength. The Christian Church could be revived tomorrow if it abandoned its present dreary penchant for once a week lecturing from the pulpit, and organized itself on the basis of free-floating emotively interacting groups with a religious bent and of a size approximating therapy groups.

The role of groups in motivation goes beyond religion, work, and study. Almost every activity engaged in with any regularity is associated with some form of motivating group. A man who may play squash, or sail, or play chess infrequently will do so regularly in a group setting. The discussions before and after matches, as well as the excitement of competition, provide higher levels of motivation than would otherwise exist. Within the group emotive links are intensified, greater emotional excitement is generated, and higher levels of motivation are established.

9

MOTIVATIONAL MILIEUX

The group of people or area of society from which a person derives his values constitutes a motivational milieu. In tribal society the tribe itself acts as the motivational milieu, providing the reservoir of values and the machinery to pass on those values. In civilization, an individual is exposed to a number of often competing motivational milieux: the family, the work group, study group, and worship group. Generally, one will predominate at any time and be seen as the group to which the person owes his primary allegiance.

The family is the first motivational milieu that most people encounter, and it is here that the basic values of society, together with essential information, are imparted. The motivating relationship is a vertical one; the adults pass their values down to the children. There is virtually no responding upward movement of conditioning, and little of information. The effectiveness of the family as a conditioning unit depends to a great extent on the amount of time that members spend in the family setting, on the size of the family, and on the respect shown to the family institution by society. In the early stages of Roman history, as in nineteenth century European countries, the sense of family remained particularly strong. Members located much of their activity in the family setting; eating, worshipping, studying, and finding recreation. These communal activities allowed ample time for emotional interaction and the formation of strong values.

Moreover, a large family, of the order of six members upwards, provides a more effective motivational milieu than a small family. Societies where family life is highly regarded, as for example in Catholic and expatriate Chinese communities, are generally characterized by large families. There is a cause-effect interaction between family size and the values that are held. Other factors obviously come into the picture, but as a rule a large family tends to be more effective in imparting values, and incidentally in generating values directed towards family life. That is, it represents a more effective conditioning unit than a small family. In contrast, where families are small, or where for social reasons the members spend little time in each other's company, or where the family is not particularly highly regarded by the society, individuals tend to find their motivational relationships within their peer group. Examples are Samoan society, some cultures of ancient Greece, and increasingly, Western society. The vertical motivational relationships of the family give way to horizontal motivational relationships with the peer group, allowing a two-way flow of values and information.

Vertical motivational relationships characterize cultures with intensely internalized values—in other words, those that are inner-directed. Because they are strongly internalized, such motivational patterns are most usual in static societies, or societies under military and economic stress, where high levels of motivation are necessary. Highly competitive societies are usually inner-directed, generally through the medium of the family. Horizontal motivational relationships characterize cultures that are more co-operative than competitive, and where the sense of siege, whether due to economic factors or to hostile neighbours, is less acute. Since the values are not so rigidly internalized and at times are scarcely internalized at all, a culture of this type enjoys greater possibilities of change. Conversely, it may be less able to handle external aggression because the level of motivation is lower. The widely discussed generation gap is largely the result of the change from vertical to horizontal motivational relationships that has taken place over the past thirty years. Parents possess, in general, strongly internalized values, often associated with religious beliefs. The values of their children are group acquired, less dogmatically held, and more adaptable to group mores. Conflict between the old and the young generation is inevitable. Not only is there a bigotry-mechanism clash between the content of values, but the modes of transmission are also at variance.

While Western society has for a long time shown a high regard for the family institution, this attitude is changing. Religious leaders and those concerned with the moral health of society argue that the decay of the family imperils the culture, an assumption that reflects their values rather than being based on any empirical evidence. Most of the functions of the family are being passed to social instrumentalities, and as an institution the family is of declining importance. Indeed, the restoration of the family to the position it held in the nineteenth century could well endanger the West. Emotive-mechanisms associated with strong family life are in effect values for conservatism; a strong family life leads to firmly internalized, and hence inflexible values. As a result, societies that continue with the same values for long periods generally display a high regard for the family and family life. This may be good, but it may limit the possibility of adaptation to new circumstances. Significantly, religious groups that have most to gain by conservation of values tend to be most adamant about the need for a strong family life. It is a matter of record that many cultures do survive with only the most nominal family life and family contact.

Beyond the family there exists a number of motivational milieux associated with particular activities, particular emotional types, and cultural and racial groups. These milieux range in size from the small work group through large religious and political organizations to the largest and generally least effective milieu, the nation state. Milieux associated with occupation have already been mentioned. They include businessmen's associations, student groups, trade unions, professional associations, and military units.

An instance of milieux associated with emotional types is the homosexual sub-culture. Groups involved in this culture form through the operation of bigotry-mechanism, and both specialize and intensify homosexual values. Since these groups generally feel themselves—and indeed are—persecuted, particularly strong group ties can result, the group providing emotional support for those who cannot adapt to conventional society.

Another socially rejected group, the criminal, is also associated with a specific motivational milieux. Almost all criminals are members of specific criminal groups, ranging from gangs of Western delinquents or Chinese-Malay secret societies to the organized families of the Mafia. These groups act as motivational milieux, conserving, intensifying, and transmitting the values associated with criminal activity. Within the criminal sub-culture a value-reversal phenomenon takes place: things associated with approbation in normal society, such as the police, law, and respect for property, are linked with denigration and contempt; things usually condemned, violence, fraud, and criminal cunning, are linked with approbation. Criminals rarely see themselves as perpetrating evil; they simply exist within a milieu that reverses the values of normal society. A particularly well-organized crime is a "good" crime, an act that aids the police is a "bad" act. Similar value reversals are found among extremist political groups and militant racial minorities. Rarely do extremists see their anti-social behaviour as evil; their milieu simply changes the emotional connections of such acts as sabotage, terrorism, and killing. Clearly, behaviour originating in these values can only occur when a group has been formed to provide emotional support for its members, and when the group has evolved an ideology or group consciousness capable of sustaining activity.

Other examples of milieux with values foreign to the bulk of society are beatnik, hippie, and avant-garde sub-societies. The counter-culture, in its ideal, contains values such as non-competitiveness, non-acquisitiveness, sexual liberalism, and permissiveness towards drugs. It is rarely realized that this sub-culture, both in its values and in its trappings, turns to Asian society rather than to the West for inspiration. Superficial aspects such as the wearing of blankets, chunky jewellery, body painting, and smoking through the fist, are endemic to India and to a lesser extent the Middle East. Marijuana has long been widely available in the New World, but hashish and chillums are relatively new. Sexual liberalism has developed dramatically in the West over the past fifty years, but group and experimental sex emerged under the influence of Hindu eroticism rather than Lawrence and Freud, despite the present Indian reaction into prudery. Sex-orientated pop groups look to the temples of Konarak and Khajuraho rather than to the sentimentalized eternal love of the crooners. The rejection of material possessions, of the pursuit of status, and of rationalism-empiricism, together with a return to mysticism and the revival of interest in the supernatural—the new Aquarian Age—all draw on Eastern culture. None would have developed without the example of the Indian peasant, the Hindu *sadhu*, and the Buddhist monk. Hippies are neither the first symptom of social decay, as the pessimists prefer to think, nor simply the spoilt offspring of affluence. They are contagious carriers of cultural shock, importing Eastern values into Western society.

All social deviant groups, homosexual, criminal, and hippie, arouse strong reactions of hostility within conventional society. In the case of criminal groups this is rationalized as fear for personal safety and property; in the case of homosexuals it is manifested as disgust and a contempt for weakness. Hippies arouse a more ambivalent, and somewhat voyeuristic reaction, but are still considered a threat to conventional society. There is an assumption that they owe it to the world not only to produce but also to consume their fair share, and that by failing to do so they represent an economic menace. These rationalizations, while containing some truth, are manifestations of bigotry-mechanism; criminals, homosexuals, and political extremists sin by possessing values substantially different from those of the economically directed middle class. Not infrequently, the hostility they arouse is accentuated by suspicions that their values may be more successful than those of the majority.

Motivational milieux, whether associated with economic role or personality type, act to internalize and intensify values, and persist for considerable periods. In addition, there exist transient milieux associated with reflective behaviour. Examples are panicked or hysterical crowds, political rallies, revivalist meetings, and sports gatherings. A crowd acts in effect as an emotional amplifier. The emotive displays exhibited by the leaders are accepted by the more responsive members of the gathering and retransmitted until virtually the whole assembly displays the same emotional response.

The earliest and most basic motivational milieu is the tribal group. This milieu is associated with racial group or subgroup, a fact that limits its expansion to natural population growth. Over most of the world the tribal group and tribal alliance have been superseded by the nation state, a motivational milieu associated with territory rather than race, and characterized by considerable variation in ethnic make-up. The most highly developed motivational milieux are completely ideological; they are associated neither with a particular racial group, as is the tribe, nor with a particular territory, and possess, at least in theory, a universal appeal. Examples are Buddhism, Islam, Christianity, and Communism, or more strictly the institutions, churches, and parties that husband and promulgate these doctrines. At times an overlapping of two types of milieux can occur. Much of the present friction in Africa reflects the fact that competing European powers divided the country into political territories which bore no relation to tribal distribution. Most Africans still see their first allegiance as with the tribe, and are largely unaware of, or uninterested in, political boundaries. Often one tribe will be distributed over a number of political territories, while traditional enemies are yoked together in hurriedly assembled nations. Motivational milieux fail to correspond with the political units created to represent people, with the result that civil wars, secessional movements, and insurrections are common. In Europe, by contrast, there has been a continual conflict between the demands of the nation states and of ideological milieux. Universal Catholicism fragmented into national milieux at the time of the Reformation, while at the beginning of the First World War a clash of loyalties arose between the supposedly international socialist movement and the nation states. The states proved triumphant.

Not only do clashes take place between milieux at the same level and between different levels of milieux, but quite often a milieu transformation takes place as the result of such a clash. The tribes of ancient Italy coalesced into a national, and eventually a super-national, milieu as a result of warfare. This nation state, coming into collision with the older civilizations of the East, gave rise to an ideological milieu—the Christian Church. What appears from one point of view as social disintegration and the beginning of the Dark Ages can also be seen as a movement to a higher level, and more general, motivational milieu. Two tendencies coexist at present in

Western civilization: for nation state milieux to break down into retribalized groups—student activists, black power supporters, criminal groups, right-wing supporters, military groups, and business pressure groups—and for a new high-order ideological milieu with a liberal-humanist-new-left orientation to emerge, capable of eventually absorbing the nation states. Paradoxically, both movements are taking place simultaneously.

One further possibility can be mentioned in the discussion of motivational milieux. This is the parallel operation of motivational milieux of different levels. An instance is the state of Israel, which is influenced by a tribal milieu (the Jewish race), a national territorial milieu (the state of Israel), and an ideological milieu (Judaism). Similar combinations of milieux are also found in states that draw strongly on a religion for support—for example, Thailand and to a lesser extent the USA, Spain, and Italy. The Nazi party under Hitler anticipated the triple milieu of Israel by combining a mythical tribalizing, the Aryan people, with a territorial milieu, the Fatherland mystique, and the ideology of National Socialism. In consequence the Nazis could hardly fail to be hostile to the Jews; the closer the structure of motivating machinery, as distinct from content, the greater the scope for bigotry-mechanism to operate. In this case both structure and content were in competition.

10
INSTITUTIONAL MILIEUX

The motivational milieux described in the previous chapter are generally of an informal nature, often coming into existence almost incidentally to provide motivation or emotional support for the individuals involved. They stand in contrast to the institutionalized milieux evolved by modern societies, which conserve and transmit values within a formal setting. Typical examples are the educational systems of contemporary societies, religious institutions and, paradoxically, prison systems. It is worth comparing and contrasting these in detail to understand how, in fact, motivation is transmitted in contemporary society.

While the avowed purpose of schools is to pass on knowledge, their true function lies in transmitting emotive-mechanisms. Schools set up values of respect for knowledge, punctuality, and authority, for the regularity and specialization that industrial society requires. In school a child is trained to accept trivialization and boredom, to allocate particular periods for particular purposes such as study, recreation, and eating, and to defer immediate satisfaction. Exams, rewards, and punishments are the means by which this is accomplished. Without such conditioning and value assimilation a child would find it impossible to fit into the Procrustean routine of eight hours spent at the same office desk or factory bench, doing work that is at best intellectually degrading, and at worst so stultifying that it damages the personality.

As an example of what happens when such values have not been established, Australian Aborigines in the Northern Territory tend to work only one or two days a week to earn sufficient money to meet immediate needs. They have not been conditioned to regularity and time partitioning. In the same way American automobile firms hiring unemployed workers from depressed areas have noted that the major problem lies not in job training, but in motivating people to regular attendance. Unsophisticated people tend to work when they need money, and to eat only when hungry; the concept of leisure time, the few brief hours when a person is free to enjoy himself, is a product of the way the West first conceptualizes, and then compartmentalizes, time.

Other teaching institutions function in much the same way, passing on values appropriate to their membership. Apprenticeship schools, which usually take four years to teach skills that could be learnt in one, ideally develop values relating to pride in work, manual dexterity, and again, respect for authority and punctuality. Military colleges pass on values appropriate to military life involving discipline, patriotism, and a regard for weaponry. Universities inculcate values associated with knowledge as a good in itself, freedom of expression and liberalism. While these sound refreshingly enlightened, they represent no more than the conditions under which a university community can survive. Where there is censorship, or indifference to the value of knowledge, a university cannot operate.

Religious institutions are, *par excellence*, examples of institutionalized milieux. Whether represented by the Buddhist *Sangha*, by Catholic monastic orders, or by Protestant church schools, these institutions exist to pass on both the information and the values of their particular creed. This connection between formal education and the implanting of religious values is the reason education is so central to many religions, for example Roman Catholicism and Thai Buddhism. The greatest threat facing Catholicism is the breakdown of its school system under economic pressure; if the Church can no longer establish appropriate emotive-mechanisms among the young, it will in time follow Protestantism into decline and fossilization.

Paradoxically, one of the most effective institutions for passing on specialized values is the prison system. A prison inmate experiences much the same conditions as a political prisoner exposed to the most intense brainwashing. He is in a completely closed society, exposed to violence from warders and other prisoners, in a state of intense apprehension, fear, and guilt, and often subject to sexual assault. He is constantly exposed to criminal emotive-mechanisms: hatred of authority, contempt for law, admiration for violence, and a respect for criminal skill. His socialization, and hence to a large degree his survival, depends on his internalizing these values. It would be difficult, even with the greatest ingenuity, to arrange a more effective means of transmitting and intensifying criminal values. Indeed, a developed criminal sub-culture only appears where there is an established prison system. Primitive societies which punish crimes immediately, even by extreme measures such as maiming and ostracism, do not generate criminal sub-cultures, and in a sense are more merciful than the West. By returning social offenders as quickly as possible to the normal motivating field, they prevent such a sub-culture from emerging.

The case of prisoners of war is quite different to that of civil prisoners, for POWs take the motivating milieu of rank and seniority with them in their imprisonment. This provides emotional support and preserves the values that they embraced before capture. Any change in their values would necessitate their removal from this motivating milieu, and exposure to other sets of values within a stress situation.

These three motivational milieux share a number of characteristics. In all cases, to a greater or lesser extent, the individual is isolated and exposed to a degree of emotional tension, fear, or excitement. In all cases particular values or emotive-mechanisms are transmitted, often under the guise of imparting information. And in all cases the institutions depend for their survival on being able to conserve and transmit these particular emotive-mechanisms or values.

Another more subtle institutional milieu is the communications media. This acts to pass on social values, particularly those values that make the consumer society possible. Most advertising on television and in the cinema is currently reactive advertising: it no longer simply shows a new brand of cigarettes, the new season's car, a new detergent, or a better after-shave lotion; it also shows a positive human emotional response to these products—delight, surprise, satisfaction, and joy.

Intuitively, the advertising industry has discovered the importance of emotive-mechanisms. People do not react to objects, they react to emotional responses to those objects. There is no point in telling people that a soft drink is good for them, or in explaining the technical advances of next autumn's V8s. Reactive advertising, by linking displays of good emotion to the particular product, establishes it as good. Reason and explanation only distract from this end.

The same mechanism is involved in the problem of violence on the media. No degree of violence, no matter how displayed, will induce an audience to adopt values of violence. What does influence them is the emotional responses displayed towards violence by those involved in it. It is well known that television audiences do not concentrate on the dramatic action; what they do watch is the faces, and the emotional responses of the participants. Usually the reaction shown is one of the greatest approbation and approval, particularly when the villain is being beaten to a pulp or shot to pieces. This approval attaches the most moral emotional connections to violence. As ever, the reaction is not to objects but to reactions. Everything in the world is morally neutral initially; it is only when people display emotions in a particular regard that things become good or bad, desirable or undesirable.

The media administrators cannot have their argument both ways. The cigarette companies, the detergent companies, the motor manufacturers, the soft drink producers, the furniture manufacturers, the cosmetic concerns, the electrical goods manufacturers, the entertainment industry, and the food retailers spend literally billions of dollars a year on advertising, and it is reasonable to assume that this advertising is effective. The history of Coca-Cola, which owes its position to advertising on a massive scale, illustrates this. Consumer goods organizations run on too narrow a profit margin to waste money on ineffective advertising. If reactive advertising is effective when applied to consumer goods, then precisely the same mechanisms associated with violence will render violence as desirable as any consumer product.

Just as individuals disguise their own motives from themselves by rationalization, so too do societies. Pareto, who suggested just this, raised a storm of acrimony and abuse hardly rivalled until Freud published his essays on sexuality. The parallel is appropriate. For, just as many individuals could not survive if they were aware of their genuine motives, so too societies would be in profound difficulties should they ever be forced to admit the emotivist, as against the rationalist, view of society.

As regards the education system, and to a lesser extent the institutionalized religions, individuals will be less willing to submit to them when they are seen as conditioning institutions. Moreover, rationalism and the attitude that more information is equivalent to better education are themselves leading to the decay of educational institutions.

Despite the importance of its emotive content, most educationists persist in seeing education purely as an information imparting process; good education is held to be education that imparts more information more rapidly at a minimum cost. This perversity is leading to greater emphasis on computer teaching, programmed instruction, and the use of teaching machines in preference to face-to-face instruction. It will be interesting to see how many values and attitudes these plastic, fantastic lovers can impart, and what sort of emotionally desiccated student results.

As regards the prison system, the emotivist approach raises the whole problem of criminal responsibility. The question is, to what extent is society justified in punishing a person for holding criminal emotive-mechanisms when he has been placed in a situation where internalizing such values is almost inevitable? And if an offender has never been conditioned not to steal or to kill, in other words if his socializing has been defective, is it just to punish him for society's oversight? To some extent he is in a position analogous to that of an illiterate who has never had the chance to study, and is punished for his illiteracy. Indeed, it is for just this reason that society insists on rationality as the source of most criminal activity. If rationality alone motivates activity, a person can be held fully culpable for his actions; the crime is a result of an intellectual choice. But if emotional patterns are responsible for a crime, then the entire society is guilty, for it is the fault of the society that an offender was not appropriately conditioned in the first place, and it is even more society's fault should he become conditioned as a criminal during imprisonment.

The same is true of every aspect of public morality, of good and evil. Every person is to a degree responsible for every crime committed in his society, for he forms part of its value reservoir. It is not possible to prevent crime by adding contingents of police, new prisons, more efficient crime-detection techniques, and new psychiatric wards; this is to seek technological solutions to sociological problems. It is only through each person, in some way as yet unexplained and possibly unexplainable, modifying his own emotive-mechanisms that change can be bought about.

11
IMPLICATIONS FOR THE INDIVIDUAL

For the individual the motivating relationships inherent in the society serve a dual function. They provide the motivation for him to act, and they provide a psychological sense of meaning and purpose in life. Human beings display a deep-seated need for some point or sense of purpose in life. It is only too easy to be aware of the absolute, utter, and blinding futility of life examined intellectually: I work in order to make money in order to eat in order to stay alive in order to work in order to make money in order to eat in order to stay alive. Such an existence seems not only agonizing in its futility but mocks on reflection whatever aspirations a person may have. To everyone at some stage comes the realization that everything is meaningless, pointless, and absurd, that beneath the apparent solidity of everyday life and the thousand distractions invoked to make existence tolerable, there is finally and irrevocably the abyss: *habis*, end, darkness, the void, and unendurable unintelligible futility.

People have sought meaning in life in much the spirit that knights of old pursued the holy grail; they have sought it as a single entity, hoping that somewhere will be found this one thing—Purpose-in-Life—and that if they can only locate it, existence will become meaningful and tolerable. Unfortunately, as Julian Huxley has argued, purposes in life are made, not found. One cannot imagine what sort of thing a purpose in life could be, or how one would go about seeking it. Wealth, power, and prestige were rejected by the Greek philosophers two thousand years ago, largely on the grounds of their transience. Spiritual development and union with the divine ground have little appeal in a secular age. And were the purpose of life ever found, it would result in an infinite regress, involving questions of the purpose in life of the purpose of life.

There is not, neither can there ever be, a rationally apprehended single purpose in life. People cannot expect the universe to underwrite them, or to incorporate a purpose of some kind in its metaphysical structure. The sense of purpose in life people seek is emotional rather than rational; failure to find a purpose in life by means of reason reflects only the limits of what rationality can achieve. A person who claims that life lacks meaning, point, and purpose is actually declaring that he is unmotivated and lacks a sense of direction. This motivation comes largely, but by no means entirely, from motivational relationships. Where these do not exist, a person can have little impetus to act in any way, a lack of direction that is experienced as futility, anomie, alienation, and existential despair.

Failure to develop motivational relationships can occur in two ways. Some people appear to possess personality flaws that prevent them from internalizing values. Autistic children and psychopaths are the extreme cases, but there are others, like Camus's Outsider, who are simply unwilling to internalize social values, while living an apparently satisfying life. A larger group are those who could internalize social values but have never had the opportunity to do so. Orphans, children from disturbed backgrounds, and children who have never been exposed to strong or, more important, consistent displays of emotion are deprived in the sense that a person suffering malnutrition is deprived. Children denied affection never become capable of displays of affection, a particular case of emotional, and hence motivational, deprivation. The conventional wisdom now accepted is that children require lavish displays of love if they are to develop into well-adjusted adults, but they also require displays of anger, hatred, disgust, reverence, and desire. Moreover, it is essential that reasonable consistency be shown in the objects of these emotions if children are to be socialized.

People who lack motivation and a sense of purpose can remedy this by moving into a milieu where strong emotive-mechanisms exist, and absorbing them from the peer group. In so doing they illustrate the paradox of freedom. As long as they have no emotive-mechanisms of any intensity, they lack the motivation to do anything beyond maintaining themselves; they are free, but cannot act. Once strong values are developed they become capable of action, but their actions are to a large extent determined by the values of the group. These emotive-mechanisms give life meaning and lead to activity, but the activity is the individual's only to the extent that he chooses the milieu. He can act, but he is free in no absolute sense. Sartre has illustrated this paradox particularly well in his *Roads to Freedom* novels. A character who appears most free and uninvolved is in fact not free at all; he lacks the emotional impetus that could move him and give him a sense of purpose. Sartre's solution to the sense of pointlessness in life is for individuals to choose a project and to seek self-affirmation through it, but in general it is necessary to choose a milieu and seek self-affirmation through the emotive-mechanisms derived from the milieu. One can only have identity and sense of self by going beyond self.

Failure to develop a strong value system lies at the root of a great many cases of mental illness. Suicides are perhaps the most extreme and certainly the most dramatic examples of motivational failure, but drug addicts, alcoholics, and many depressives are in fact the result of a failure to develop, or to sustain, motivational relationships. Jung has commented that most cases of mental disorder reflect ultimately the need for a spiritual basis in life, but all statements with spiritual content reduce finally to statements about the emotions. The human need is more for something to believe in, some worthwhile pursuit in life, rather than for spirituality in the supernatural sense.

People lacking the emotive-mechanisms which could give their life meaning react in a number of ways. The most usual is to fall back on primary drive motivation, and to seek a sense of purpose in such basic pursuits as food and sex. The hoodlums and Casanovas who pursue sexual conquests on a score card basis and the gourmand who devotes his time to trying new, exotic, and tantalizing food are all acting on the basis of primary drive motivation. In a sense they have no alternative. The higher level and more complex socially determined pursuits are closed to them.

However, once people begin to seek primary drive satisfaction a curious thing happens. They tend to find themselves in the company of people of like interests, and again the similarity in emotional patterns leads to group formation. The gourmands compare this and that particular cheese, wine, or bread; the rockers and hoodlums compare sexual exploits, discuss the reactions of various women, and compete to "score" as the vernacular expresses it. Slowly the primary drive reactions are reflected within the group, and converted into secondary drives. People rarely eat and drink because of pressing needs, they do so from social considerations, or because it is the accepted time to do so, or because they are bored. Convention rather than hunger governs eating, to the extent that people are pleasantly surprised if they find themselves hungry at meal times.

Much the same is true of sexual needs. Despite the writings of Freud, and the elevation of sexual drives to the level of hunger and thirst, sexual behaviour is largely secondary drive motivated. Normal people can, and do, go for years without having sexual intercourse and exhibit no ill effects. Patterns of sexual behaviour show such marked cultural variation that it is impossible to accept them as innate; the fiction of the lusting beast within is simply a self-gratifying fantasy of post-Freudian thought. Given a group preoccupied to a greater or less extent with sex, an eventual intensifying and specialization of sex pursuit values takes place. The result may range from incidental promiscuity to gang rape. Individuals who would never do more than phantasize about sex individually can be motivated to almost any excess in a sex pursuit group. The point is that such preoccupied pursuit of sex takes place only in a value vacuum. It is a least common denominator of action and, objectionable as most people find it, is the consequence of failed social conditioning rather than specific malice.

A more extreme instance of primary drive refugee is the hard drug addict or alcoholic. A physiological need which simply cannot be ignored is set up, providing the addict with his sense of meaning and purpose in life, no matter how perverse this purpose may seem to outsiders. The addict devotes himself entirely to obtaining, using, enjoying, and discussing drugs. Everything else becomes unimportant. The dulling of sensitivity and the temporary euphoria are obvious factors in drug use, but are much less important than the motivation which results. T. S. Eliot once commented that in some ways it is better to do evil than to do nothing at all—at least one exists. The addict and the alcoholic do, for a time at least, exist. Anything is preferable to the anguish of utter meaninglessness.

This explains why group therapy as used by Alcoholics Anonymous and Synanon is reasonably effective in the treatment of addiction. In the intense emotional field of the group, strong emotive-mechanisms directed against drugs and drinking can be established. More constructively, other values of greater social utility can be instilled, allowing members to find the sense of purpose in life that they previously lacked, and motivating them to less destructive behaviour. In contrast to psychotherapy groups, such groups show a decidedly authoritarian bias, making the internalization of new values more probable than would be the case in a non-directional group. Psychotherapy groups are traditionally non-authoritarian and encourage members to look within themselves to find the basis of their problems. While valuable for many types of disturbances, this approach is worse than useless for people whose problem is basically an absence of emotive-mechanisms. The last thing such people wish is to be forced to look deeply within themselves, for they know there is nothing there. To be forced to contemplate a vacuum is unendurable.

A curious reversal of the use of hard drugs occurs among those who use hallucinogens, for it appears that these drugs, in particular LSD, have the capacity to break down emotive-mechanisms. This is seen in the rebirth ethic of the hippies and similar groups, who use drugs to gain liberation from the social games of society, and to achieve freedom to develop their own values and life-style. While the heavy drug users lack emotive connections and turn to hard drugs to give themselves some sense of purpose in life, the soft drug users intentionally break down their emotive-mechanisms by the use of hallucinogens and set out to establish new value systems. Hippies are a classic example of retribalization, and generally the group proves capable of providing new values, motivation, and a sense of purpose for its members. But the use of amphetamines—"starters"—and other stimulants to provide non-directional motivation indicates that these values are not always strong enough to ensure emotional satisfaction. The use of drugs to eliminate emotive-mechanisms and then to promote activity is an interesting alternative to value motivation. But it seems unlikely that society will move in this direction or even that it ever could. There is no possibility of value continuity, and continuity is essential for a viable society.

There is a fundamental clash between primary drive factors such as sex and drugs, and secondary drive values. The arguments of those who claim that society can survive with more liberal sexual mores, or that drug laws are totalitarian and pathological, miss this point. Western society has developed strong inhibitions in these areas because it senses that both sex and drugs are socially, rather than individually, dangerous. They compete with existing value schemes. Sexual feelings and drug involvement, by their connection with the primary drive levels of personality, are capable of edging out the more precariously held emotive-mechanisms; they constitute in effect a competing value system and so arouse bigotry-mechanism reactions. Moreover, a person who finds most of his satisfaction in sexual relationships rather than in consumer goods, or in marijuana fantasies rather than television fantasies, threatens the economic order. Interesting as the European experiments in sexual liberalism and the abolition of censorship are, they remain no more than this—social experiments. The interactions between society and the individual are both subtle and complex, and there is no way of predicting what long-term effects this liberalizing may have. The majority of cultures maintain strong controls on sexual expression in particular, and these must be assumed to have social utility. It is no coincidence that periods of rapid economic advance, for example in nineteenth century Britain and contemporary Russia, have also been periods of sexual repression and puritanism. Presumably the damming of sexual emotions provides the energy needed for economic development. At some stage a balance must be struck between the level of economic activity that a society needs, and the sexual freedom that it wants.

A further point regarding sexual relations and motivation:

many people quite legitimately derive much of their sense of meaning in life from emotional involvement with a lover. Russell has commented that sex is one of the most important elements taking people outside themselves, and a host of popular songs subscribe to the sentiment that a love relationship alone makes life meaningful. A love relationship can be seen as a particular group situation in which two people possess the same feelings; both share a high regard for the same two people. Positive bigotry-mechanism—the response to shared emotional attachments—binds the relationship to a degree that affection and even intense sexuality could not achieve.

In addition to primary drive and emotive-mechanism motivation, there remains one other source of activity—ego involvement as characterized by self-attaching mechanisms and the response to competition. Ego-involved motivation provides not only activity but also a sense of purpose in life. A person who embarks on an activity that does not particularly interest him often becomes more and more involved with the activity as it progresses; tension associated with the task itself provides motivation. These activities range from the most trivial—the compulsive pursuit of a mosquito—to artistic creation. Most of the routine tasks of life—housekeeping, office and factory work—fall in this category. People frequently begin a project showing little interest and become progressively more involved as it proceeds, particularly if they are in a group that can reinforce attitudes relating to the particular activity.

Competition in a field can give point to an otherwise meaningless activity. Rationally, there is nothing so pointless as sailing back and forth over the same stretch of water, tacking, reaching and running, setting spinnaker, and going about. Yet for a person sailing in a race these activities are not pointless; every movement, every tack acquires significance. Much the same response can be seen in suburban life. Many of the activities are completely meaningless, but competition with neighbour and peer gives buying the new season's car, improving the garden, and acquiring a colour television set considerable point. The same is true of status acquired through job seniority and income; the significance of these pursuits lies in their being viewed in competition with the achievements of others. If nobody showed the slightest interest in buying the current Buick or in promotion to Assistant Managing Director (Marketing), these activities would lose much of their point. It is no coincidence that competitiveness has increased with the loss of a spiritual value in work. Medieval European society exhibited far greater co-operativeness than is the case today. In that age it was still possible for a tradesman to offer up his work and skills to the glory of God, as something inherently valuable in themselves, rather than as something that simply commanded an economic return. This changed as European society came under the influence of industrialism. Urbanization and the sudden increase in population associated with the Industrial Revolution led to increasing economic competition, and this, rather than religious values, came to provide a sense of purpose in work.

Despite its considerable dynamic, or perhaps even because of it, twentieth century urban and suburban society has developed into one of the most demotivated in history. In part this is due to the relative isolation most people endure; the hermetic families in the suburbs, the countless occupants of London bed-sitters and New York single-room flats, the old-age pensioners too poor or too ill to maintain social contact. To prevent motivation it is only necessary to isolate people and prevent group formation. This happens spontaneously, unplanned and almost inevitably, in a suburban setting. Moreoever, motivation and action are almost always separated by one, and at times two or three, intermediate steps. Primitive man hunted or harvested both because these activities provided directly for his needs and because he possessed appropriate emotive-mechanisms. Civilized man works to get money in order to satisfy the emotional wants instilled by advertising, but fundamentally he is suspicious of advertising, aware that he is being manipulated for the benefit of large corporations, and that advertising claims are to a great extent nonsense. No such cynicism interrupts the primitive's motivation.

This failure of motivation shows up not so much among adults as among the young who sense that they have been in some way cheated. It can be seen among the hoodlums of run-down working-class suburbs indulging in vandalism and crime; among the allegedly spoilt children of the well-to-do, who seek excitement through drugs, alcohol, sex, and libertinism; among radical students who resolve their demotivation by retribalizing with ideologies their parents find anathema. While these activities arouse self-righteous anger, they represent little more than a reaction against a life experienced as pointless because it is unmotivated.

In the discussion of happiness it was suggested that happiness derives from three areas of experience—creative activity, affectionate relationships, and sense usage—and that this schema represents a polar organization of human experience, possibly the most useful for investigating the individual's relationship to his world. The area closest to a person is represented by creative activity, that is, by ego-involved behaviour. The next circle represents affectionate relationships, while the last is associated with sense usage. The same polar arrangement of categories is useful in considering motivation. The ego-involved forms of motivation—self-attaching mechanisms and the spur of competition—represent the most immediate and in some ways the most personal area of motivation. If they have not been discussed at length, it is not because they are unimportant, but rather that there is little to be said about them. Affectionate relationships, the second source of happiness, are intimately bound up with emotive-mechanism motivation and values. A person incapable of responding to emotion or of fitting into a primary group of some description can never show any degree of secondary drive behaviour. The importance of this source of motivation compared with others is that it alone makes societies possible.

The third source of happiness, sense usage, is associated with primary drive motivation. Hunger, thirst, and the avoidance of discomfort all impinge through the senses. But while sense usage is an important source of happiness, primary drive motivation is of little significance in a civilized setting, for most of its functions have been assumed by the more flexible secondary drives. The importance of happiness itself—the pursuit of happiness—as a source of motivation remains far from being clear; the general belief is that it is all-important, while here it has been considered as insignificant compared to other sources of motivation.

Emotive links can be established in three ways. They may develop from personal experience, as in the case of fear of fire;

they may reflect the responses of others, as occurs in a crowd in panic; or they may be internalized as socially trained attitudes and values. In this multiplicity of sources lies the origin of emotional conflict.

For a person to experience a sense of conflict, at least two sets of emotive links must be operating simultaneously; it is possible for present experience to conflict with socially imparted values, as for example when sex is found to be not disgusting but enjoyable. It is also possible for experiential values to clash with reflective responses, as when a person rejects the reactions of a crowd on the basis of his own past experience; and for internalized values to clash with reflective reactions—cases usually considered as issues of conscience. However, it appears impossible for responses of similar source to clash. The most recent experience is generally the one that predominates, and if fire was found tomorrow to give pleasure, this would be accepted. Reflective values are strictly transient, so that no possibility of a clash exists. Deeply internalized values may just be able to clash with other internalized values, but eventually, as with brainwashed prisoners returned to their own society, one set of values decays in favour of another.

12

IMPLICATIONS FOR SOCIETY

If the establishment of values is important for the individual it is absolutely vital for the survival of a society. At the worst, individuals can find motivation in primary drives and ego involvement, although they will be the poorer for the lack of socially acquired activities. But the survival of a society depends absolutely on its members being motivated in quite specific patterns of behaviour. It is usually assumed that the industrial state, and indeed every society, operates on a combination of enlightened self-interest and inertia, but this is hardly the case; the existence of internalized values alone ensures a society's continuation. Moreover, it is these values or emotive-mechanisms that give each society its distinct character. The material assets and equipment that a society possesses, the works of art and the social institutions, even the basic economic organization, are little more than manifestations of social values. The pyramids, cloisters, coliseums, cathedrals, and city walls; the temples, harbours, bridges, factories, memorials, cenotaphs, cemeteries, canals, power stations, and shrines—these represent the enduring expression of emotional values, much as a coral reef represents the permanent excrescence of long-decayed polyps. The richness and diversity of a culture depends in the last analysis on the richness of its social values.

For a society to endure it must be able to transmit its emotive-mechanisms virtually unchanged, just as the survival of a species depends on its being able to transmit its genetic code in a scarcely altered version. Creatures that produced off-spring of a random make-up would become extinct, since all the advantages gained in the course of evolution would immediately be lost. Indeed, it is possible to argue for the existence of a pre-biological selection in which only molecules capable of reproducing themselves unchanged survived to give rise to organic life. In the same way, pre-social evolution produced methods of transmitting social values intact as a prerequisite for social life. A culture that is indifferent to this, and which neglects the task of transmitting its values, will in time disintegrate.

Every example of a civilization in decline is, in part at least, an example of a society no longer able to transmit its value system. And symptoms conventionally taken as indications of decadence can be readily seen as the failure of the society to establish motivation in its members.

The civilization of post-second-century Rome is conveniently taken as a paradigm of social disintegration, being characterized by phenomena appearing in all cases of social breakdown. These are the concentration of economic power, increasing militarism, sexual preoccupation, a decline of the state-linked religion, the growth of esoteric religions, the disaffection of minorities, and an increase in bureaucratic organization.

With the exception of economic centralism, these factors represent sociological changes that are inevitable once a culture loses the capacity to motivate its members. Increasing militarism represents the passing of political power from civilian to military groups, as the military are the one faction whose values, the product of rigid military discipline, remain intact. In the closing stages of Roman civilization the army was responsible for making and breaking successive emperors, different sections of the armed forces even putting forward rival candidates for imperial power.

The larger part of the population, by contrast, lacked the disciplined framework of the army and hence the opportunity to internalize strongly held values. The worship of the family gods of the hearth had previously been complemented by state polytheism, a change representing the shift from tribal to state organization. Initially the values that supported the state were associated with, and transmitted within, this polytheism. With the growth of a slave and foreign national proletariat, military expansion, and a more sophisticated population, the state religion proved incapable of providing emotional support. As a result its adherents turned to more individualistic, world-denying, and emotional creeds within which they could retribalize: Christianity, Mithraism, and the mystery religions. People for whom religion held no attraction turned to primary-drive motivation as a substitute for the lack of secondary social drives, finding distraction in sexual extravagances, gluttony, and the monstrous displays of the circus.

This failure to transmit values involved the existing Latin population less than the new immigrants. Following the establishment of the empire, Rome drew into its society large groups holding values foreign to the traditional Roman values of discipline, authority, religious piety, and self-control. In particular, the barbarians who entered Roman society in its final stages shared no common heritage with Roman citizens and felt no allegiance towards the established institutions. Additionally, as the breakdown of social institutions continued, the thinkers, innovators, and entrepreneurs were alienated, which robbed the society of its creative energy. Because sociological motivation had grown ineffective it became necessary to construct a large, unproductive, and finally inefficient bureaucracy to ensure that the state continued to function.

The parallels with contemporary European society are obvious. In Rome the concentration of economic power proceeded in the first and second centuries as large landholders forced small farmers from their holdings, and as slave-operated factories drove self-employed artisans out of work. In contemporary society, large business organizations, benefiting from the economies of scale, have continued to increase their share of the market at the expense of smaller companies. The five hundred leading corporations of the United States, for example, increased their share of the market from 55 per cent in 1958 to 64 per cent in 1968.

Christianity played the same role in Western European society that classical polytheism played in Rome, providing the transmission equipment for values and emotional support for its members. Like classical polytheism, Christianity has become so involved with the formal institutions of the society that it is no longer able to provide emotional support for individuals. A number of esoteric emotional religions—spiritualism, mysticism, Westernized Buddhism and Hinduism, and the Aquarian creed of the counter-culture—are emerging to replace it. The belief in magic, witchcraft, and every form of superstition is more prevalent among fringe groups now than at any time for a hundred years, an apparently paradoxical situation in an age as technically sophisticated as the twentieth century.

Again, as was the case two thousand years ago, people who cannot find emotional support in more esoteric religions tend to resort to sexual extremes, alcohol, and drugs as a means to make life endurable. The hypersexuality of Western Europe has arisen partly as a result of commercial pressure, partly in response to the scientific work of Freud, Kinsey, and others, and partly in reaction to Victorian puritanism. Europe has experienced successive reactions from puritanism to licence and back to puritanism, but the present preoccupation with sex, pornography, and deviation exceeds in degree and universality anything since the passing of Roman civilization. This sexual preoccupation is less a cause of social disintegration than a sensitive indicator that a value vacuum is forming.

It is useful to draw a distinction between organic and inorganic, or institutional, societies. Organic societies are typified by tribal cultures, where social functions such as the care of old people and of orphans and the decisions about property rights and government are the province of social values. Primitive societies care for the old, the orphaned, and the less fortunate because the societies hold values that protect these people. Highly developed cultures, by contrast, develop institutions such as orphanages, old people's homes, hospitals, and legal systems, so replacing the operation of values with specialized institutions. The welfare state is the prime example of an institutional society in which virtually all specialized functions are delegated to particular instrumentalities. Administrative bureaucracy, characterized by hierarchic centralized control, assumes the role once played by universally held values in controlling and ordering the society.

None of these factors—economic concentration, militarism, changes in religious belief, sexual preoccupation, alienation of minorities, and growing bureaucracy—by themselves need be particularly significant. Considered together they indicate a trend remarkably similar to that existing in the final stage of Roman civilization. A case can be made for this being the declining stage of Western civilization, but, as argued below, there remain major differences between this society and that of Rome, differences sufficient to invalidate whatever conclusions the more pessimistic social thinkers may be tempted to draw.

Yet while predictions of social disintegration may seem a little premature, most of the social changes causing concern in Western culture—the generation gap, the alienation of minority racial and social groups, the emergence of a powerful criminal sub-culture, the loss of respect for law and civil institutions—can be traced to a failure to transmit social values. In contrast to tribal societies, few major civilizations have developed permanently effective machinery for socializing the young while allowing sufficient flexibility for value evolution. Each civilization is the product of innumerable responses to the challenges it meets, responses that involve adopting socially useful values. But civilizations are by their nature in a state of flux. The values that a civilization evolves tend to become maladaptive as the society itself changes, or otherwise to decay once the original challenge has been removed.

This cycle of growth and decay in the history of civilizations may not be entirely regrettable. Macaulay suggested that the barbarian assault on Rome prevented the empire from entering a long period of stagnation such as afflicted Chinese and Egyptian civilizations in their final stages. But the breakdown of a civilization, and the loss of values that follows such a breakdown, may lead to a more barbarous and inharmonious way of life than tribal existence.

History is sociology in time. Just as the behaviour of contemporary societies can best be interpreted in regard to sociological factors, so the history of a society can be understood in these same terms. Moreover, history provides a far more valid check on theories of social dynamics than does comparative sociology, for social interactions take place over long periods and entail long time lags. Sociology can provide only still photographs, as it were, of a society at a particular period; a sociological history is capable of providing data on the long-term interaction of values, the growth and decay of ideologies, and the social utility of values, motivational milieux, and spiritual equipment. Any theory of how societies operate must finally stand or fall on the evidence provided by history.

The type of motivational milieu or set of milieux that a society possesses is closely related to the society's structure. The history of Western society illustrates the changes that take place in the shift from a simple tribal culture to a more complex society. In the case of the tribe, the whole society represents the motivational milieu; in pluralistic industrial society a number of religious and economic milieux coexist or compete within the larger milieu of the state organization. Each milieu is associated with particular types of spiritual equipment such as religious ritual or the state education system, and the transition from one type of equipment to another, for example from religious ceremony to church schools to state schools, signifies a change in milieu, and hence in values.

Motivational milieux are associated with the structure of a society, but it is the values of a society that determine its quality and behaviour. It has been argued that values are capable of evolving to meet changing social conditions, and that successful societies are those that have developed values appropriate to their setting. Historical study of a culture provides information about the type of emotive-mechanisms held at a particular stage, the growth and decay of values, and, most important, the social utility of these values.

In practice, it is difficult to discern exactly what type of values exist in a society at any period and their actual distribution. It often appears that values that have a considerable influence on a society are held only by a select minority such as Roman patricians or nineteenth century British imperialist administrators. The types of values present find expression in literature, religion, political discussions, and the formal history of an age, but an analysis in these terms requires considerable insight. It is difficult to be certain of the values that exist in a contemporary Western country, more difficult, even for a trained anthropologist, to determine the leading values of primitive cultures, and impossible to be certain of the values that underlay past societies. Yet it is these intangible, vague, and indeterminate factors that condition to a great extent every aspect of history.

A society's view of its formalized history is inherently subjective, but this in itself offers advantages in determining the nature of its values. An imperialistic state emphasizes its national conquests, wars, and victories out of all proportion to their actual historical significance; a society based on religion emphasizes events of a religious or spiritual nature; one with an economic outlook tends to emphasize events of an economic nature. All tend to preserve the memory of these events in ceremonies, celebrations, and memorials. The history that members of a society are taught represents an element of spiritual equipment, used to pass on values and attitudes of a particular type. Additionally, the events that a society emphasizes in its history tend to be those that have traumatized the society. Events such as a conquest, a nuclear attack, a potato famine, or a religious reformation produce changes in values rather than immediate changes in the political balance or the economic structure of a culture.

The subjective nature of formal history results from factors over and above its role as spiritual equipment. In examining history, people almost invariably concentrate on aspects that have relevance to the present and ignore elements unique to the age under study. History, even in the most skilled hands, can no more be neutral than the structure of a novel can be neutral. It is always necessary to make some sort of selection among source materials, and this selection generally reflects the interests of the present rather than the views that the society of the time held. Christian historians have combed the records of ancient Rome with diligence in search of references to the life of Christ. Contemporary historians examine the records of the Middle Ages for those trends that were to determine present day society: the new technologies and inventions, the changes in economic organization, the emergence of nation states. These are often aspects that the Middle Ages considered of no importance even when conscious of them. No doubt the aspects of contemporary society now rated important will be ignored by future historians preoccupied by features of the age that we are hardly aware of.

History describes by implication the development and selection of a society's values. These may evolve within a society, but are often imported from other cultures or taken over by subject people under foreign domination. Improved communications have had a considerable effect on the spread of emotive-mechanisms, both within societies and from foreign cultures. Except in times of war, tribes had little tendency to acquire foreign values, because of the natural barriers of geography, language, and the strength of established custom. Modern societies encourage both the physical movement of people—tourism, educational exchange schemes, and immigration—as well as increased verbal communication. Hence every society is increasingly aware of what is happening in other parts of the world and more inclined to borrow values and ideologies that may prove useful. This has resulted in more rapid value selection than ever before.

Another aspect of values that historical study illuminates is their extraordinary persistence. Where the spiritual equipment of a society is well developed, value systems can be transmitted for hundreds of generations without substantial change. This is normal in tribal societies, but also occurs in the more highly developed civilizations. The value system of Judaism became incorporated substantially unchanged into Christianity, and hence into the secular Western tradition. The value system of Hinduism has survived for approximately four thousand years, displaying little change over the latter two thousand years. The value systems that maintained ancient Chinese and Egyptian civilizations endured for over two thousand years.

History provides information on the growth, selection, persistence, and decay of values. More important, it provides data on the social effectiveness of sets of values in particular circumstances, and of the ways in which values serve particular societies. These values influence both the internal adjustments that an equilibrium-society makes and its success in competition and conflict with other societies. A highly motivated society with a strongly held ideology will generally prove superior to less motivated societies, other factors being equal. Indeed, a technically unsophisticated society that is highly motivated will often prevail against a more sophisticated but less motivated society, a fact instanced by Vietnam and in a hundred contemporary guerilla campaigns, revolutionary wars, and secessional movements. The preoccupation with material means in warfare could only occur in a highly technological society. In the same way, only a very materialistic society would conceive of the end of war as the destruction of material plant and equipment, the mentality behind the bombing of Coventry, London, Dresden, and Hiroshima. Wars are conflicts finally between competing value systems, and the end of war is the destruction of value schemes and motivational milieux rather than the destruction of people or things. The destruction of a motivational milieux, such as befell the North American Indians and the Australian Aborigines, is far more final than the destruction of equipment, which can usually be made good in a few generations.

A sociological approach to history provides a framework, not unlike the Marxist economic framework, within which historical events can be understood. The sociological approach, moreover, is far more general than the Marxist, which finds its appropriate application in societies that are economically advanced and which have an organization based primarily on economic functions. All societies are characterized by sociological factors—values, ideology, motivational milieu, and spiritual equipment—and can be understood through these factors, whereas only economic societies are amenable to analysis in economic terms. Thus history represents the final test of any theory as to how societies function. If a theory explains particular historical phenomena, this serves as evidence in its support. If it is incompatible with the findings of history, even though it may explain aspects of contemporary society, the theory is probably false. In this sense history and sociological theory are complementary. History provides data for the theories of sociology, and the means for verifying those theories. Sociology provides the models and conceptual schemes within which history is intelligible.

13
THE TRUE AMPHIBIAN

The amphibian is an animal that has not solved its evolutionary problems. Descending as it does from the fish, it retains most of the characteristics of the fish's body structure, imperfectly adapted to life on land. Its legs pivot from the side of its body so that its weight is carried on inefficient cantilevers rather than on struts. Its permeable skin limits it to moist habitats. Its soft-shelled eggs contain virtually no food and so must be laid in water. And because the amphibian has not evolved a constant body temperature mechanism, it cannot survive extremes of heat and cold.

These limitations were overcome by succeeding life forms. The reptiles developed an impervious skin and the amniotic egg, allowing them to survive in even the most desolate regions. In addition, the later reptiles brought their legs directly under their body, achieving greater mobility by virtue of their increased structural efficiency. The mammals developed a constant body temperature mechanism, making them independent not only of moisture but also of temperature. By evolving the device of gestation, the mammals also afforded the young a greater chance of survival. These developments gave the mammals a range and flexibility not available to the amphibians, so that today they range over virtually the entire earth.

The human race now finds itself in the same type of evolutionary impasse as that which trapped the amphibians, but in this case it is the evolution of behaviour, rather than biological evolution, that has trapped it. The formation of emotive-mechanisms worked excellently for the higher primates and proved satisfactory for primitive tribal man, but in the macro-societies represented by civilization, scale alone prevents the formation of emotive-mechanisms common to the whole culture, even if this were desirable. The *ad hoc* solution—retribalizing within the civilizations—has proved a millennium-long disaster without parallel in evolutionary history. Groups generate non-rational values that motivate and support their members, but there is no way that rational concern for the whole civilization, the human species, the natural ecology, or even the condition of the physical environment can be involved. The gap between rationality and emotion provides the flexibility necessary to pursue ends in a non-tropistic way. The price is that rationality cannot influence the formation of values.

It is here that the circle cannot be closed. Rationality cannot motivate. Motivation cannot be mediated by reason. Marx asked who shall educate the educators, but the question is rather who shall condition the conditioners. Plainly the social group does, but in ways that result at best only in the survival of that group. It is a trite truism that human nature does not change, trite because the ambiguity of terms leaves the statement empty. Human nature is both unchanging and infinitely changeable. The values and ideals of different cultures show extreme variation, yet the mechanism by which these values are developed and adopted is the same in all cultures. Computers operate with vastly different programmes, but the means by which the programmes are accepted are the same.

Arthur Koestler has suggested, following Paul MacLean, that most social problems are the result of the coexistence of several levels of the central nervous system, the lower inherited from the reptiles, the second being a heritage of the mammals, and the neocortex, in its highest development, being a distinctly human attribute. But it is not necessary to seek the problem in physiological mismatches or in the inadequacy of the more primitive sections of the central nervous system. Most human behaviour is socially determined, and it is in the interaction between individual and society, in the grey area covered neither by individual psychology nor by studies of society, that understanding is necessary.

There are two possible avenues of development. The first is the evolution of new values, new emotive-mechanisms, new emotive dispositions more adaptive to large-scale societies. The evolution of new values, however, requires new groupings and new patterns of social organization, for it is only in new groups and interest blocks that value evolution will take place. The geometry of social organization and the question of who is in face-to-face contact with whom are fundamental determinants of the values evolved.

More radical than the evolution of new value schemes is the possibility of developing new behavioural mechanisms to modify and mediate emotive-mechanism behaviour. It is difficult to see how such new mechanisms could arise or what form they would assume, but the history of animal behaviour has been one of increasingly flexible and more adaptable behavioural mechanisms, and there is no reason to believe that the development has ended. The insects could never have imagined emotion or reason as behavioural mechanisms; we are unable to imagine what form future behavioural mechanisms could possibly take. Certainly, once the human race develops these new mechanisms, it will have gone beyond *Homo sapiens*, for the species is distinguished not by wisdom, as it likes to think, but by its modes of motivation. At this stage, discussion trails into science fiction and speculation. It is impossible for humanity to be concerned about what it might become, for that condition will no longer be human. Despite Shaw and Nietzsche, the human race has as little interest in its descendants as our primate ancestors had in us. Yet it is the change taking place now that will determine the descendants of man and indeed the future of terrestial life, for virtually every other species has specialized itself into an evolutionary dead-end.

PART THREE

KNOWLEDGE AND UNDERSTANDING

14

CHANGING ATTITUDES TO KNOWLEDGE

Two thousand years have seen major changes in the way the human race views knowledge. Not only has its domain been extended following an explosive growth of content, but attitudes to knowledge itself, to what it is and how it functions, have also changed. A continuing interaction has taken place; growth in content has influenced views of the abstract quantity knowledge, while these changes in attitude have in turn determined its domains. These shifts in attitude to knowledge display three aspects: a change from static to dynamic views of the world, leading to views of knowledge itself as evolving and changing; changes from a constitutional to a functional approach to phenomena, leading to a functional as against an absolute idea of knowledge itself; and an awareness that there exist very real limits to what can be known about the world.

Every discipline undergoes a change from static to dynamic world-view in the course of development. Early pre-Copernican astronomy embraced a world-view that was entirely static. For Dante and his contemporaries no change ever took place beyond the lunar sphere; change and decay were characteristic of the earth alone. The planets and heavens had been set in motion by the hand of God and, with the exception of such portents as meteors and comets, were expected to continue unchanged until the day of judgement. The Copernican and Newtonian revolutions left the static world-view largely intact. For Newton, God had set the planets moving in their respective orbits, after which the law of gravity could be expected to maintain the system in motion indefinitely. It was only when questions of the origin of the solar system were raised in the eighteenth century, followed by the realization that the stars, and indeed the galaxies, were evolving, that the importance of flux was fully realized.

A similar change occurred somewhat later in the field of geology. Before the nineteenth century, discussion of the origin of geological formations had been necessarily reconciled with the Pentateuch, resulting in a static world-view of the earth's surface. With the possible exception of erosion, the present configuration of mountains, rivers, plains, and oceans reflected faithfully the original creation. It was not until the work of Buffon, Hutton, and Lyell forced the time scale of creation far beyond the biblical limit that the importance of change was fully appreciated. Darwin's contribution to biology involved much the same insight; species are not immutable, new species are constantly evolving while others are disappearing. The same change in attitude has now penetrated the social sciences; whereas seventeenth and eighteenth century thinkers such as Hobbes, Locke, and Rousseau assumed that human nature was invariant, the emphasis now lies on the variety and variability of human nature rather than on its constancy. In technology, where conditions of flux are usually more obvious, it is still true that most disciplines began with a static-world conceptualization and only slowly moved to the more complex world-in-flux view. The science of statics, of forces in equilibrium, preceded the study of dynamics. The theory of steady-state DC circuits preceded the more complex theory of AC circuits, which involves current growths and decays. Steady-state fluid flow and heat flow phenomena were analysed long before the more complex, and to a large extent still unanalysed, transient flow cases. Even the Special Theory of Relativity dealing with constant velocity systems preceded the General Theory which describes accelerating systems.

Just as the focus of knowledge has shifted towards changing phenomena, so knowledge itself has come to be seen as an entity in flux. For the ancients, in so far as there was a concept of knowledge at all, it was of an unchanging entity. All knowledge was recorded in sacred books or in the writings of philosophers; only gradually was it realized that the content of knowledge was expanding. When the area of comprehending is small, it is far from obvious how much lies outside it. As the area grows, both the margin with, and the extent of, the unknown becomes more apparent. Beyond simple growth in content, however, it is now clear that other cultures have had quite different ways of seeing knowledge, and of conceptualizing the world. The attitudes that the Greek philosophers held towards knowledge differ from those current. Future ages will no doubt hold quite different attitudes again.

Changing attitudes to knowledge are further characterized by the shift from constitutional—and in a sense absolute—to operational or analogue knowledge. Philosophers such as Plato held that if only a person could go beyond the veil of illusion, beyond the limitations of the senses, it was possible to really know the nature of the world. For Plato, this involved escape from the Cave and the shadow show of illusion. It lay in apprehending the unchanging ideas, of which all things in the material world are insubstantial reflections. All imperfectly drawn triangles reflect the idea of the triangle; all beds reflect the idea of the bed. To know anything important about triangles or beds, it is necessary to go to the idea and investigate its properties. This is the foundation of *a priori* theories of knowledge, that is, theories that reason alone provides worthwhile knowledge about the world. Platonic attitudes to knowledge persist in European idealism. Other branches of philosophy, notably British empiricism, while largely rejecting *a priori* reasoning, maintain much the same attitude: once it has been established, knowledge is an immutable quantity.

While most philosophy retains the idea that knowledge is fixed and absolute, science has taken an approach that is more pragmatic, less ambitious, and ultimately more fruitful. What is true of science is even more true of the technologies. Ignoring the question of what, in absolute terms, a quantity is, both have chosen to ask how it functions and what it does. Among the most fundamental quantities of physics is energy, but questions as to the composition of energy, or what it really is, go unanswered.

The same is true of physical entities such as gravitational, magnetic, and electrical fields, of matter and of the properties of matter. The most that can be done is to describe how they behave, and how they relate to other quantities. They are defined in functional, rather than constitutional, terms.

Quite generally, it became obvious to scientists in the seventeenth century that they were posing the wrong questions in asking what things really were. Or more strictly they probably never realized they were asking the wrong questions; they simply abandoned problems of the absolute nature of reality to the philosophers, and asked questions that enabled them to advance their particular disciplines. These questions proved to be functional questions. This is perhaps the major difference between science and philosophy. Philosophy generally assumes that all questions have meaningful answers; science has concluded that some questions are useful and some are not. Moreover, no way exists of knowing beforehand which type of question will be useful, just as there is no way of knowing beforehand what categories are applicable in any given study.

Intellectually, functional approaches are far from satisfying to people who desire to know the ultimate nature of reality. Two lines of argument exist, however, one philosophical and one based on common sense, indicating that such knowledge is in the long run unattainable. The philosopher Berkeley developed the theory that the external observed world is illusory, and that the sense data on which beliefs are based exist only as ideas in the mind of God. Stripped of the need for God, this philosophy has since been taken up by J.S. Mill, among others, and christened phenomenalism.

The basic tenet of this philosophy is not that the world is real or that it is illusory, but that nothing can ever be known about its fundamental nature. The classic example involves a person seeing a red object. In discussing the object seen, all that can be said is that it has properties which reflect light of a particular wavelength. The light itself is not inherently coloured; it has a particular frequency. The cones of the eye send specific nerve messages to the brain, but these messages are uncoloured.

These intermediate steps involved in acts of perception mean that the most anyone is entitled to do is to claim the existence of red sense data within the visual field. In other words, there is a shift to functional as against constitutional description. The thing-out-there functions to cause certain perceptions on the part of an observer; no one can say what it really is, but only what it does.

An equally persuasive argument involves the nature of analysis. Enquiries into the real nature of a thing lead logically to questions of its composition; these lead in turn to the same questions asked of its elements and so on through an infinite regress. Moreover, and just as significantly, the analysis of an object into its components reveals nothing of its real nature. A house is more than the total of all bricks, mortar, tiles, timber, and plumbing; it is these elements in a definite arrangement. A molecule is more than the sum of its atoms; it is these atoms in a specific configuration. The insight that Gestalt psychology brought to the social sciences extends to all knowledge. The parts and the arrangement, the figure and the field are equally important.

The implications of phenomenalism and the limitations of analysis have forced science to adopt a functional, rather than a constitutional, approach. It is no longer useful to ask what energy, matter, red, or magnetic fields are, but only what they do—what effect they have. The same applies to knowledge itself. It does not make sense to ask what knowledge is, for the same reasons that it does not make sense to ask what energy or matter are. It is only useful to ask what it does.

One further view of knowledge not so far discussed is the direct unitive type of knowledge claimed by most branches of mysticism. This approach has been anathema to Western thought not so much because of the anti-mystical, anti-religious prejudices of most thinkers, but because of the disproportionate prestige accorded to rationality and the belief that knowledge itself is fixed in its nature. Pure reason, however, has less power and range than supposed by classical Greeks and eighteenth century thinkers. If the nature of knowing itself is evolving, as it demonstrably is, then there is no reason why it cannot move into areas of direct intuitive awareness. The suggestion may be unwelcome to people raised in the Western tradition, but it cannot be ruled out. The present reaction against reason and empiricism into mysticism may represent no more than emotional needs, but it may have much wider implications. It may represent a more developed and powerful approach to knowledge.

Further shifts in attitude to knowledge followed the realization that quite definite limits exist to what can be known. These limits are of two kinds: technical and practical limitations resulting from limitations of equipment and intellect; and absolute limitations that appear to be involved in the very nature of the universe.

Limitations of tools and equipment circumscribe both what can be known and the accuracy with which it can be known. An example is the measurement of the length of an object; even using the most sophisticated techniques, involving beams of coherent light and interference phenomena, length cannot be measured beyond an accuracy related to the wavelength of light. In the same way, the smallest object that can be seen through a microscope is limited by the wavelength of the light used; objects smaller than this simply do not register. Techniques such as the use of ultra-violet microscopes and electron microscopes extend the range of observation, but eventually a limit is reached. The indirect approaches used in high-energy physics allow the effects of smaller particles to be seen, but even these techniques have limitations.

The very act of measuring or observing a phenomenon often affects the thing observed. Measurements of temperature require heat flow into the measuring equipment, resulting in a minute temperature change. Measurements of voltage and amperage also change the value of the quantity measured. These difficulties can be met to some extent by the use of null methods, but only in rare cases can they be completely eliminated. Observations in the biological or social sciences are even more subject to experimental interference. The act of observing social phenomena inevitably changes the phenomena; people do not behave in the same way when an observer is present as they would in his absence. Animals do not react in an experimental setting as they do in the wild state.

The finite capacity of the human mind also limits what can be known about the external world. Expansion of knowledge in any field, whether it be sub-atomic physics or biochemistry, requires a thorough grounding in the work that has gone before, but knowledge is now growing exponentially, so that every ten or fifteen years it doubles in content. A point must be reached, even with the most sophisticated techniques of abstraction and the use of electronic data banks, where a person cannot learn everything known in a field in his lifetime.

At this stage, the S growth curve of knowledge will begin to flatten out. Even ignoring this difficulty, the point is being approached in such sophisticated studies as sub-atomic physics and mathematics, where the development of new concepts, new intellectual models and appropriate ways of thinking are simply beyond human capacity. The human mind is, after all, born to a particular world, and there must be limits to how far imagination can span.

These limits involve shortcomings of techniques and the finiteness of human intellect; obviously they can be extended a long way. More serious are limits on knowledge that appear to be inherent in the nature of the universe itself. One much-quoted example is Heisenberg's uncertainty principle. Developed to deal with phenomena at the sub-atomic level, this principle states that all descriptions of nature retain some irreducible uncertainty. If the position of an electron in its orbit is known with precision, its speed cannot be definitely known, and vice versa. The greater the accuracy with which one variable is established, the less accurately can the other be determined.

A similar difficulty has emerged in relativity theory. Einstein's major contribution to physics was to replace facts or data as the fundamental basis of knowledge with the act of observation. This change in emphasis is still to have its full impact, particularly in the social sciences where the act of observation—the interaction between observer and object and their relationship—is more important than the simple fact observed. Einstein pointed out that the only way to compare the times of events at different places was to utilize a message from the event to the observer. This message, for example a ray of light, must take finite time in its passage. In consequence, the absolute time and space of Newton yield to the here-and-now of each observer. Events that may appear in one sequence to one observer appear in a quite different sequence to another. Any attempt to determine the real sequence of events or the absolute interval of time between two occurrences is foredoomed; the nature of the universe is such that these things cannot be known.

What is worse, a similar difficulty has emerged in the field of logic itself. The construction of any formal logical system requires a general proof that contradictions cannot appear within that system. It is not sufficient to see whether contradictions eventually arise; it is necessary to prove initially that they cannot do so. However, in 1931, the logician Kurt Gödel demonstrated that any logical system of any richness must contain propositions that are not provable within that system. In consequence, no system of logic can ever be guaranteed consistent; neither can it be guaranteed complete. The formalist attempt to develop logical systems within which all discussion of truth and falsity are subsumed is in its very nature condemned to failure. Subsequent work by Church and Turing point to the same conclusion: not only are there truths about the universe that cannot be known, but the logical systems used for analysing propositions cannot be guaranteed secure.

These changing approaches to knowledge, the move from static to dynamic, from absolute to functional, and the growing awareness of limitations, are all interdependent. If there are absolute limits on what can be known or proved, then it is pointless to hope for absolute knowledge, for such knowledge would be capable in theory of being complete. Similarly, if ideas of knowledge itself are slowly evolving, there cannot be absolute and eternally true knowledge. And if knowledge has become purely the investigation of constructs, it has absolute limitations.

15

METAPHYSICS OF KNOWLEDGE

Every claim to know or to understand something involves an underlying metaphysic. This metaphysic forms the final appeal against questions of how we really know what we know; a defence against objections that we can never be sure of anything.

The earliest metaphysic lay in reference to authority, either in the form of religious writings or the works of past sages. It is easy today to be critical of medieval thinkers who based their world-view on the revealed word of the scriptures, but in fact they had little alternative. When a person is raised within a hermetic intellectual tradition, it is almost impossible to break out of it. Most radicals depend on the impact of ideas and attitudes from outside their milieu to liberate them from the received world-view, and in medieval times such cross-fertilization was lacking. Moreover, faith rather than knowledge then held the higher prestige, whereas the reverse is now true. Ultimately there is no way to adjudicate between the competing claims of knowledge and faith; a reasonable person *knows* that the claims of knowledge precede those of blind faith, while a religious person living in the Middle Ages had absolute *faith* that in faith alone lay salvation.

This reference to authority went far beyond religious belief. The reverence in which the writings of Aristotle were held is almost incomprehensible today, when every thinker must be prepared to face his critics in the arena. But the tendency of medieval scholastic thought was to accept that the ancients knew everything worth knowing, and that this knowledge could be retrieved by combing ancient manuscripts with sufficient diligence. This attitude, together with an excessive deference towards religious authority and a penchant for *a priori* reasoning, made intellectual progress impossible. Russell has commented that Aristotle was the greatest intellectual disaster to befall the human race, but the fault lies less with the unfortunate Greek than with the attitudes of the Middle Ages. This deference to authority is characteristic of most religion-based societies, and appears, reasonably enough, inimical to both science and the belief in progress. The more fundamentalist Islamic countries and the strongly Catholic areas of southern Europe and South America are those in which the scientific approach has made, and can be expected to make, least headway.

Descartes is generally regarded as the founder of modern philosophy. Perhaps his most important achievement was to overthrow the excessive deference to authority which had shackled and frozen medieval thought. Resolving to accept nothing on the basis of authority or convention, he finally came to his celebrated proof of his own existence—*Cogito, ergo sum.* This Descartes accepted as true because of its inherent lucidity and clarity. Accordingly he took the approach that those statements which strike an observer with particular clarity are in fact true. This is Descarte's clarity metaphysic of knowledge: a statement is true if it is seen with particular lucidity and immediacy.

The clarity metaphysic of knowledge underlies, implicitly or explicitly, most modern philosophy. Often its presence goes unnoticed because the truths it supports are so obvious as to require no justification. The rules of logic and the syllogistic form are to be found in this category. It is taken for granted that every object can be put into categories of the type A or not-A, red or not-red, round or not-round, mortal or not-mortal. There is no middle range undistributed between A and not-A. Similarly we take it for granted that if A then B, if B then C, hence if A then C is invariably a true argument form. The reason for holding these perfectly reasonable views is that they are seen with particular clarity; they seem so self-evident that only people of dubious sanity could question them. Yet multi-valued logic is being seriously explored by logicians. Every statement need not be true or not-true.

A clarity metaphysic is particularly suited to the fields of logic and philosophy where categories are clearly drawn and arguments are distinguished by simplicity and directness. But the material world is neither simple nor clear cut; it is characterized by complexity, pluralism, overlapping categories, and indeterminate boundaries. As such it does not lend itself to a clarity metaphysic of knowledge. What is seen with particular clarity—for example, that a heavy weight falls faster than a light weight—is quite liable to be wrong. And statements not apparent with particular lucidity may nevertheless be true. Science has accordingly gone its separate way, developing not only its own methods and techniques but also its own justifying metaphysic. To a degree science seems unaware of just what sort of supporting metaphysic it is employing, being more concerned with extending its particular disciplines than with investigating its foundations. In particular it is apparently unaware just how far its basic point of appeal differs from either that of philosophy or of the medieval world.

Science draws upon a consistency metaphysic to support its claims to know. This takes two forms: consistency with previously established knowledge held with reasonable agreement, and consistency between experimental observation and explanatory hypothesis. Invariably, there is greater willingness to accept new ideas, new theories, and new knowledge where these are consistent with what has gone before. Where there is a dramatic clash between old and new theories, the new is either completely wrong-headed, or a major change in understanding is at hand. Such have been the theories of Copernicus, Newton, Darwin, and Freud, but for the most part scientific development represents a continuity rather than a series of revolutions, an evolutionary growth rather than an erratic sequence of starts and stops. The essence of the empirical method is not simply that information about the world derives from the senses, but that theory and observation must be compatible. Its underlying, unspoken metaphysic involves consistency.

The difference between a consistency metaphysic and authority and clarity metaphysics is that the latter two require a firm ground to build on. In the case of authority, this ground is the revealed documents themselves. For clarity metaphysics it is the psychological awareness of the immediacy of certain truths. Given these grounds, a body of knowledge can in theory be built up much as a tower is built on firm foundations. But these approaches are singularly vulnerable as the history of Christian dogma shows. Once the foundations are attacked, the entire structure crumbles. Consistency-based knowledge, on the other hand, is assembled not like a tower but like a space station. It does not much matter where one begins building so long as the resulting structure holds together. And as it has no vulnerable foundation, parts of it can be destroyed without affecting the structure as a whole. The consistency metaphysic has turned up in other areas besides scientific knowledge. The most noteworthy is jurisprudence, where the validity of new laws and interpretations depends on their consistency with precedents. It has been realized intuitively that there is no fundamental basis on which law can be built up, that it is a matter of convention, usage and to a large extent social utility. Unless there is to be reference to an absolutist religious framework, which fortunately is no longer the case, all that can be asked is that jurisprudence be internally consistent.

16

KNOWLEDGE AS MODELS

Aware that it can never arrive at an ultimate understanding of reality, and that what information it possesses relates only to how things function, science has developed a particular view of knowledge. It regards knowledge as an infinite number of analogue models, which may be operated on to give information. These models parallel the world in the aspect under investigation, but they are not the world. And since all arguments from analogy are logically invalid, models cannot be extended with confidence beyond the field in which they were developed.

There is nothing new in the idea of knowledge and information being viewed as models. Maps are, in effect, two-dimensional models of three-dimensional terrain, providing information on altitude, vegetation cover, habitation, roads, water courses, and resources. By the use of these models people are able to work through in analogy programmes that will yield a particular result. They can plot a trek, plan the exploitation of minerals and timber, anticipate possible difficulties, and act with reasonable confidence on the results. As might be expected, the model is basically functional; it allows people to act. Knowledge about the nature of the terrain is relevant only in so far as it permits some interaction with the world. Marine charts, star charts, and weather maps all play a similar role. They allow people to act in a particular way on the basis of information supplied, and can often be understood only when the conventional coding is known. Nor need maps be of the two-dimensional form familiar to the West; the Pacific Islanders used three-dimensional maps of cords and wood, not unlike a cat's cradle construction, to provide information on the location of islands, their approaches, reefs, and swell patterns.

Nor are maps and charts the only conventionalized models in common day use. Engineering drawings, circuit diagrams, economic graphs, and so forth are analogue models. So too are impressions on punched cards, magnetic discs, and in ferromagnetic memory banks.

Among the most useful models now available are those provided by mathematics. It is possible to set up mathematical analogues in almost any field and to work through these models to obtain results applicable to the world. The advantage of mathematics is not simply that it quantifies with accuracy, but that it has an enormous richness of operators. These include simple arithmetic operations such as addition and subtraction, those related to rates of change such as integration and differentiation, and the more recondite operators of vector calculus. Moreover, mathematics provides a tremendous number of functions—algebraic functions, sine and cosine, hyperbolic sine and cosine, and logarithmic functions, each with unique properties. The use of mathematical operators with these functions allows almost any aspect of the physical world to be modelled.

The nature of mathematical models illuminates the doctrines of *a priori* knowledge held by many Greek and Continental thinkers. The best example of such knowledge has always been mathematics, because mathematics appears to yield information independent of experience. It is known that $2 + 2 = 4$ or that $\int 2x dx = x^2$ without ever having to add items together or to measure minutely the area under a graph. Hence it was long believed that pure reason could by itself establish all worthwhile knowledge. The work of Locke and Hume has largely discredited the notion of *a priori* knowledge for contemporary thinkers. Most philosophers have struck a compromise, agreeing with the British school that while most knowledge is derived empirically, knowledge in the fields of mathematics and logic is genuine *a priori* knowledge.

This view weds two quite different uses of the word *knowledge*. Knowledge of the world, as suggested above, lies in having operative models that parallel the behaviour of the world in some way. The knowledge of mathematics, and to a lesser extent logic, involves rules worked out to a certain convention in accordance with internal consistency. Different systems, based on a variety of conventions, give widely differing results, as can be seen when the deductions of Euclidean geometry are contrasted with those of the non-Euclidean systems. Rules that apply in one area do not apply in another. That $a \times b$ equals $b \times a$ is axiomatic in standard algebra, since the rules are defined in this way, but it is not true once imaginary numbers are introduced. The internal consistency of mathematics is not a philosophical problem but the defining characteristic of the discipline. Mathematics is the science of pattern, and to ask why it is consistent is to ask a meaningless question. If it were not consistent it would be folklore, fable, and fantasy rather than mathematics.

Nevertheless, it is the application of mathematics to the world rather than its internal consistency that causes most confusion. Obviously, two pebbles added to two pebbles make four pebbles, and buildings can be constructed with confidence using Euclidean geometry. This induces people to believe that all phenomena mirror some underlying mathematical order, a Platonic notion rendered explicit by scientific enquiry. This is simply not the case. Since the relationship between mathematics and its application to the world is that of an analogy, there can be no way of knowing beforehand which model is useful in any study. Arithmetic, which we seem to come to intuitively, is simply the branch of mathematics dealing with discrete, finite objects. It is this group of objects that the human race were first, and still remain, most interested in.

But $2 + 2 = 4$ is not true of drops of water, not true of distances, is not true of sub-atomic particles, and is not true of microbes. Had the human race been aquatic, they would probably have begun with some form of finite arithmetic, as well as with quite different basic units to mass, length, and time. And had they been historically more interested in distances than in solid objects, they would have developed vectors ahead of simple arithmetic. The appropriate mathematics for a particular field is discovered by intuition, curve fitting, and trial and error. Often branches of mathematics developed in one area turn up quite unexpectedly in another. Vectors, which deal with distances, also find application in electrical theory. The mathematics of chance, developed to aid gamblers, finds application in genetic theory.

Every technology has developed models that prove useful in its particular field. These models represent conceptators or thinking-within-mechanisms and allow the data of the particular field to be handled in a way that gives results. In some cases the models bear an apparently direct relationship to the physical world; in more complex cases the elements of a model have no physical significance. Often the models represent quite new ways of looking at or conceiving the world, and of handling data.

An example is the field theory, developed by Faraday, but implicit in the ideas of Newton. Before the discovery of gravitational, magnetic, and electrical fields it was held as an article of faith that there could be no action at a distance. Objects had to be in contact before they could affect one another. The idea of a field as some type of continuous change in the nature of space, extended over a considerable distance, freed physics from simple mechanistic thought. It became possible to handle new data and to view the world in a novel and more flexible way. Mechanics had earlier developed its own conceptator involving the interrelated concepts of mass, length, time, force, energy, momentum, and power. These appear so basic to the contemporary mind that it is difficult to appreciate the novelty they had when first developed. It was not even clear in the seventeenth century that mass—ponderability—was one of the important qualities of matter; gases indeed appeared to possess no mass. A similar group of interrelated concepts are those of potential, flow, resistance, and capacity. These appear in electrical theory, in fluid flow, in acoustics, and in thermodynamics. They are as fundamental to technology as the mechanical conceptator and the field conceptator involving intensity, charge, and energy. All share the characteristic of being conceptual models into which variables can be inserted and manipulated to give results.

Dimensional analysis is another conceptator which at first sight appears to have even less connection with the material world. Developed to handle complex problems in heat and fluid flow, dimensional analysis assembles variables into dimensionless parameters and operates on them, instead of on the original data. Problems of heat flow may involve densities, conductivities, flow rates, temperatures, viscosities, and heat rates. Such an accumulation of variables renders a problem practically insoluble by direct means, but by grouping variables into a small number of dimensionless parameters, dimensional analysis makes the manipulation of data possible. These parameters have no physical significance and are purely artefacts of convenience. Dimensional analysis is a tool, incidentally, which has never been adequately explored outside a small area of engineering. Its use in physics in particular could prove most fruitful, particularly when applied to non-dimensionless constants.

Thinking-within-models—conceptators—range from the purely physical to the purely mathematical. Many problems in engineering are most readily solved by constructing a distorted physical model and testing it. If the behaviour of wave movement and sedimentation in a harbour is to be determined, a distorted model is built and tested. Other problems may be set up on analogue computers, which use the analogy between electrical systems and mechanical, thermal, fluid, and acoustic systems. There is no difference in principle between representing behaviour on a physical model, on an analogue computer, or in mathematical equations. All are models, and all represent an understanding of the real world.

A further method of modelling only recently coming into general use is the computer simulation study. Digital computers process information under the control of a programme written in a particular convention, and translated internally into machine instructions. In simulation studies, this programme is the model. It may describe the financial operation of a large corporation, the stress distribution in a bridge, the flow of fluids in a complex pipework system, or indeed any one of an almost infinite number of phenomena. It is possible, once the programme has been established, to feed any set of variables into the computer as data and examine the result. These data may involve the innumerable permutations of cash flows, taxation rates, and expenses involved in a corporation's operation, the infinite variations of loads due to traffic and weather imposed on a bridge, or the flows and pressures applying in a pipework system. Once the simulation model has been tested it is possible to optimize the final result; if the model is valid over its range, the final selection will be the best that can be made. No matter what conditions apply subsequently, the case has been anticipated.

The use of computers for on-line control and data processing differs somewhat from this, but the principle remains the same. Data, in the form of a binary code in most machines, represent information about the real world; the programme represents an operation of some type. In simulation studies it is a model, in data processing it is instructions for handling data, and can still be considered an operational model. On-line computers represent a different case; forming a feedback loop, they represent part of the world rather than being knowledge about the world.

The distinction between a computer's programme and the raw data is an important one. It represents the difference between understanding as against knowing, between comprehending a field and simply knowing something about it. We understand something if we have a model of some kind that allows us to make predictions and anticipate possible developments. For example, we claim to understand the movement of celestial bodies because we have a mental and mathematical model of the Copernican solar system operating under Newtonian laws. We understand the plurality of animal species, the distribution of fossils, and the complexity of organic life because we have a Darwinian model to operate within. We understand the behaviour of chemical substances because we have a Daltonian model incorporating discrete atoms with specific valencies and invariable mass. These models apply only in the area for which they were developed. Newtonian models break down when relativity effects become important; Darwinian models break down in human society where the effect of natural selection is insignificant compared with other factors; the hard eternal atoms of Dalton are seen as a fiction when one comes to the field of nuclear physics. But within their field the models are useful and allow us to make sense of data.

Data, on the other hand, are known rather than understood. Astronomers before Copernicus had recorded the positions of Mars, Jupiter, and Saturn; chemists had known long before Dalton that a particular weight of one chemical reacted with a particular weight of another to give a definite weight of a third. These were facts. They were known but they were not understood.

All facts—that rainfall is ten inches per annum, voltage is 240 volts, Paris is the capital of France—are capable, in principle, of being inserted as data in a computer programme. They are also capable of being inserted as the value of a variable in a Russellian logic statement. Every phenomenon that we claim to understand can be represented by models and, in principle, described by a computer programme. Any item of relevant data, any fact, can be fed into the programme and processed to give significant results. It is a simple matter to write a programme describing the behaviour of the solar system, and then insert the current positions of the planets as data. With the programme and data the positions of the planets at any time in the past or future can be determined. Conversely, it would be impossibly difficult to write a programme describing the operation of natural selection, even for an isolated island, but theoretically it could be done. The characteristics of animal species, weather, and vegetation would be fed in as data, and evolutionary trends predicted. In practice, random effects would make any results obtained all but meaningless.

Understanding involves having an operative model of the world; facts or data represent models of conditions capable of observation. There is clearly a gradation between the two, and in the case of some low-level hypotheses we say both that we know and that we understand a particular occurrence. More usually, however, there is a marked distinction between knowing something and understanding it. Viewing knowledge in its wider aspect as involving models eliminates the distinction between hypothesis and established fact. A hypothesis can be seen as a tentative model explaining the facts; if the final knowledge in which we feel confident is also regarded as a model, the only difference between the two lies in the degree of substantiation. Furthermore, this approach reinforces the idea that all knowledge is functional knowledge; it allows us, at least in principle, to operate within the world. By manipulating the model, certain effects corresponding to the behaviour of the world are produced, and these can be acted on. There can be no absolute knowledge of what the world is—only of how it operates.

As all understanding of the world can be reduced to operative models, it is only reasonable to assume that knowledge itself can be viewed in this way. This is not to say that knowledge is a model, but only that it can be treated as such. The concept of recursion is involved; the idea of knowledge as models is itself a model—a way to visualize and to handle it. And just as other models—Copernican and Darwinian—cannot be extended with confidence beyond the range in which they were developed, so knowledge as a model is a model which cannot safely be extended beyond its inspiration—twentieth century knowledge. The representation is not held to be true for all times and all places, but only a viewpoint enabling the concept to be used. As more sophisticated approaches to knowledge are developed they will replace the model concept.

17

LANGUAGE AS A MODEL

Despite the advances in mathematics, cybernetics, and analogue constructions, the major example of modelling remains language. Indeed, language is so much a part of human thinking, and so taken for granted, that it is not obvious that, in using language, people model. This is not the only function of language. As suggested previously, language is one of the most potent agents of social conditioning. It serves to express emotion. It is one of the major mediums of artistic and aesthetic creation. It is also a medium of play, delight, and recreation. But wherever language is used in speculation, providing information, in planning, philosophy, or analysis, it can fruitfully be viewed as a modelling medium.

Words serve as symbols. The word *rose* stands for a flower of a particular type, the word *grow* symbolizes a process of a certain kind. The use of such symbols is taught both ostensively, by pointing out examples of roses, and by the use of language itself—the meaning of words is learnt from the function they serve. The sentence "A rose grows in my garden" represents a model of a situation in the physical world. The information could as well be conveyed by a papier mâché model, or a photograph, but language has the advantages of convenience and of being able to communicate abstract information. Its range is as wide, theoretically, as the body of communally shared concepts. It is capable of conveying information about events far in the past and at enormous removes in space. The speculative use of language involves constructing verbal models of a situation and working through these analogue models. This may be as mundane an activity as planning a day's business itinerary, and as recondite as thinking through an abstract problem in science or philosophy. Just as knowledge itself is best understood with reference to its function and behaviour, so language can only be discussed on the basis of what it does rather than what it is. Wittgenstein was the first philosopher to insist that the meaning of a word lay in how it was used rather than in some inherent property of words or language. This is a scientific as against a philosophical approach.

The use of language to model the world has two considerable drawbacks. The first hinges on categories, the second on operations. There are, in theory, an infinite number of ways to abstract the external world into categories, an infinite number of sectioning planes, as it were, that can be taken through the complex of reality. The process of formulating categories is to a great extent an artificiality, even when categories correspond to fundamental distinctions, as for example animal species. There is no hard and fast distinction between variants within a species and species themselves, nor can there be; a criterion is generally decided upon, in this case interbreeding, but these criteria are never absolute. There is always the problem of marginal cases; at some point blue shades into green, conglomerates merge into sandstone, metals grade into non-metals. Consequently the concepts used in language always involve a degree of uncertainty. This uncertainty is an inherent property of language. Verbal concepts cannot be precise.

A more serious drawback to language as a modelling medium lies in the operators it uses. The rules of grammar are such that language does parallel or mimic the world to a large extent, but these rules must fulfil their own linguistic ends besides paralleling the world. In this lies the difficulty. It is never possible to know whether a verbal argument is valid or not from its structure alone. For example, it is true that if A is greater than B, and B is greater than C, then A is greater than C. It is true that if A includes B and B includes C, then A includes C. But it is not true that if A can beat B at chess, and B can beat C at chess, that A can beat C at chess. Neither is it true that if A fears B and B fears C, that A fears C. There are an infinite number of such cases, and no way to tell from the grammar alone if the model is a true portrayal of the situation.

The reasons for this difficulty lie deep in the history of language itself. Language developed at a time when the human world-view was static in nature. Neither society nor the physical world evinced any change from generation to generation, and deep within the structure of language this attitude still lies dormant. In consequence, language is adequate to handle states and situations that are not time involved, such as the "greater than" and the "inclusion" cases mentioned above. But time-involved phenomena and actions such as "fears" and "beats" are processes rather than situations, and do not lie happily within the ambit of language reasoning.

These two drawbacks to language, difficulties with imprecise categories and difficulties in knowing when the structure of an argument parallels the world, render it unsatisfactory for many purposes. It is particularly suited to data-rich disciplines in which a large amount of not closely related information must be stored—history, geography, biology, geology, anthropology, psychology, and their related disciplines. It is less useful in disciplines that consider processes, in particular physics, engineering, and chemistry. In these fields mathematics or some form of synthetic symbolism such as used in chemistry are more useful.

18

THE PARADOX OF PHILOSOPHY

The discipline that has been the most resolute user of language models is technical philosophy, and, not surprisingly, it is technical philosophy that has been the greatest victim of the shortcomings of language. Because of its failure to see, and to guard against, the problems inherent in using language for speculation, philosophy has involved itself in a host of difficulties that are more apparent than real and introduced problems that have no relevance to reality. This has been particularly true of its sub-discipline, formal logic.

Like language, formal logic developed at a time when a static view of the world prevailed. This is reflected in its content, which embraces the relations between classes of objects and the relations between propositions. Inclusion, exclusion, and partial inclusion typify relations between classes of objects; contradiction, contrariety, and identity are among the possible relations between propositions. The category of red objects is entirely included in the larger family of coloured objects, and excluded from the category of green objects. The proposition "All men are mortal" contains within it the less sweeping assertion "Some men are mortal", and contradicts the proposition "Some men are not mortal". These relations, both between categories and between propositions, can be represented on diagrams showing the shared or excluded areas, schematic representations that are only possible because the situations are not time involved.

Because of the static nature of language, both logic and language arguments are powerless to handle phenomena involving change and flux. All that can be done is to represent a situation in the initial stages by one logical relationship and in its final stage by another, in a manner reminiscent of stills from a movie film. There is no way to represent the change itself by a logical relationship—logic simply was not and is not designed to handle this function. And arguments that relate to change have historically presented the greatest difficulty to logicians. Hume pointed out quite correctly that causation is not a logical relationship and drew the reasonable conclusion that it represents no more than a psychological disposition. He could have remarked with equal justice, "So much the worse for logical relationships!" The difficulty lies in trying to use intellectual tools that are inappropriate to their task. Ironically, science is now dispensing with the concept of causation in favour of statistical probability, just as logicians are really getting their teeth into the problem. Causation, like most concepts of science, is an intellectual construct, justified only when it proves useful. To ask what it is, rather than what it does, is as futile as asking what knowledge is.

The restriction of logic to static-world cases is a serious drawback. More important for philosophical inquiry is the fact that language, as a medium, does not lend itself to rigour. The imprecision of categories and the inability to know when an appropriate verbal model has been used mean that it is impossible ever to develop a watertight, significant argument when language is used as the medium. The classical proofs of God's existence, refined by Leibniz, were refuted by Kant. Kant's arguments for the non-reality of space and time have in turn been refuted. Even Descartes's esteemed proof of his own existence contains logical flaws. This is the inevitable consequence of using language as a model.

There never has been and never can be a logically watertight language argument which is informative.

A number of modern logicians, among them Bertrand Russell, have attempted to overcome the drawbacks of classical logic by recasting propositions in a form inspired by mathematical functions. But these still retain the problems of imprecision of concepts, and are still limited to static-world cases. Moreover, if knowledge can be validly conceived as a model, then every conceivable variant of the model must be set up and examined if an argument is to be guaranteed valid. As the logician Alan Turing has shown, no mechanical procedure can be devised by which every possible case can be covered.

In general, philosophy has suffered from a tendency to assume categories and approaches rather than develop them pragmatically. Many of the most original philosophers have also been mathematicians, and while Pythagoras, Zeno, Leibniz, Descartes, and Russell have made outstanding contributions to philosophy they have also endowed it with a tendency to *a priori* reasoning, simplification, and an ivory tower detachment from the material world. This detachment is representative of a mathematical rather than a pragmatic approach. Science works to establish the categories and methods of operation that are appropriate in each particular field. This can be done only by trial and error and is often the most exacting part of any research. Once the machinery has been set up, once the appropriate concepts have been developed—mass, length and time, Reynolds and Prandtl number, field strength and pole—the remainder is usually relatively easy. The difficulty lies in finding the patterns of thought, as it were, appropriate to the particular field. In contrast, philosophy has approached every enquiry with the assumption that the methods it uses—logic, analysis, and deduction—are appropriate. Indeed, it rarely occurs to philosophers that there could be other methods. Like convinced medieval Christians insulated from heretical influences, the majority of philosophers have isolated themselves from the intellectual advances of science, and even more so of technology, and they find a curious satisfaction in their solitude.

The methods and operations of logic form conceptators just as mathematics, dimensional analysis, chemical equations, and the mechanical, field, and flow schemas form conceptators. But the scientific conceptators were developed for certain fields and only give useful results in those fields. Logic was developed for no particular field and is assumed to be applicable in every field. The suggestion that it is only useful in certain areas, and that even then there is no way of knowing initially which areas, would be rejected by most logicians.

Assumptions of the same type are held about categories. The classical qualities of essence, existence, and extension, and the Platonic notion that real world objects partake of the qualities of ideas, have reappeared in modern metaphysics. The problem of universals and of how particular objects partake of qualities such as redness and roughness are of this type. They assume particular categories, rather than attempting to establish what categories are most useful in a particular case. Moreover, it is simply not true that every question capable of being asked has meaning; to ask how properties inhere in an object or what sort of existence universals have is as sensible as to ask what is the colour of E-flat, or what shape is integration.

Another example of simply assuming a particular approach to be appropriate is the recent philosophical adoption of analysis. Impressed with the power of analysis, first in chemistry, then in physics, philosophy now approaches many of its problems by way of analysis. I have heard knowledge analysed as attitudes, attitudes analysed as predispositions to act, and so on *ad infinitum.* None of this is significant. It simply reflects the assumption that analysis is the best way to go about an investigation. It is only one way, and then only to be justified by results. In short, virtually all the problems of philosophy, whether in metaphysics, logic, or ethics, are strictly non-problems. They reflect the imprecision of language as a device for thinking within, the use of categories and patterns of thought that have never been proved appropriate to their task, and assumptions about the relationship of language to the world which are untenable. It seems doubtful whether there is one problem in philosophy which has any substance at all beyond verbal confusion.

This lack of contact with the experienced world, this failure of relevance, has had a debilitating effect on philosophy itself. Possibilities that do not go beyond themselves decay, and this has happened to philosophy. Increasingly, university philosophy departments are subject to total internal reflection; one thinker refines an old theory to remove an apparent difficulty, another picks minute flaws in this approach and advances his own theory, and so it goes on. Within the departments, in the pages of *Mind* and *The Journal of Philosophy*, at higher or lower levels of sophistication, the same pursuit is seen—theorizing for the sake of theorizing, but theorizing that is completely divorced from the world. Few question whether the pursuit is worth while, or whether anything is ever contributed to intellectual advance or the enrichment of the culture.

This sterility has forced philosophy to resort to other fields for intellectual nourishment. Locke's development of empiricism is highly rated by academic philosophers, and rightly so, but Locke simply codified what practical scientists since the Renaissance had done as a matter of course. Non-empirical attitudes persisted only because philosophy carried the fossilized *a-priori* approaches of Greek thinkers within its structure. The same borrowing underlay Hume's investigation of causation. It characterized Mill in his writings on scientific method, particularly in regard to his four canons and his theory of induction as a logical operation opposed to deduction. The canons of scientific investigation—method of agreement, method of difference, and so on—only codified the common sense that scientists had long used. Induction as a logical relation is a myth, and reflects a complete misunderstanding of how scientific advance takes place. There is no logical process by which one can proceed from innumerable observations to a general hypothesis. Hypotheses are invented by a leap of imagination; they are the result of insight and intuition rather than logic, and their development can be more appropriately studied by psychology than by philosophy.

This borrowing from the sciences continues today. Many philosophy schools have inaugurated courses on the philosophical problems of relativity and even the new notions of uncertainty and indeterminacy raised by quantum mechanics. By such interest, the philosophers claim, they are helping the scientists to clarify their concepts and eliminate sources of error. This justification fails to appreciate that the concepts used in science are purely intellectual tools, to be used when helpful and discarded when no longer relevant. There is nothing absolute about them. If the scientific community seems at times less than enthusiastic towards the proffered aid, it may be that they have troubles enough without introducing confusions latent in philosophy. Psychology, the most recent discipline to borrow heavily from philosophy, is still bedevilled by attitudes, problems, and concepts absorbed from philosophy of mind, and which philosophy has long since abandoned.

The methods of philosophy have been extended to the related disciplines of ethics, aesthetics, theory of education, and economics. With them have gone the drawbacks of philosophy—the imprecision of language as a medium, the assumption of methods and categories, and an unwillingness to develop approaches relevant to the phenomena being studied. Ethics, taken in its technical sense, is the language of morals. It does not attempt to arbitrate on right and wrong, good and evil, or where a person's duty lies; that is the province of morality and religion. Ethics pursues the much less ambitious task of analysing the concepts employed in moral discourse, investigating their relationship one to another, and examining the validity of moral arguments. Mill, writing at the end of the last century, regretted that ethics had made no progress comparable to the developments in science, but this failure is due less to a lack of effort than to a failure to understand the particular nature of moral statements. Ethical thinkers are now well aware that moral injunctions are peculiar, but how peculiar has largely escaped them.

All usages of the word *red*, for example, have elements in common; they refer to objects that transmit or reflect light of a particular wavelength, or to light of that wavelength. The same applies to the majority of sensible properties such as shape, texture, and size; objects sharing a common description have some property in common. It does not apply to the concepts employed in ethics, whether used in a moral or in a non-moral sense. A good penknife, a good map, a good house, a good action, a good car have no property in common. A good penknife may be sharp, durable, and portable; a good map accurate and detailed; a good house may be durable and pleasant to live in; a good action one in accord with agreed moral principles; a good car one that is comfortable and pleasant to drive and which exhibits sound handling qualities. The fact that evaluative words refer to no single property has been dignified by the term *systematic ambiguity*. Some thinkers have accordingly drawn the conclusion that since there is no property common to all praised or condemned objects, these words must refer to common attitudes rather than to qualities.

Hobbes, the great realist of philosophy, was among the first to take this approach. He held that all evaluative terms simply described a person's emotional response to an object; good and bad, right and wrong can be simply interpreted as "I like" or "I do not like" a particular object or action. The modern school of emotivist thinkers, typified by Stevenson, take this position.

The emotive-mechanism theory, outlined previously, supports the emotivist stand. However, not only are evaluative words used to describe a person's response, they also serve to communicate the response, and to aid in social conditioning. Assumptions that the terms *good* and *bad* describe some property of an object illustrate the extent to which philosophy has been misled by its verbal bias. Implicit in its approach is the assumption that the relation of language to the world provides information about the world. From this standpoint it is easy to assume that objects described by a common adjective share some inherent property, some element of composition or history. This is simply not the case. The application of verbal labels to objects may have no significance at all. It may indicate emotional attitudes to them—holy, good, bad, threatening—or it may indicate some teleological property, that is, some direction or capacity to fulfil possibilities in the future. Beliefs that all properties are either constitutional or historical, that they represent some aspect of make up or history, are unfounded.

Ethics also provides an excellent illustration of the rationalistic and verbal bias of Western thought. It is constructed on the assumptions that human behaviour is largely rational in nature, and that the ideal framework for discussing moral questions is a rational one. Furthermore, ethics considers only the verbal content of moral discussion, whereas a large amount of the communication carried out in a moral context is non-verbal. Facial displays, body movements, stance, tone of voice, and gestures all play a part. The individual, from earliest infancy, learns to read these reactions and subconsciously attributes more weight to them than to verbal content; the youngest child is aware of hypocrisy when he meets it.

This abstraction of verbal content from its moral context invalidates any conclusions ethics may be inclined to draw. The abstraction of phenomena from a situation is one of the more useful tools of inquiry, but it must be handled with care and justified on the basis of results. In the case of ethics, verbal abstraction completely distorts the picture and offends against the holistic approach most fruitful in the social sciences. As a result, ethics has become not only impoverished but trivialized. There are few fields which make duller reading than ethics, and few which seem to have less relevance to everyday life.

What is true of ethics is even more true of aesthetics. This foundling discipline not only assumes a framework of rationality but also presupposes that something worth while is to be gained by analysing the process of analysing works of art, and inspecting the process of inspecting the aesthetic experience. A knowledge of artistic techniques and methods is essential for an artist, but this can only be learnt by imitation and developed through practice. It is the province of art schools. Realistic criticism is also desirable, but this represents finally a personal response, based on a knowledge of the art form and an intuition of what the artist is trying to achieve. This criticism may also take into account the possibilities that the medium itself can fulfil and where it is headed. Internal and external criticism go hand in hand. By contrast, aesthetics attempts to force a basically non-rational experience into a frame of rationality. It comes prepared with the intellectual tools of philosophy, the second-order study of artistic criticism just as ethics is the second-order study of moral discourse. At some stage it is worth questioning whether these disciplines are really necessary.

19

NEW PHILOSOPHIES

For Greeks living in the classical period, philosophy embraced almost every aspect of human knowledge. Aristotle and Plato discussed political theory, logic, ethics, metaphysics, sociology, biology, geography, and theology. Socrates, as represented by Plato, saw the role of philosophy as a general inquiry into human life, experience, and conduct. In this comprehensive tradition the area defined by technical philosophy—logic, metaphysics, epistemology, and ethics—constituted only a small part of their speculative interest.

Classical philosophy was preserved by Islamic civilization during the Dark Ages and introduced into Western thought by scholastic philosophers in the twelfth and thirteenth centuries. Aquinas brought the Aristotelian approach to philosophy into Christian thought, beginning a tradition that is still alive today.

The Scholastic school, however, took over only as much of the classical tradition as was compatible with Christian thought. Scientific issues and questions concerning religion, raised by Aristotle, were ignored, as most were already authoritatively answered in the Old Testament. Thus the areas of philosophy that the Scholastic philosophers concentrated on—logic, metaphysics, epistemology—were largely the areas that could coexist with Christian belief.

Descartes was instrumental in freeing philosophy from the limitations imposed by Christian orthodoxy, although the development of his own philosophy involved the need for a deity. By the seventeenth century, however, the physical sciences had developed independently of philosophy and were never to return to the framework of classical thought.

The history of philosophy in general since the seventeenth century has been one of a continual narrowing of interest and of an ever closer inquiry into the limited areas held to be its appropriate province. It is true that philosophy has, since the work of the empiricists, inquired into the nature of scientific knowledge and the general methods of science. It is also true that the philosophy of history and of religion and political philosophy are studied intensively, but this extension does not result in any genuine enlargement of the role, as against the subject matter, of philosophy. In all these sub-disciplines the subject matter is simply considered as branches of knowledge, and the role of philosophy is seen as criticism of the methods of history, political theory, and religion. Little of what philosophy says in these areas appears to feed back to the disciplines involved, partly because philosophers rarely agree among themselves on any issue and partly because scientists are untrained in, and uninterested in, philosophy. Moreover, the philosophies of religion, science, history, and politics were treated, if in embryonic form, by classical philosophers, so their present study represents little extension of the role of philosophy.

The charges made against academic philosophy in short are these: its academic base has trapped it in an area of social irrelevance; it is ineffective in its purported role as a critical study of other disciplines; it does not function as a storehouse of ideas as it claims; it does not train the intellectual or critical faculties; and unlike older philosophies it does not result in any enrichment of the culture to which it belongs.

These points are worth considering in detail. Academic philosophy develops by the ever more detailed examination of old arguments and the investigation of past questions. It was previously suggested that most problems of academic philosophy lie in the nature of language itself and in its limitations as a modelling medium. There can never be logically watertight arguments for any philosophical position, not even for the belief that there can be no logically infallible arguments. In consequence, no matter what conclusions a philosopher arrives at or what position he takes on an issue, it is always possible for later philosophers to criticize his work and advance alternative interpretations.

Philosophical inquiry, particularly academic inquiry, is inherently conservative. Every generation of students is trained in the ideas of previous major philosophers, a training that represents a considerable investment in time and effort.

There is no incentive in any part of the academic tradition for a philosopher to branch out into new areas or to extend the variety of roles that philosophy could play. It is because of this that the questions raised by Plato are generally those that still preoccupy academic philosophers. Philosophy consists largely of the intensive study of past intellectual schemes, to the exclusion of any attempt to consider what role philosophy could or should play in modern society. There is no incentive to pay any attention to the contemporary world and no reason for philosophy to be relevant in any sense.

Philosophy's claim to provide critiques of other disciplines, especially the sciences, rests on the implicit assumption that its methods are more valid or more reliable than are the methods of the sciences. There is no question that logic in particular, by elucidating confusions, ambiguities, and empty concepts, does at times perform a useful if negative service. But the most that logic can do, and generally all that it claims to do, is to bring out confusions in verbal discussion. Where writings about physics wander into metaphysical vagueness, as do some of the popular works of Eddington for example, a philosopher such as Stebbing has every right to intrude. But no logical system can ever be guaranteed either consistent or complete, so that logical criticisms are always suspect. Furthermore, philosophy with its reliance on verbal models or conceptators can never constitute a basis for criticizing disciplines which use alternative models such as mathematics or chemical formulae, so the role of philosophy in criticism is limited.

A further claim made by apologists for philosophy is that it acts as a storehouse for, and as a source of, new ideas. Ayer has characterized philosophy as a kind of intellectual maelstrom, continually throwing out new insights, approaches, and ideas. In fact, however, philosophy has proved deficient both as a source of new ideas and as an intellectual reservoir.

In the last century at least, philosophy has given rise to virtually no new idea, no new way of conceptualizing or dealing with the world, and has provided no new insight into reality, the nature of the world, or the human condition. It has been the scientists—Darwin, Huxley, Planck, and Einstein—who have influenced the way individuals view the world, providing not so much new information as new patterns of conceptualization and new ways of thinking about the environment. Similarly, it has been the writers, poets, artists, social scientists, and religious leaders who have influenced man's vision of man and the human condition. Lawrence, Beckett, Eliot, Picasso, Frazer, Freud, Malinowski, and Jung rather than the academic philosophers have conditioned the way in which Western man views himself. Russell's popular writings have been influential but lie outside the academic tradition. Mill has had considerable impact, but as an economist and politician rather than as a philosopher. The existentialists have attracted widespread attention in Europe, but more as writers than as philosophers, and their work is, in any event, largely disparaged by English-speaking philosophers.

Not only has philosophy failed to have any impact on Western culture, it has also been highly deficient in its role as a reservoir of ideas. The academic tradition has always been highly selective about which thinkers it has been prepared to treat seriously and those it regards as inconsequential. A list of major philosophers bears very little relationship to those names that have made the most important contributions to human thought.

More significant is the number of leading thinkers who are dismissed out of hand by the academic tradition. This is often the case with people who are pre-eminent in other fields, although frequently their intellectual contributions have been outstanding. Jaspers is almost alone in treating Buddha, Confucius, and Christ with the degree of seriousness usually reserved for major Western philosophers.

However, there are other major religious thinkers such as Zoroaster, a number of Old Testament prophets, Muhammad, some Hindu and Buddhist seers, and the major philosophers of ancient China who have been virtually ignored. Indian and Chinese philosophy are only now entering Western universities, and it will be some time before their fertilizing effect is felt, but this is no reason why major Hindu, Chinese, Hellenistic, Hebrew, Christian, and Muslim thinkers should not be treated equally on merit. Technical philosophy is now as antipathetic to religion as it was once eager to accommodate it, with the result that most thinkers who have been concerned with religious questions are ignored.

Philosophy shows a similar reserve towards thinkers who have been primarily concerned with science. Purely scientific theories such as the theory of gravity or of evolution have little relevance to philosophy, but there have been a number of outstanding thinkers who have considered the nature of science in the abstract and its effect on man and yet have not been taken seriously by philosophers. Francis Bacon, Buffon, Vico, T.H. Huxley, and Teilhard de Chardin, to name only a few, have been prominent in the history of ideas but ignored by academic philosophy.

Thinkers who concentrate on the literary medium to publicize their ideas can expect little better, although there have been significant exceptions. Montaigne, da Vinci, Camus, Schweitzer, Aldous Huxley, and Dostoevsky have all had important comments to make about the human condition, but have generally been ignored. The point is not that thinkers who are primarily religious, scientific, or literary in their interests should be studied in academic philosophy, but that most of what is most original, important, and interesting in human thought is excluded from technical philosophy.

The claim to improve the powers of reasoning and to sharpen the critical faculty is one made at various times both for Euclidean geometry and Latin grammar. It has long been the justification for inflicting these studies on adolescent schoolchildren, despite psychological evidence that skills gained in one area do not carry over to another. This same argument is used to justify a training in academic philosophy; that the skills developed in analysis and in logical argument will benefit a person in all intellectual activities. Logic and language analyses of a situation are, however, only one of a number of possible ways of modelling the external world. Logic is linear and concerned with deductions from given postulates to particular conclusions, a process diametrically opposed to intuition and creative thinking. People trained in the rigorous deductive modes of thinking have rarely achieved any originality in their ideas, nor have they had the capacity for lateral thinking or non-deductive insight.

Contemporary philosophy largely fails to do what is claimed for it. In addition, it has never considered taking on two functions that Western society urgently requires, but for which no equipment at present exists. These are the studies of conceptics and of teleology.

Each scientific discipline has evolved particular techniques for dealing with the material in its domain. These are all fundamentally modelling techniques which simulate a particular aspect of the world by the use of thinking-within-mechanisms or conceptators. The most widely used conceptator is language, but language lacks precision and the capacity to quantify with accuracy. Logic began as a more systematic and precise use of language, but is now moving off in pursuit of that most prestigious of all the sciences, mathematics. Mathematics itself represents an alternative modelling medium, as do block diagrams, chemical notation, dimensional analysis, computer programmes, and graphs.

While each discipline has unique conceptual tools at its disposal, there is curiously little exchange of conceptual equipment between disciplines. The content of physics, chemistry, engineering, mathematics, economics, and logic are known to anyone with a reasonable education, but the intellectual tools used in each study are rarely appreciated. Indeed, most people assume that all use much the same methods.

This failure to realize that different disciplines use very different methods has prevented any large-scale exchange of techniques taking place. It is true that statistical methods and computer simulation studies, pioneered by the physical sciences and the technologies, have spread to the biological and social sciences, but there remain at least a score of powerful modelling methods which have rarely been employed outside the discipline that gave rise to them. What is required is a central discipline—conceptics—which would function as a storehouse of intellectual models and approaches, provide a framework within which cross-discipline comparisons could be made, and afford the basis for developing hybrid techniques. Such a study could be developed within the existing field of epistemology. It would require contributions from experts in a number of fields and necessitate people learning how various disciplines approach their subjects, rather than studying the content of each field.

Conceptual models are not the only item that could be profitably exchanged between disciplines. The classical causal chain approach of early physics has given way to holistic field conceptualizations in many studies. At the same time, the concept of cause itself is being abandoned in favour of statistical probability. Even the concept of determinism has been questioned in quantum mechanics. These changes in conceptual approach tend to appear first in the more sophisticated sciences, and only slowly to percolate down to less developed studies. A separate study of the concepts, ideas, and approaches used in each field would increase the speed at which less advanced studies became aware of more sophisticated conceptualizations, even if these proved of no particular value. The contrast between the conceptual methods of a sophisticated field such as physics and the methods used in economics, for example, is startling.

The need for a separate teleology, a science of ends, is developed more fully in the following section. It is, in a sense, the central issue of this book. A developed teleology is required both to provide a critical apparatus for comparing systems of ends and to allow people to make rational decisions. Post-Renaissance philosophy made intermittent attempts to develop schemes of ends, but the majority became caught up in system building; it became more important to find support for particular values than to develop a systematic machinery of inquiry. This resulted in philosophies that supported Christian beliefs, as did those of Locke and Leibniz, or that supported particular political views, as did the writings of Hobbes and Hegel.

As technical philosophy withdrew from the discussion of ends in the belief that this was not its proper concern, literature assumed this function. Virtually all recent discussion about the meaning of life, about ends and values, has been carried on in literature, either in the contexture of novels, plays, and poems or more directly in essays. There are few major works of literature that do not, implicitly at least, discuss moral choice and the importance of a meaning in existence. But this concern is and must be secondary to the artistic function, just as structural engineering is secondary to sculpture and paint chemistry is secondary to painting. It has never been the purpose of literature to develop a body of ideas, intellectual operators, or attitudes about ends. Even the essay is primarily a personal and literary venture; its relevance to the world is always secondary.

Any attempt to draw discussions of ends together must deal with very diffuse material: drama and poetry going back at least two millennia, novels and short stories spanning at least four centuries, two and a half thousand years of speculative philosophy, and the doctrines of ends contained in all the major religions. Teleology, assembled as a unified study, would have the advantage of bringing together all the ideas about ends so far formulated, both as regards content and the methods used in their different developments. It would contain material from literature, religion, philosophy, the social sciences, and the technologies, allowing a cross-fertilization of ideas, comparative study, and cross-criticism. The very richness of the material and the diversity of approaches and doctrines would force the development of evaluative techniques. It would no longer be sufficient to accept or reject the ideas of human ends in Buddhism, Christianity, utilitarianism, liberalism, existentialism, and Marxism; it would be necessary to develop methods for evaluating these views, for comparing them, and not least for examining the effects that particular views of ends have had on particular societies. The importance of teleology would lie in forcing people to take the questions of ends seriously rather than dismiss them as the irrelevant by-product of religion and philosophy. It is argued below that once an evolutionary framework of thought is adopted the possibilities of a thing—where it is tending and what ends it is capable of fulfilling—are as important as its properties. Physics and chemistry take questions of composition very seriously; archaeology, geology, palaeontology, and cosmology are just as concerned with the past history of things. Nowhere is the question considered of where things should go in the future, of what ends could or should be sought in particular fields, of what methods are to be used in evaluating ends. Yet the potential ends of an object are properties quite as important as its history or composition.

Two minor branches of philosophy are at last becoming aware of this defect. Existentialism, the European philosophy associated with Sartre and Merleau-Ponty, differs from most modern philosophies in being strongly teleological and in attempting to turn philosophy back to questions of human existence. Its metaphysic is enthusiasm; it values intense experience and whole-hearted commitment above contemplation. Its atomistic individualism is characteristically French. Each person is exhorted to choose his own project and to find salvation or satisfaction through involvement, a doing-your-own-thing ethic that has a considerable attraction for the intellectual young. Building on Hume's insight that factual statements cannot legimately give rise to normative statements, Sartre shows that the properties of an object—a knife for example—provide no guide as to how that object should be used. But beyond encouraging people to find their own project, existentialism has little to say. It provides no guiding principles for what type of ends to follow, nor does it provide an apparatus for evaluating ends.

Humanism bears the same relationship to existentialism that British empiricism bears to Continental idealism. Like existentialism, it is concerned with ends and human life rather than the problems of technical philosophy, but it brings a more pragmatic, down-to-earth approach to its subject. As a philosophy, humanism has not yet seen the systematic development of which it is capable, something that may not be a bad thing. But in its intellectual credits—Russell, the Huxleys, and Ayer have been among its prominent spokesmen—its potentially wide appeal, and its concern with ends, it shows more promise than any contemporary branch of academic philosophy. It seems possible that a humanism directed towards constructive social change, a radical humanism, could provide the most useful intellectual framework for contemporary Western society.

A developed society needs a body of philosophical speculation in the sense that it needs a literature or even a technology. Indeed, the decline of religious faith, with the consequent failure to see that the problems raised by religion were real, has made the need for a general philosophy even more imperative. Academic interests, quite unwittingly, have appropriated Western society's birthright, and, by specializing in purely technical questions, have emasculated and trivialized philosophy.

Philosophy in its more general sense is the whole body of human speculative thought that lies outside science. Possibly a new term should be developed for general philosophy—*speculacy*, for example—to distinguish it from technical philosophy. Within the larger framework of general philosophy would fall the conventional studies of academic philosophy, together with conceptics and teleology. Intellectual tools are as important to a society as its technical tools, but at present the only intellectual tools to be taken seriously, to be studied and taught, are the intellectual tools relating to science. A broader total philosophy, by developing tools for use in thinking beyond the realms of science—in mysticism, in religion, in personal relationships, in individual experience—would not only enrich Western culture but vastly increase its chances of survival. Past cultures have decayed not only from physical and sociological causes but because they have lacked the intellectual equipment needed to understand their condition.

PART FOUR

POSSIBILITIES AND ENDS

20

MECHANISM AND TELEOLOGY

There are two ways of explaining an event. The first is by way of the forces acting from behind, the dynamic causes of which the event is only the final result. The second is in relationship to intent, aims, and desires. The first is described as a mechanistic explanation, the second as teleological.

The question why an army marched, for example, can be answered in either of these two ways. In mechanistic terms it can be explained as a result of economic conditions, changing population pressures, and the loss of arable land. Teleologically, it can be explained in terms of the commander's plans and his desire for conquest and glory. In general, mechanistic explanations are found to apply in science and in relation to inanimate phenomena; teleological explanations are associated with human behaviour. One characteristic of primitive thought is that people tend to seek teleological answers to questions involving natural phenomena. Objects are assumed to possess a primitive soul, an anima, which impels them to act. Bodies fall because it is the nature of their anima to seek the ground; plants grow because of an inherent desire or will to reach upwards. The success of science has hinged to a great extent on its substituting mechanistic for teleological explanations. There seems no way in which it could have been known initially that this was the appropriate or even the most fruitful approach; it simply turned out to be so. The posing of mechanistic questions led to the construction of a useful body of knowledge, while the assumption of anima, intelligences, angels, or other end-seeking minds associated with a phenomenon proved unproductive.

As a result the teleological approach with its interest in ends has been largely abandoned in science. Even the social sciences, which deal with phenomena where ends would appear to be relevant, have tended to take a mechanistic approach. Psychology considers human behaviour as functions of motivating mechanisms: the unconscious, social conditioning, childhood events, and other influences acting on an individual. A similar approach can be found in sociology, anthropology, and history. Even though human beings clearly do possess wills, desires, and an idea of the ends they seek, the social sciences have found it more rewarding to study behaviour as a product of pressures from behind. Aims and ends have assumed a secondary importance. Moreover, the ends that human beings aspire to can generally be explained in psychological terms. Ideals do little more than rationalize social pressures; aims and purposes reflect the values of the culture.

Nevertheless, the emphasis on mechanism to the exclusion of teleology has had an unbalancing effect on modern thought, for it has resulted in a general disregard of the question of ends. Mechanism as an intellectual approach is associated with means, while teleology is linked with issues of ends. Contemporary science, the product of causation and mechanistic thinking, cannot provide insights where questions of ends are involved, nor can it provide information about how the capacity it provides is to be used. This is not its province.

Every culture possesses a body of teleological lore, a codified set of rules laying down social behaviour and the appropriate ends of its members. For most cultures, this teleological code is contained in religion. As the term is generally understood today, religion is held to be the study of supernatural phenomena and miraculous events. Religious instruction in its attenuated Western form represents little more than Old Testament folklore and New Testament history, so the misconception is not surprising. But in fact the study of the supernatural is the province of theology. Religion is concerned with the complex of problems of man's duty to man, to nature, and to God· of the point, end, or meaning in life; and of the basis of moral judgements. Religion can survive without a belief in the supernatural, although supernatural sanctions strengthen it, and the emotions of worship and reverence reinforce its values.

The West is probably the first culture to endure without a generally held body of religious belief. This is a source of undisguised delight to rationalists and humanists who have tended to ignore the emotive content of the higher religions in general, and the richness of emotive-mechanisms that they contain. The popular explanation for the decline of religious belief is that the growth of scientific knowledge destroyed it, once people were ignorant and prepared to accept the dogmas of religion, now they are more sophisticated, educated in the sciences, and reject religion. In fact, the matter is nowhere as simple as this. Both religious and non-religious attitudes are compatible with scientific learning. Bertrand Russell was agnostic, Aldous Huxley was a mystic, Einstein was deistic; all were men of scientific learning and temper, yet held widely differing religious attitudes. The conventional reasons why Christianity failed, and why most other higher religions are losing influence, are certainly important, but as always these represent only rationalizations for the true causes of failure. Christianity declined in the West because it became incapable of providing emotional support for its adherents.

Hume put an end to moralizing, and in particular to religious moralizing, when he showed that it is logically impossible to derive an 'ought'—a value statement—from an 'is'—a statement of fact or alleged fact about the world. The fact that God created us does not logically entail the injunction that we should follow God's will in everything, even assuming that we can know God's will with certainty. Even if God is visualized as the absolutist despot of the Old Testament, it is still possible to defy him and accept the consequences. A person of outstanding pride, or one who felt that his duty lay in disobedience to divine injunctions as did the mythical Prometheus, is all but committed to defying God or the gods and accepting the consequences. Moreover, the analogy of God the Father has never been consistently explored by Christian thinkers. A wise human father would prefer to see his offspring go their own way in independence once they had reached maturity. Presumably an infinitely wise divine father would be even more prepared to see his charges become independent.

It is unfortunate that Christianity, Judaism, and Islam have become so deeply involved with temporal events and explanations of natural phenomena, for this has left them particularly susceptible to attack on the basis of their factual information. Medieval Christianity accepted a limited time scale for the creation, a Ptolemaic universe, and particular creation of animal species. These beliefs have all been refuted, and because the factual beliefs of Christianity are so interwoven with the normative material—moral codes, values, and the framework of ends—the latter have also been discredited. It has been possible to minimize the damage by claiming allegorical significance for Biblical stories, and this is the approach taken by most modern apologists and by Protestantism in general. Religions that do not attempt to anchor themselves in a particular historical time and do not aspire to explanation are far safer from the disruption caused by new knowledge. In this respect, mysticism and the Eastern religions, which locate themselves outside the temporal frame, have a marked advantage over the time-involved religions of the West.

As with their factual information, so with their values, the major religions have allowed themselves to become trapped in a particular temporal setting. They have developed, or assimilated, particular sets of moral injunctions appropriate to particular periods. While many moral rules have social utility in any society—for example, prohibitions on murder and theft *within* the society—many have become maladaptive or irrelevant as society evolved. A society in a process of accelerating change will find more and more of its absolute prescriptions becoming irrelevant. More important, the established religions provide no precepts to accommodate new problems, nor is there an intellectual format within which the questions of ends can be examined. Significantly, it has been the theologians rather than the philosophers or social scientists who have suggested the most promising approach. Since the world is now too complex to lay down absolute prescriptions for every set of circumstances, theologians have proposed a situationalist approach to morality. That is, they have attempted to develop criteria for judging rather than to construct a body of absolute prescriptions. Where these criteria are consistent and sufficiently broad, they can be used in lieu of atomic prescriptions.

If some policy on ends is desirable for individuals, it is even more essential for groups and organizations. Business corporations, political societies, and governments, while not immediately interested in moral questions, are vitally concerned with ends. All have, admittedly, their own ideas of ends, usually representing the attitudes common to the particular type of organization: the business corporation pursues profit as its end; the political organization sees its end as implementing a particular programme; universities devote themselves to acquiring and transmitting knowledge; religious organizations see their end as proselytizing. Organizations as much as individuals are all to a degree trapped within their ideology. Yet inevitably the question arises: After this, what? Business organizations find themselves involved in charitable work, job retraining, pollution control, and providing amenities for the community, whether from self-interest or altruism. The political party finds itself with social responsibilities beyond its original programme. Universities undertake extension work and service activities. Religious organizations, becoming more willing to accommodate erstwhile rivals, find it necessary to redefine their aims as new demands are made on them by society. These organizations, faced with an increasingly complex world and a lack of consensus on major issues, now find that some means of evaluating ends is becoming essential. It is no longer a luxury, but something that must be developed. Economics serves to a limited extent, but economic considerations themselves are a suspect criterion, for they finally rest on a particular ideology.

Confusion among societies and organizations reflects the uncertainties of individuals. Many questions, both moral and non-moral, present themselves. How to judge between conflicting ends? What criteria are valid? How to know which direction to take? How to know the good from the bad, and, accepting that these are emotionally charged counters, how to judge whether this loading is worth while, valid, or relevant? And recognizing *good* and *bad* as purely emotive terms, how to develop evaluative concepts and programmes that allow us to discuss these terms? In other words, by what criteria can a person judge the emotive values of his society? These are the central problems of ends.

Over the last thirty years a general concern with ends and criteria has become noticeable in the West. Part of the impetus has been the psychological need for reference points, an almost anguished cry for some meaning, purpose, or direction in a largely secularized life. But its source also lies in the sudden realization of the immense power made available by science. Science, the citadel of mechanism, has provided tools of a power undreamed by earlier generations, but all tools are potential weapons, just as all weapons are potential tools. Science has no normative content, no built-in values, and provides no information about how this new power may, should, or must be used. Even the uncertain use of *may*, *should* and *must* shows how tentative the whole discussion has become. The problem of values and ends is pressing and immediate for, in the cliche of the age, man has the economic and technical power literally to reshape the face of the earth, to destroy every species of animal life, and potentially to change even his own consciousness and genetic structure. The search by an individual for a purpose in life may be dismissed as a psychological pseudo-problem. The search for criteria of ends for the society cannot be.

Hints of this new teleological thinking have begun to appear even in science. Teilhard de Chardin has suggested that, while determinism is appropriate for studies of the inanimate, it becomes diminishingly applicable in the biological sciences and even less useful in the social sciences where teleological factors are present. Support for this can be found in a tendency for the social sciences to turn more to statistical and probabilistic approaches and to neglect mechanism and determinism. Teilhard de Chardin's comments could be dismissed as the special pleading of a religious mind unwilling to accept the elimination of free will, but they merit attention nonetheless. The movement away from determinism and causation is general throughout the sciences.

As suggested, science has found that the most useful approach lies not in examining an object's constitution, but in asking how it functions and what it does. The classical definitions of energy, force, and field are the results of this functional approach. From a functional definition of a concept—what it does—it is only a short step to ask where things are going, that is, what end they serve or what purpose they fulfil. The proviso is that the term *purpose* is used not in the sense of human or divine purpose, but indicating potential direction. Science has traditionally answered questions of composition—what an object is made of and how it is made up—on the basis of its history and its relation to other objects and phenomena. There is, however, no predetermined list of the questions that science may or can ask. The potential uses of a thing or the directions that it is taking are as much properties as its history and composition. Once a dynamic, as against a static, world-view is accepted, both history and potential direction must be considered in investigating a phenomenon.

The clearest example can be found in evolutionary theory. Once the history of organic life is envisaged on Darwin's analogy, as a branching tree, the question inevitably arises where the various branches are tending. Paradoxically, the answer in most cases is—nowhere. Most species have worked themselves into evolutionary dead ends. Without a major change in the condition of the globe, an ice age, or the disappearance of the dominant type, man, it seems unlikely that further biological evolution will take place in the near future. Even the human species has stabilized as far as its organic structure is concerned. Sir Julian Huxley has suggested that biological evolution has given way to psycho-social evolution, which from now on will be the dominating force in history, an idea supported by emotivist theories. Nevertheless, no matter what form evolution takes, evolutionary thought still raises questions of direction and ends and makes them relevant to science. This would be even more the case should man become capable of controlling his own evolutionary development.

21

THE VARIETIES OF ENDS

Before attempting to develop a general approach for evaluating ends it is worthwhile enumerating the various types of ethics, or systems of ends, that have been held in the past. As in many fields the Greeks were the first to set out competing beliefs in a systematic way and to provide cross-criticism. Writers such as Aristotle ranked the ends that men pursue in a hierarchy which reflected their own personal values and prejudices; at the lowest level came the pursuit of pleasure and wealth, ranging through higher pursuits, such as fame, to a life dedicated to pure contemplation. Among the major philosophies of ends developed, first by the Greeks and then by European thinkers, are hedonistic ethics, wealth- and fame-seeking ethics, contemplative and intellectual value systems, the aristocratic and totalitarian ethics, life-reverence, and humanism.

The vestiges of puritanism still colour any attempt to justify the pursuit of pleasure. However, for a Greek thinker such as Epicurus the pleasures to be found in life included intellectual pleasures, the enjoyment of good company and good conversation, appreciation of music, art, literature, and natural beauty as well as the so-called lesser pleasures of food, sex, and drink. A hedonistic philosophy readily degenerates into a worship of gross sensuality and into selfishness, but it can also lead to a life devoted to the nominally higher pursuits of art and the intellect. As with pleasure, the veneration shown to wealth as an end varies from culture to culture. In the late eighteenth and early nineteenth centuries, the pursuit of wealth required no justification and no apology; wealth was all but equated with moral rectitude. It proved that a man embodied the virtues of hard work, thrift, and ambition. The change in attitude towards wealth, from the "eye of a needle" doctrine to laissez-faire competitiveness, illustrates how successfully social values have evolved to serve social needs. That the pursuit of wealth is embraced with a little less enthusiasm today, despite the almost Fitzgeraldian adulation still shown the very rich, indicates a further change in values, reflecting again changing social conditions.

A wealth ethic reflects a society entering a stage of sudden economic growth. A fame ethic on the other hand reflects a militaristic or politically expanding society. A high value was placed on fame and honour at the time of Athenian expansion, during the sovereignty of Imperial Rome, and in nineteenth century England. Its social utility under these conditions is obvious. It is only where there are campaigns to be waged, lesser races to be dominated, empires to be extended, and famous victories to be won that fame and honour are relevant. They provide the spur to military conquest and to the extension of empire. Fame may admittedly result from scientific and cultural pursuits, but in these cases fame is generally incidental to success in the particular field, rather than the primary incentive. A variant of the fame ethic is the power-seeking ethic which maintains that men inevitably seek power, and that this pursuit should be either contained or exploited for the good of the society. This preoccupation with power characterized nineteenth century state-directed thinking, one reason why nineteenth century philosophers such as Russell paid it so much attention. The distribution of power within a society remains the central issue of politics, but the pursuit of power as an end in itself is becoming less reputable.

Towards the end of his *Nicomachean Ethics*, Aristotle attempted to show that the only occupation open to God was pure thought and contemplation. Accordingly, this was the highest end that human beings could aspire to. This belief in the higher value of thought and intellectual achievement, as against more worldly pursuits, persists if often unstated among the intellectual community. A quite different value system, best described as aristocratic, was put forward by Friedrich Nietzsche at the end of the nineteenth century. He held that the end of society and culture was the production of the superman, and that to this end any sacrifice of lesser mortals was justified. Nietzsche's views have been widely misrepresented, even where they have been understood, both by Nazi propagandists and by hostile democrats. Both have attempted to interpret him from the standpoint of their own ideology. The aristocratic ethic is fundamentally different from the totalitarian, although in the Nazi credo the two were synthesized. All organizations make greater or lesser demands on their members, but a totalitarian organization, be it a religion, a state, or a secret society, demands the complete sacrifice of members to the organization. The end, in this case, is the organization. This type of morality will emerge when a group or society is under considerable stress and, even though repugnant to democratic society, has social utility. It is doubtful whether Russia or China, for example, could have been industrialized without a totalitarian ideology, and eventually the more chaotically underdeveloped countries such as India may be forced to adopt totalitarian values. The opposed ethic, humanism, takes the view that individual human beings alone are the only end to be considered. This attitude is not new, having appeared in Greek thought and in late Roman Stoic philosophy. Kant in his ethical writings stated that human beings should never be viewed merely as means, but also as ends. Formal humanism reflects an age that is nominally individualistic, and which places a high value on the person rather than the group. Albert Schweitzer developed a related ethic of reverence-for-life, under the influence of his experiences in Africa. In his view it was not simply human life or some section of humanity that should be viewed as an end, but all life in whatever form.

These ethical systems all possess a number of characteristics in common. To begin with, all reflect to some extent the social needs of particular groups at a particular stage in their history. Hedonism, contemplativism, and humanism reflect individualistic ideals, and tend to emerge in periods when people have a certain degree of leisure and independence. Fame and aristocratic values reflect militarism and imperialism. A reverence-for-life ethic can be expected to emerge at a time when wildlife and biological resources are becoming scarce. Totalitarianism reflects the condition of a society or group fighting for existence and demanding the complete loyalty of its members. As all ethics reflect emotive-mechanisms, there is no logical way in which they can ever be ruled right or wrong. *Right* and *wrong* are terms reserved for statements of fact; they have no truck with value systems. All that can be said is that one likes or does not like a certain ethic, but this represents little more than a personal reaction to it. Most Westerners dislike the Nietzschean and totalitarian ethics, but where these are widely held they are held because of quite definite social pressures. These may be the desire of a particular group to maintain power, or they may reflect the attitudes of the society as a whole, particularly a society that is encircled by hostile forces and denied the standing it believes to be its due. In such a case, totalitarian values may develop within the society in order for it to survive. There is no need for them to be imposed by the rulers as a sort of confidence trick; cultures develop the emotive-mechanisms that meet their needs.

Again, all existing ethical systems are directed towards one particular end. This may be the personal pleasure or happiness of the individual, or the well-being of a particular group such as the aristocrats or the organization. This notion of a single final point to which actions are directed reflects a static world-view. Even with the broadest moralities such as humanism or life-reverence one is tempted to ask: What then? The eternal good of the particular end may be impossible to achieve in practice, but if it ever were achieved, then what is the next step? Is a new value system to be developed, or does action stop? Clearly, what is needed is not a given "point-end" to work towards, but a direction to take. In mathematical terms, point thinking is replaced by a vectorial approach. In this way, not only is the change from static to dynamic world-view made, but a continually renewing criterion is possible. Having reached end 1 it is possible to go on to end 2 and so on, since vectors can be extended to infinity. This approach implies the use of criteria rather than the laying down of predetermined ends, and indeed many ethical thinkers have attempted to develop just such a criterion, or family of criteria. These range from the simplistic "biggest is best" criterion to the sophisticated consistency criterion first used by Kant.

It could be claimed that few people today are naive enough

to argue that size is a workable criterion of value. Nobody seriously believes that a twenty-foot-long automobile is inherently superior to a compact model, that a six-decker novel surpasses in merit a slim volume, or that a B52 is necessarily better than a smaller aircraft. Yet this is true only where material objects are involved. In the more abstract field of organizations, for example, people prove less certain in their attitudes. A giant conglomerate has certain advantages of scale over a small company, and these are sufficient to induce people into a *de facto* "biggest is best" judgement. Once the subject is something as abstract as an economy, there is no doubt that biggest is best. A trillion-dollar economy is vastly superior to a billion-dollar economy simply because it is bigger. The "B52 argument", for want of a better name, applies where people want it to apply.

There is a variant of this argument which is both more persuasive and more subtle. In essence it can be traced back to Plato. Bigness may not be best, but what of the fourth dimensional analogy of size—persistence? In a world where everything is subject to transience and decay, it seems reasonable to place the highest value on those things which endure. Carried to its logical conclusion, the only things that finally have any value are those which are eternal. The Christian Church, notably in its early world-denying stage, adopted just this view. Everything on earth passes away: achievements, wealth, beauty, love, material possessions. The only goods not subject to decay are spiritual goods to be accumulated in Heaven, outside time, where moth and rust corrupt not. Hence, it is argued, spiritual goods alone are worthy of attainment. This attitude is found in many other higher religions, and generally reflects a pessimism towards, and an abnegation of, the material world. Ultimately, the argument is invalid, for to claim that a thing has no value because it is transient is equivalent to claiming that it is valueless because it is not infinite. Nonetheless, it remains a persuasive doctrine particularly for those disillusioned with the material world.

In general, systems of moral criteria show a not unexpected parallel with the metaphysics used to support knowledge. The authority basis, the clarity basis, and the consistency basis have all appeared at one time or another. The use of authority as a basis for ends and moral values needs no elaboration; indeed most people would assume that authority, presumably religious authority, is the only basis that a prescriptive morality can assume. A clarity metaphysic for value systems and morality can be developed as readily as for knowledge. However, instead of claiming that people know certain facts because they are seen with particular clarity, it is claimed that certain values are held to be true because they are known with particular clarity, or felt with particular immediacy. Rousseau with his emphasis on the individual conscience was one of the first thinkers to formalize this approach. Just as Descartes with his emphasis on knowledge through clarity liberated philosophy from the dead hand of Aristotelian authority, so Rousseau liberated morality from Catholic authority. Even the Protestant emphasis on a return to the Bible was paradoxically a liberation, since as many interpretations can be placed on the holy word as there are interpreters. The result has been to destroy Protestantism. The clear light of conscience, which since Vatican 2 is now penetrating even Catholicism, militates against centralism, absolutism, and the monolithic structure that once characterized the Church. Its tendency is to further the individualistic, competitive, atomistic character of the present age—to fragment doctrine and to increase uncertainty. When every man is his own prophet, there can be no absolute morality; the value system equivalent of Babel then exists.

Kant was the first philosopher to appreciate the power of consistency in developing value schemes. His well-known principle of universalizability stated that one should act so that, in principle, one's actions could be extended to the whole human race. Murder and lying are obviously rejected on this principle, because if every person committed murder there could be no morality, and if everyone lied, all vows and information would be useless. The consistency approach tacitly assumes social utility, which is the only reasonable approach to value systems once a universal religious belief is lost.

22

CRITERIA FOR VALUE SYSTEMS

Previous attempts to construct systems of ends have presumed that an ethic must be true for all times and all places. In fact, precisely the opposite is true. Just as knowledge and understanding represent models that are applicable in particular fields at a particular time, so value systems represent operators or criteria that have social utility for a particular time and place only.

Consequently, any proposed value scheme must be consistent with the recognized laws and injunctions of the period. Many laws are the product of particular vested interests and power groups; special taxation laws, discrimination against minorities, religious laws, and trade regulations are examples. Many, however, such as prohibitions on murder, rape, and theft, are of such long standing that they must be assumed to reflect essential conditions for the survival of a society. In addition, the value system of a society must be consistent with its factual beliefs about the world and with the way in which these beliefs are ordered. A culture which believes that the world was created by the devil, or that matter is evil, must embrace a code of ends compatible with this belief, and reject the material world as far as possible. A culture which holds, as the Hindu does, that life consists of infinite returns and recycles, will embrace a value system both minimizing the importance of this life and attempting to find escape from, or accommodation with, the infinite recurrence.

Western culture now interprets its universe implicitly on Darwin's branching tree model. Reversing the analysis carried out by the physical sciences, it is impossible not to see sub-atomic particles coming together to form approximately one hundred varieties of atoms, the atoms in turn coming together to form some ten million or so known molecules, these molecules in particular arrangements forming a tree, a rock, a cloud, all the manifestations of the physical world. One type of atom, carbon, has the ability to form long continuous chains and closed rings. From this simple property springs the whole field of organic chemistry, reproduction, organic life, and Darwin's tree of evolution. At some stage intelligence arose, and this gave rise to highly organized societies, science, and art. Whether we are aware of it or not, this is the way we now see the world. It has been so ever since the publication of *The Origin of Species*.

Since we arrange factual information in this way, any value system must be compatible with this outlook, even if not based on it. Stephen Toulmin in *The Discovery of Time* has argued that the only temporal frameworks available, from history to cosmology, are the steady state, the recycling, and the evolving. Parallel to these are the particular value systems associated with them; the eternally true Christian "steady-state" morality, the Hindu morality which is static within a recycling framework, and the evolutionary or self-modifying value system. The latter is the only one capable of accommodating a continually developing society.

Any new value system proposed for Western society must accept these conditions. It must be situationalist rather than prescriptive in regard to moral decisions, and vectorial rather than point-directed in regard to non-moral decisions. It must be capable of developing within itself rather than claiming absoluteness and infallibility, and it must be compatible with the evolutionary model of the physical universe.

Most cultures make a clear distinction between means and ends. Some elements are usually accepted as ends, others are always considered as means, while most can be seen as either means or ends, depending on the circumstances. Historically, everything that this culture has held to be a valid end has moved, or is now moving, into the category of means. Wealth is the paradigm of this. During the industrialization of Europe, wealth was seen and accepted as an end in itself. If one sought money it was not necessary to find further justification; money was an end sufficient in itself. But as material standards of living have improved wealth is increasingly justified in terms of what can be done with it. The same shift in attitude is now taking place with regard to sex, consumer goods, and even knowledge. Thirty years ago the attainment of a sexual conquest appeared justification enough; now it needs the justification of contributing to a "deep personal relationship" if it is to be acceptable. The accumulation of consumer goods, even under the constant prodding of the advertising industry, could not continue forever without verging on the absurd. Current advertising concentrates less on the simple act of ownership and more on what can be achieved through the manifold miracles of production engineering. "Lead the good life", "get up and go", "towards a better tomorrow", and "a new world awaits you" are the constant strains of the advertising media. Owning a houseful of cluttering artefacts is no longer enough; they must be used in some constructive way if they are not to appear ludicrous. In the same way, scholarship and the accumulation of information as an end in itself now commands scant respect; information is seen as both a means and an end, both tool and yield.

This blurring of the distinction between means and ends has been in progress for at least fifty years, and there is every reason to assume that it will continue. To some extent this reflects the breakdown of the rigid categories of cause and effect which is now taking place in science. As determinism and the causal principle become not so much invalidated as irrelevant, the corresponding distinction between means and ends becomes less significant. Both represent the move from a simplistic single-line view of phenomena to a holistic field attitude towards the world.

The eighteenth century represented causation on the single-line billiard ball model used by Hume: A causes B and B then causes C and so on. This simple model is still useful in elementary fields such as mechanics, but once disciplines such as electronics and biology are encountered, it rapidly becomes useless. Cause-effect feedbacks enter the picture. A causes B but B simultaneously interacts with A and with C and D. A holistic or field representation of a phenomenon, as against a straight-line representation, becomes essential. It becomes impossible to abstract particular interactions and examine them in isolation.

Just as it is no longer possible to distinguish absolutely between cause and effect, so it is becoming less certain which things are to be regarded as means and which as ends. A thing that is the means towards certain ends will be affected by those ends, and these in turn contribute to the original means. For example, the wealth a person accumulates allows him to improve his education, his health, and his standing in the community, but these in turn allow him to further advance his wealth. These means-ends interactions are the rule rather than the exception in human life and social affairs. They completely invalidate any attempt to rule on which elements are means and which are ends. This means-ends confusion can be eliminated by accepting that the traditional distinction always was insupportable. It belongs to an age that attempted, quite reasonably, to simplify the world in order to understand it, and which interpreted it from a static rather than a dynamic viewpoint. It can be resolved by changing the perspective, by admitting that every element in the world can be viewed as both means and end simultaneously. Kant's moral dictum is thus extended to the entire organic and non-organic world.

This leads in turn to equi-valuing. Every possibility in the world is, in principle, quite as legitimate an end as any other. The qualification is that some give rise to other possibilities, whereas others destroy or limit other possibilities. In order to act with consistency, the only possible injunction is this:

Act so as to maximize the number of simply enumerable possibilities.

This is the possibilities value criterion.

This does not pretend to be a logically valid deduction of a value system. Such a deductive programme is impossible on three counts:

1. There can be no logically watertight proof of anything, much less the arguments for a value system.
2. Values are associated with emotive-mechanisms and emotional states. As such they finally analyse into emotional expressions—*I like*, *I hate*, *I revere*, and so on. Logic has no conceivable truck with statements of emotional content.
3. If a logically watertight eternally true value system could be formulated, it would be incapable of development. It is im-

possible to conceive of a system that would be applicable to the civilization of Hammurabi, to the present day, to the world four thousand years hence, to computers and finally to all intelligent life throughout the galaxy. Yet this is implied by those who seek logical proofs for value systems.

Another objection to the demand that logically valid proofs be advanced for any ethic is that science itself has long abandoned this type of approach. Nobody attempts to deduce a scientific theory logically from the observed data, or even to induce such a theory. A hypothesis is constructed by a process of intuition and then tested against the experimental data. In the same way, there is nothing in the data of received moral values, or anything else, that allows a value system to be deduced. All that can be done is to construct a possible value scheme, again using intuition and imagination, and to examine the moral precepts that result.

This having been said, there remain monumental difficulties in justifying the possibilities criterion. The injunction to maximize is the most suspect; it savours of the best-of-all-possible-worlds mentality, and of an optimism and opportunism that is now unfashionable. However, a value system is necessarily involved with directions, and the only way to derive a direction is through maximizing or minimizing some element. Simply arranging the world as a system of branching possibilities leads nowhere.

23

DISADVANTAGES OF THE POSSIBILITIES ETHIC

A possibilities ethic has advantages and disadvantages. Among the disadvantages are problems of levels and of numeration, and logical problems. None prevent the criterion being used, but they do make it a less tidy tool than it might otherwise be.

It has been pointed out by many thinkers, often in rejection of the Victorian era's optimism, that there is no logical reason to prefer being over non-being, no way to show that it is better that things exist rather than not exist. A world in which there is a multitude of things can never be proved better than a world in which there is nothing. Consequently, there is no reason to do, or not to do, anything, and in particular no reason to optimize possibilities. This is the familiar problem of motivation, this time decked out in logical attire. But as rational processes cannot motivate behaviour, it is only reasonable to expect that logic cannot accord any value to being or to non-being as such. In fairness to logic, the question is far more complex than this. To ask whether a value can be placed on being raises not only the question of valuing and involvement with motivational problems, but also problems associated with the nature of being itself. These are considerable.

Being, as it has now become clear, is not a property in the sense that redness or solidity are properties. To say that an apple is red and solid conveys quite definite ideas about it, but to add that it exists contributes nothing to the information. There have been numerous attempts to solve this problem, in particular Russell's use of his Theory of Descriptions, and the restatement of propositions in a functional form with existential quantifiers. None of these approaches has been entirely successful. The problem appears to hinge, once again, on inappropriate models and ways of thinking about the world, although it is much easier to assert this than to prove it. Probably the readiest response to the "cannot logically value being" objection is to reject logic and its associated modes of thought as irrelevant in this connection. Being entails modes of thought associated with the static world-view. It relates to the question of what a thing is. Once the intellectual approach moves to the functional—what a thing does—all the classic problems involved with being vanish. This is as true of modern existentialism as of Scholastic philosophy.

Beyond the logical objections there are difficulties in actually applying the possibilities value system. The first concerns an old philosophical problem—that of numeration. In order to choose between alternative paths of action or alternative ends, it is necessary to count the potential results that accrue. But the number of possibilities in any area depends entirely on how the situation is described. A rose bush is one bush, a dozen flowers, a hundred leaves and twigs. A hand is one hand, five digits, over a score of bones, and a million cells. Even if the likely results of several courses of events can be determined, there is no way to agree on how many possibilities are involved in any instance. This problem is more apparent than real. The possibilities criterion is only a construct to allow choice between competing courses of action. Provided the description is consistent for the various programmes of action, there is no difficulty. Even though alternative courses may yield quite different results, these developments can usually be described along comparable lines, the results enumerated, and a decision made.

More serious is the problem of varieties and levels that possibilities thinking involves. If one had to choose between two courses of action, one of which destroyed, say, a thousand giraffes with little to be gained, and one that left the giraffes unharmed, the only reasonable course would be the latter. If, however, one had to choose between a thousand giraffes and a lesser number of giraffes with zebras and deer included, one would be tempted to choose the variety, even though the total number of animals was smaller. If one had to choose between this variety and the development of a completely new level of possibilities, such as intelligence, then the latter choice would probably be made. Difficulties are encountered in deciding what degree of variety compensates for what number of possibilities, and how much weight to give a completely new level, such as the advent of life, intelligence, or art.

It is possible to develop quite elaborate frameworks in which to consider possibilities. For instance, linear developments at one level could be set against *evelopments*, or non-linear developments, and some method found of weighing the results. A motor vehicle is a linear descendant—that is to say, a development—of the horse-drawn carriage, which in turn descended from animal transport; the service station is an evelopment of the motor vehicle, without which the former would not have come into existence. Human beings are linear descendants of a now extinct primate which in turn developed from the reptiles, the fish, and single-celled life. Intelligence, on the other hand, is not a straight line development of anything but an evelopment. It is brought into existence almost incidentally, and tangentially to, biological development.

Probably a quite elaborate calculus of ends, not unlike that proposed by Leibniz for moral questions, could be developed, but the effort seems hardly worth while. In practice, people rarely calculate the particular results that are likely to spring from particular courses of action; rather, they develop an intuition as to which is likely to be the most fruitful, the most enriching, or the most far-reaching course of action. Instead of refining and sharpening the criterion, it is more useful to generalize it.

The main contribution of a possibilities ethic lies in the attitudes it involves, the approach it implies, rather than in any minute calculation. The injunction can thus be restated:

Act so as to give rise to the greatest variety of ends.

The more serious objections to the possibilities criterion are those that apply to Bentham's hedonistic utilitarianism. It fails on counts of fairness, and it fails on counts of suffering. It is possible to have a course of action that demonstrably maximizes possibilities and leads to higher levels, and which is still manifestly unfair to many people involved. Where great suffering would be caused, the only way to accommodate this is to allow for the diminution of possibilities brought about in those who suffer, an attitude that few humane people could accept. Fairness and the minimizing of human suffering can be written into the possibilities criterion as boundary conditions, but at the expense of elegance. These drawbacks are far more serious than any logical or philosophical objection, for finally a value system must justify itself in its effect on people's lives. If it cannot, it has failed even though its logic be impeccable.

24

ADVANTAGES OF THE POSSIBILITIES ETHIC

Against the disadvantages stated at the end of the previous chapter, the possibilities criterion has significant advantages to offer. To begin with it is recursive; it is capable of calling itself. Other value systems point to a predetermined end, such as happiness, the superman, the state, but are unable to make reference to themselves as the subject of a value system. The possibilities criterion is capable of being applied to itself, just as it can be applied to any object, activity, or condition in human life. If it is the value system that gives rise to the greatest number of possibilities, then there is good reason for adopting it. If it can be shown that another value system gives rise to a greater richness of human life, or to more possibilities, then there is good reason for adopting the alternative scheme.

As a result the ethic fails safe; in political phraseology, it keeps its options open. Adherence to such value schemes as the totalitarian or aristocratic not only excludes other ethics at the time but may prevent them ever developing. An aristocratic ethic, for example, could result in the elimination of all lesser beings, leaving only the supermen as survivors. If this happened, alternative ethics could never arise. As the possibilities criterion would tend to leave the largest number of alternatives available, it would provide the greatest opportunity for other schemes to develop. As a matter of interest, several of the value schemes described are already subsumed by it. In particular, humanism and the life-reverence ethic of Schweitzer are limited cases of the possibilities ethic.

Because of its emphasis on levels, itself a result of the branching tree model, this ethic is capable of continually refining its criteria. In practice all criteria, in no matter what field, are developed by trial and error, and later codified into a social consensus. Generally there is some sort of ideal, some agreed set of properties by which the field is judged, these generally reflecting past prejudices and experience. We expect a mother, for example, to show certain qualities of patience, affection, and discipline in rearing her children. In addition, we also examine the things that the mother's qualities have determined—in this case, the behaviour and personality of the children. If the children have turned out well as judged by accepted standards, we agree that the mother has been a good mother. Obviously, the results obtained at the derived level tend to modify criteria at the basic level. It could be that a woman whom neighbours judge as lax, slovenly, and inefficient will still bring up children who are acceptable according to the prevailing standards. In this case, assuming that the mother has been the major determining influence, it will be tempting to modify the original criteria by which she was judged.

Judgement is thus made of the mother both as an end in herself—as a mother on the basis of agreed criteria—and on the basis of the things she has given rise to—the personalities of her children. And the results at the derived level constantly modify the thing-in-itself criteria. This type of dualistic judging is applied, implicitly or explicitly, wherever one level gives rise to another. In practice almost all judging is concerned with multiple levels. There is a continual modification of criteria going on at any time between different levels. The final appeal is made not simply to results, as the pragmatist thinkers would suggest, nor to the innate qualities of the thing being considered, as moral purists would desire. The interaction between the two, and the continual modification of criteria are all involved. This approach turns up in ethics, in art criticism, and in almost every field where judgements must be made, and where one element gives rise to others.

Another consequence of the possibilities ethic is that, in its terms, it does not make sense to go beyond a certain point in any pursuit. It is not possible to say that one cannot go beyond any limit, because further progress is always possible, at least in theory. Similarly, one cannot say that people must not go beyond a certain point, for this is no more than an emotional expression of one's own feelings. There is no adequate language at present to express value recommendations, but probably the most satisfactory way is this: that it does not make sense to do a certain thing. It is agreed for instance that health and financial security are desirable and worthwhile ends, but the person who pursues health and physical fitness to the fanatical extent of a Mr Universe, and the businessman who pursues wealth to the single-minded exclusion of everything else are in fact limiting possibilities. By their absolute determination to have or to do one thing to the exclusion of everything else they lose everything else, and risk losing even the thing they most desire. The Mr Universe physique finally runs to fat and its proud owner finds that he has nothing in compensation. The wealthy business entrepreneur finally discovers that he is left with nothing to fall back on except wealth. The golden mean and the middle way find their justification in a possibilities ethic. At some point the phenomenon of diminishing returns always becomes significant. At this stage, the only sensible course is to cease the single-minded pursuit of particular ends, and to use them as means to other ends. Otherwise, there is not only a reduction of total possibilities but the inevitable risk that the original end will be lost.

It was suggested in the first section that creative activity integrates personality. This type of feedback applies to all human activity and to all human institutions, whether legal, educational, financial, or artistic. Any institution that goes beyond itself, fulfils other possibilities, and gives rise to new developments tends to maintain its dynamic and perpetuate its existence. Those institutions that are intent only on maintaining themselves and which lead nowhere stultify in the manner of Parkinsonian government departments. A readily imagined model is an electrical cable only maintained in good condition for as long as it conducts electricity. Once the flow of current is shut off, the conductor begins to corrode. There is no reason why this effect should appear at the human and, to a lesser extent, the biological level; it is simply a matter of record that it does. No corresponding effect can be found in the inanimate world. Generally, those people and institutions which go beyond themselves to fulfil other possibilities retain their own dynamic and integrity. Those which turn inward to protect themselves decay. In a very real sense there is no alternative to unselfishness, even where that unselfishness may be turned to bad ends. One can only have self by going beyond self.

I sometimes wonder if this is what T. S. Eliot meant when he wrote that possession can only be achieved by dispossession, and that to arrive at what you are involves going through the way in which you are not.

A more penetrating thinker, Jesus Christ, originated the idea two thousand years earlier, when he pointed out that those who would have life shall lose it, and that only those prepared to give up their lives shall live fruitfully. The imposed deification of Christ, apparently unsought, has been unfortunate for, by promoting Christ from the ranks of great ethical thinkers to spiritual dogmatist, it has prevented serious examination of his ideas. Even now people are only just beginning to understand what Christ was saying. It will probably be centuries before his ideas are fully appreciated, in the sense that the ideas of Socrates or Kant are appreciated. It would please neither the humanists nor the Christians if Christ came to be regarded as the greatest humanist thinker of all time.

These are the advantages of a possibilities ethic as applied in practice. It is consistent, both internally and externally; it allows the continual modification of criteria between levels, so that dogmatic value judgements are unnecessary; it is situationalist rather than prescriptive; and it avoids excesses. Because evaluations are seen as operators rather than as absolute prescriptions, the split between knowledge and values is partly eliminated. Understanding requires operators that allow people to act and which relate to things already in existence. Evaluations require operators that allow people to act but which refer to things that may come into existence. Both are functional interpretations; we are interested in them for what they do, rather than for what they are. The main argument for a possibilities value scheme, however, lies in the fact that it is already presupposed in large areas of life. Legal codes implicitly accept it. Practical decisions are usually made on this basis. Even artistic and aesthetic judgements are affected by it.

25

POSSIBILITIES IN PRACTICE

Legal systems, as Hume realized two hundred years ago, have social utility. They evolve to meet the requirements of a society and, where they are adequate, reflect the underlying needs of the society. All laws on which there is a widespread consensus can be looked at from the point of view of their effect on possibilities. Murder, theft and rape, arson, and the destruction of property all result *prima facie* in the diminution of possibilities. Where this is not true, as for example, in mercy killings, judicial executions, abortion, and Robin Hood type robbery, the society becomes less certain of its values.

The severity of the crime and the emotional reaction that it produces reflect the possibilities involved. The assassinations at Sarajevo and at Dallas were rightly considered far more serious than the killing of a mentally deficient child, because they encompass far more possibilities. This raises the possibility of a completely situationalist approach to law and jurisprudence. As society becomes more complex and interdependent, the number of purely prescriptive laws will increase in something approaching a geometrical progression. The USA is the most complex and rapidly developing society on earth, and not unexpectedly has the greatest number of laws. With increasing complexity, the developed countries will finally involve themselves in the sort of legal bureaucratic strangulation that now paralyses India. The alternative is to shift to situationalist laws, prohibiting for example anything that diminishes the possibilities of another person, rather than framing particular laws against murder, assault, rape, harassment, and so forth. The qualities of the victim—that is, his potential possibilities and the reduction of these possibilities—would need to be considered along with the seriousness of the crime. Such a programme would be incredibly difficult to work out, but may eventually be the only alternative to an infinitely complex atomistic legal structure.

The possibilities viewpoint also brings together the two main approaches in the technical field of ethics: the utilitarian, associated with the British empiricist school; and the intuitionalist, which is related to Continental idealism. Utilitarians such as Bentham, Mill, and G.E. Moore judged the value of an object or action by the final result produced. For Bentham this end was human happiness, plain, pure, and simple; for Mill, other goods such as justice were introduced; while Moore carried this further, introducing still other ultimate goods, such as benevolence and compassion, and arguing that all moral values ultimately depend on the extent to which they contribute to these goods. Clearly the final ends sought reflect social values and are logically unsupportable. They must be accepted on faith. The intuitionalists, typified by the English philosopher Sir David Ross, took the opposite approach. They held that certain actions were inherently good in themselves, almost independent of the results produced. Acts of benevolence, justice, and compassion require no justification by way of happiness, welfare, or any other result; they are in their very nature good, although exceptions can be allowed when moral acts give rise to obviously disastrous results. Considered on the basis of possibilities both the inherent nature of the act itself and the result produced—the next level of possibilities—are equally important. The derived possibilities modify the criteria used for the thing in itself, and this modification proceeds through a continual interaction at various levels. It is not necessary to accept criteria on faith; instead, a picture of the total pattern, a holistic conception of the field, is obtained and the consequences, including fed-back possibilities, considered.

Judgements made in art, quite as much as in other fields, can be considered from a possibilities viewpoint. One piece of dogma that the Western world does take very seriously is art for art's sake. This would appear to make art the one great exception to a world in which every other item can be viewed both as means and end. The *art for art's sake* doctrine has social utility in that it prevents art being trivialized as religious and political propaganda. There is, however, the attendant danger that art which is intransitive, which goes nowhere and fulfils no possibilities, will result and lead to stagnation.

In point of fact, the periods that have exhibited the greatest creative energy in art have not seen art as its own end. They have used art, either consciously or unconsciously, as a means towards some other, and in their view, higher end. In the eleventh to thirteenth centuries the architectural style that was later to be known as Gothic developed in France, and spread through Europe. Yet the anonymous tradesmen and artisans who created the Gothic structure of Chartres had nothing further from their minds than an *art for art's sake* doctrine. Such an idea could only occur in an extremely individualistic and self-conscious age. The Gothic masters saw their work as an offering praising and glorifying God.

In the Renaissance a quite different outlook found its expression in a totally different art. Reacting against ten centuries of retreat into mysticism and religion, the Renaissance set out to re-explore the physical world through the twin media of art and science. It was only when an absolute accuracy in depicting the world made further progress impossible, and photography made it irrelevant, that the search for new directions became essential.

Some of these new directions have already become apparent. Expressionists such as Munch sought to use art to express their own feelings rather than to explore the external world. Blake in his etchings and paintings explored the mystical and metaphysical aspects of the world. Cézanne used landscapes to explore the relations of colour and form, a departure that began the present development of abstract art.

The movements in the plastic arts are reflected in the literary arts. The novels of Austen, Lawrence, and Tolstoy represent, like the paintings of the Renaissance, attempts to investigate the world and in particular the psychological condition of the characters. The inward turning novels of Kafka and Virginia Woolf represent, like the paintings of Van Gogh and Munch, attempts to explore and express the artist's own psychological state. The fold-in prose of Burroughs parallels the exploration of pure media found in abstract and kinetic art. Because literature is the art form associated with the central means of communication—language—it has traditionally performed a twofold function. It has not only served its own ends as an art form; it also carries the weight of much thinking on the human condition, world-views, ideals, and value systems. This has been generally to the advantage of literature, but it also means that people's ideas about existence are dispersed through an incredible range of material. Information on crystallography or biochemistry can be located immediately in a library. When it comes to finding what people believe about life, it is necessary to go to the plays of Euripides, Shakespeare, and Shaw, the essays of Montaigne, Huxley, and Russell, and the novels of Hardy, Lawrence, Dickens, and Sartre. And traditionally, philosophers from Plato to Berkeley and Sartre have turned the compliment to literature by using its forms whenever they wanted to communicate their ideas to a wider audience.

One of the most vital contemporary art forms, if one that is somewhat ignored, is architecture, and it is no coincidence that architecture more than any other branch of art has been concerned with ends and the direction it is taking.

Furthermore, much of the most original thinking about human ends, the good life, and desirable environments is being done by architects and town planners in the more specialized architectural journals. A person who designs a building or a city must at some stage ask himself what sort of life these works should contribute to, what should be the relationship between man and environment, and what the good life means. It is in architecture rather than in philosophy or the social sciences that these questions are being pursued with most originality.

Traditionally there have been two approaches to art criticism. One examines the work as a thing in itself and makes no references to where it fits into the genus or how it relates to other works of art. The other considers the work within its genus, relates it to its predecessors and sources of inspiration, and compares it with similar works. Most good criticism combines the two approaches. The first approach corresponds to the thing-in-itself evaluation mentioned above, but because of the excessive deference shown to the *art for art's sake* doctrine there is usually little consideration of next level possibilities.

Hence there is none of the feedback, none of the constant modification of criteria, found in other fields.

Nothing could be more unfortunate than for art to be judged on its social impact, its contribution to human happiness, or its furtherance of the revolution; but unless some notice is paid to the possibilities that art gives rise to, unless it is seen as part of the larger picture feeding back insights and awareness to the human race, then it will eventually atrophy. Great art, as Shaw avowed, is always propaganda. Artists are people first and craftsmen second. And whether an artist works towards the end of social protest, as did Dickens, Zola, and Baldwin, or towards investigating his own soul, as did Woolf and Rimbaud, or with the aim of understanding the whole perplexing problem of man and life and destiny, as did Shakespeare and Euripides, the art is always pointed in some direction. It cannot exist in a vacuum.

Art, science, religion—these are the three major areas of possibilities, the evelopments, that the human race has given rise to. Significantly, all are returned possibilities. It is as if Teilhard de Chardin's noösphere is, with the advent of intellect and emotion, attempting to close in on itself.

One set of possibilities not yet mentioned in this discussion are human relationships. It is probable, even granted other intelligent life in the universe, that there exist nowhere else relationships quite like those between members of the human race. As such they are uniquely worthwhile ends in themselves. The relationships that people now enjoy are, we feel, inherently more rich and varied than those of primitive people. It is to be hoped our descendants will discover varieties of personal relationships that are more complex, more wide-ranging, and more interesting than those of contemporary society.

There is another type of relationship whose implications have never been fully explored. Science fiction writers have tended to appropriate the phenomenon, or apparent phenomenon of parapsychology as their own, but have done little more than use it as machinery in stories depicting contemporary people using parapsychology to solve contemporary problems. If such a power does lie latent in the human mind, and can be developed, the resulting culture will be more foreign to us than we are to a bees' hive. The work of J.B. Rhine and other researchers and the body of anecdotal evidence provide more copious evidence for the existence of parapsychology than the Greeks possessed for the existence of electricity. They could never have imagined a civilization that depended on electricity for its power and its communications, just as people are now unable to imagine a society dependent on parapsychology for its energy and communications.

Given that psychic powers exist, it is possible to picture the universe as a vast four-dimensional cobweb of communication between intelligent minds, stretching as far back, as far ahead, and as distant as there are minds to receive and transmit. Because this communication web extends unbounded in time, it is in effect eternal. Because there must be energy of some kind associated with the communications, this standing wave, as it were, contains infinite energy. And because every sort of awareness or information is transmitted, it is effectively all-knowing. Infinite, eternal, all-knowing, and all-powerful—these are an interesting collection of properties.

PART FIVE

ECONOMICS AND IDEOLOGY

26
THE NEW RELIGION

Behaviour, it is suggested, has its origin in the emotions rather than in rationality. Values are acquired from the society to which a person belongs, are internalized, and thereafter acted on whenever situations arise where they are relevant. These values are capable of evolving to serve social needs. Successful groups evolve adaptive values which serve the ends of the particular society; groups that have less useful or adaptive values lose membership to more successful groups or, in extreme cases, are eliminated entirely. Values consequently tend to serve the interests of the group as a group rather than to promote the well-being of members of the group or of society as a whole. Given two groups, one with a set of values that furthers the group interest at some cost to the individual, and a second with values that favour its members at the expense of the group, the first will invariably prevail over the second.

Groups and societies are held together by their shared values. Members of the group see those with similar values as "us" or "belongers" and those with opposing values as "them" or "outsiders". This is as true of tribal societies as of modern political associations. Most schemes of values are to a degree in competition; even when not in direct conflict they are still seen as rivals. In consequence there is always some hostility between value systems, the hostility being greater where the value systems are closely related. Catholicism is close to the Christian heresies in the content and structure of its beliefs, with the result that considerable hostility exists between them. It is reasonably remote from Buddhism and Animism and, while hardly tolerant, displays less hostility towards them than to the heresies.

The motivational milieux which transmit values range from tribal groups to nation states to pure ideological associations. The first two are associated with racial groups and territory respectively; ideological milieux are theoretically independent of both race and territory. Historically there has been a progressive movement away from the restrictive tribal and national milieux to the more general ideological milieux, reflecting the fact that the wider the appeal of an ideology the greater its chance of survival. Such wide-ranging milieux are represented today by the ideologies of Christianity, Hinduism, Buddhism, Islam, and Communism, complexes of values which together count most of the world's population in their membership. These emotologies have the capacity to evolve, both changing in their emphasis and giving rise to new emotologies. Protestant Christianity, a branch of Catholicism, has in the last two hundred years given rise to a secular variant which is proving the most potent ideology yet developed. This is economic thought, or to distinguish it by a particular name, *economism.* Evolving in nineteenth century Europe to accommodate the particular needs of that society, it first spread to North America and thence to most of the developing world.

The structure of economism closely parallels that of Protestant Christianity from which it developed. Hard work and individualism remain as primary virtues, but welfare replaces salvation as the final goal. Like Protestantism, economism has both informative and normative content, but beyond this the two part company. The informative content of Christianity includes the creation myths, Hebraic history, the life of Christ, and the work of the early disciples, particularly Saint Paul, in spreading the gospel. The normative content includes the Ten Commandments and the doctrines of the prophets and of Christ. The informative content of economism consists of the whole body of modern economic theory. The normative content is typified by the injunctions and exhortations delivered endlessly by members of parliament and successful businessmen; produce, consume, develop the country, maintain a higher growth rate, increase foreign trade—all reasonable good sense, but in the final analysis no more firmly based than the Ten Commandments or any other religious set of injunctions.

It is widely accepted, at least in the West, that Marxism has the structure of a secular religion. Like Freudian thought, Marxism has taken over more of the underlying framework of Christianity than its founder ever realized. There is the same fundamental struggle of good and evil, the same promise of final victory and the millennium. The dialetic and the laws of history replace God, while the true prophets are Marx, Engels, and Lenin rather than the Biblical figures. Yet Marxism itself is a heretical deviant of mainstream economism, having the same relationship to it that the major heresies have to Catholicism. The major difference between the two lies in the degree of centralized control they advocate and the machinery of capital accumulation they propose; Western economism, or capitalism, holds that the business corporation is the appropriate institution for capital formation, while Marxism holds that this role belongs to the state. This general doctrinal similarity makes antipathy between them inevitable.

All successful emotologies have social utility. This is particularly true of economism, whether in its mainstream form, or in the Marxist variant. Earlier societies had little conception of productivity, economic growth, or business activity as being things desirable in themselves. There were simply no emotive-mechanisms applying to these concepts in the societies of Imperial Rome, Ancient China, or medieval Europe. Wealth itself was regarded as highly desirable, but this is a naive value compared with the range of economic values developed in the West. The existence of these emotive links ensures that the large-scale economies of developed countries continue to operate. Such economies depend on the level of motivation, which in the USA and Western Europe is very high, possibly so high that the economies cannot be controlled. The reason that the underdeveloped countries remain underdeveloped is not so much shortage of capital or of resources, important as these are, but the lack of appropriate emotive-mechanisms. They remain poor because they are economically unmotivated.

Every society requires certain spiritual equipment to pass on its values. This spiritual equipment has attained a sophisticated level in the West in the form of higher education, business schools, and innumerable magazines from *Time* and *Newsweek* to *Fortune* and *US News and World Report*. They spread the true gospel, endorsing the emotive links that make a highly motivated economy possible. Their informative function is secondary to their emotional and motivating content. An indication of the importance of economic values is provided by the history of Japan and Germany after the Second World War. The physical plant of these two countries had been effectively destroyed. They were fortunate in having a supply of capital to hand, largely obtained from the United States, but more important was the fact that their motivation, in the form of emotive-mechanisms, and their knowledge of business techniques remained intact. These allowed them to reconstruct their economies at a remarkable rate, to the extent that Japan is now the world's third economic power.

By contrast, the underdeveloped countries of the world, even when provided with a comparable supply of capital, have not been able to achieve a similar rate of development. To some degree this is due to a shortage of trained managers and a lack of technical knowledge, but to a far greater extent it reflects a lack of motivation. The emotive-mechanisms that provide the drive for developed economies do not exist in economically backward societies.

Japan and Germany, to return to these examples, not only possessed a value system that promoted economic growth, they also retained the spiritual equipment to ensure that these values were transmitted. The Japanese in particular have been quick to realize the value of education, for education does more than simply transmit information, it also serves to pass on emotive-mechanisms. As in European countries the same use has been made of business magazines and the media to transmit economic values. In this respect, however, the Japanese have failed to exploit one major opportunity. Information is as much a commodity as any consumer item, and there exists a major market in Asia and the Pacific for an English-language Japanese "*Time Newsweek*", with a world outlook providing spiritual equipment for Asian economic growth.

27

THE ARTICLES OF FAITH

As an ideology economism has a number of substantial advantages. It has a clear set of ends, a precisely enunciated teleology, which many other value systems lack. These include economic well-being, development, and a high standard of living—terms which in the final analysis mean a good deal less than might be supposed, but which remain nonetheless highly persuasive.

In addition to having a precise teleology, economism has developed an elaborate machinery for measurement, and this in turn allows it to rule between alternative programmes of action. Assuming that a sum of money becomes available for investment, it is possible to estimate the life cost of, for example, a dam and of a thermal power station, to estimate the expected return on these two alternatives by quite sophisticated techniques, and finally to choose the course that gives the higher return on investment. Clearly, this is a special case of the possibilities criterion, but in this event wealth is the concern rather than the number of possibilities. Economism represents a consistent system of thought so long as the final goals—increasing gross national product and maintaining a high level of productivity—are accepted. If these are rejected the entire framework crumbles. And, as suggested previously, no single end in life can be argued for logically, even where this end is economic welfare.

The articles of faith of economism form a loosely interwoven set of attitudes, rarely defined explicitly. Implicitly, however, they have been enunciated in innumerable addresses by public servants and businessmen, in a variety of economic textbooks, and in the repeated morality tales, most fortunately with a happy ending, which grace the pages of the weekly news magazines. Briefly, they can be summarized as follows:

1. Basically all behaviour is economic in nature.
2. Well-being depends absolutely on economic factors. Where productivity is high, and the economy is expanding, people will be well off. Where the economy is underdeveloped or stagnant, people will be badly off.
3. Because of this, an indefinitely expanding economy is desirable.
4. This expansion is to come from natural population growth, and more immediately from the development of new technologies. Hence the close connection that economism draws between knowledge and economic policy.

These four items of economic faith are all open to objection. Marx was, above all others, the economist who held that behaviour is primarily economic in its basis, to the extent that he made economics fundamental to his system. The economic organization of a society forms its substructure. Social organization, politics, religion, ideas, art, and the numerous other aspects of a culture simply reflect the underlying economic substructure; they represent the superstructure. Marx wrote at a time when economic concerns were the primary interest of Europeans, and his approach reflects this interest. But quite simply economic considerations play nowhere as large a part as Western society believed and still tends to believe. The primitive who builds himself a house is not indulging in an economic activity; he is indulging in an activity that is primarily carpentry and manual labour. The person who plants and cultivates his own food crop is not indulging in economic activity; he is following an agricultural pursuit. The person who makes his own clothes is engaged in a tailoring occupation; he is not immediately interested in economic processes as such.

Economic factors are present whenever trading and an exchange of goods takes place, but even trading in unsophisticated societies tends to be more of a social pastime than an economic pursuit. The market-place is the social centre of the village, haggling and bargaining are more directed at scoring off other traders than at achieving an economic advantage, which may in any case be ridiculously small. And after the bargain is struck, more often than not refreshments will be served. Trading, buying, and selling are, in such societies, social rituals with certain forms to be observed. The economic component is often rather small.

If a person examines his own behaviour over a period, it is surprising how small a part economic factors actually play. In work, recreation, and travelling, the main determinants are more often social and psychological than economic. Most people find some satisfaction in their work, a certain enjoyment in their recreations and personal interests. Economic considerations are usually present, but this is no reason to make economic issues the primary concern. Religion, ideas, the unconscious mind, and biological factors all play at least as great a part in life as economic issues, and there is no justification for assuming that any of them are primary.

That most aspects of welfare are basically economic is an idea that could only be taken seriously in an economic society. A religious society would assume that all good and worthwhile things were primarily associated with religious belief; a sociological society would assume that all goods were basically involved with social and psychological factors. It was suggested previously that the goods necessary for a full life include health, economic security, freedom, education, social acceptance, activity, affection, and a good environment. Some of these items are economic, or have an economic component, others are basically social or psychological. It is possible for people to be well off or badly off in a highly developed economy, and equally well off or badly off in a very primitive society. The poor-but-happy myth, and the idea that the poor had a particular virtue by dint of their poverty, died with the onset of industrialism. It has now become an article of faith held with equal tenacity that people cannot be well off without economic development. This attitude is socially determined and holds social advantages for Western culture; if people did not believe that their well-being depended on economic factors, they would lack the motivation required to maintain the society. In the same way, if members of a religious society did not believe that their religious behaviour was essential for present or future well-being, they would not engage in the religious activities essential for the society to function. In each case welfare is defined in terms which the society is particularly able, or allegedly able, to provide. An economic society defines welfare largely in economic terms as goods and services; a religious society views welfare in terms of particular spiritual conditions.

The need for a continually expanding economy is an item of faith held with almost fanatical tenacity by most economists and by the majority of politicians. A few economists are beginning to question in the pages of technical journals whether growth is a true need or nothing more than a fetish, but for the most part it retains its almost hypnotic sway. The reason is not hard to find. For businessmen, growth in the economy means that sales will inevitably rise, that profits will improve, and that the scope and size of their business will expand. These are such unquestionable benefits that it hardly seems reasonable to ask whether they can be achieved, or even whether they are really worth while.

Most economists hold that two factors contribute to economic growth. These are (*a*) natural population increase and (*b*) improvements in technology and methods of production. Conservative politicians and business interests tend to look more to population growth to provide economic growth and expanding markets. Liberal politicians and labour interests, on the other hand, show more interest in technical development to increase output, so that the wealth available to the population is increased, such increase being achieved if possible without unemployment.

If real economic growth, independent of inflation effects, is simply a matter of providing the same goods and services to a larger and larger population, there seems very little to be gained. There is no advantage to be had in increased population as such. Indeed, the world's aggregate population is probably too high by a factor of ten, despite the existence of large relatively uninhabited areas. A large population is no automatic guarantee of wealth. The poorest areas of the earth are generally those with the greatest population—India, China, Pakistan, Indonesia, areas of Africa and South America. It seems paradoxical that economists in developed countries are calling for population growth as a means to greater wealth, while the more populous countries are desperately poor.

Moreover, a neo-Malthusian consideration enters the picture. Malthus's original concern was that food supply, which must increase in arithmetical progression, would eventually prove inadequate for a population which increased in geometrical progression. Improvements in food-producing techniques have deferred this problem to the extent that many developed countries have huge indisposable gluts of food, but even if the problem of food production could be deferred indefinitely there remains the more pressing problem of support technologies. Where population density is low there is little difficulty in providing the essentials to life for the population. As the density increases, the cost and complexity of support technologies increase at a geometrical rate. Larger water catchments, more elaborate dams, larger pipelines, and more complex pumping plants become essential for the supply of drinking and process water. The transport system required becomes more complicated and expensive, necessitating elaborate highway systems, more expensive railway installations, containerized and bulk-handling port facilities, and vastly more complex airport equipment. High-rise office buildings require air-conditioning, elevators, and electrical services that are not required in low-level buildings. Much of this expenditure returns to the economy, but the fact remains that the facilities required by a growing population, simply to maintain the level of amenity, increase out of proportion to the population. The wealth to provide these services must be obtained somewhere, presumably from the higher levels of economic activity made possible by increased population.

If economic growth is to come not from population expansion but from increased productivity—the most persuasive of economic phrases—major questions still remain. Increased production means in the long run that more people are working harder and longer to achieve more. Productivity evokes images of new and improved techniques, better machines, and more efficient methods, but as a matter of hard fact these new machines and technologies involve, even if indirectly, more work rather than less. Just as a housewife, surrounded by a galaxy of sophisticated labour-saving devices, finds that she spends at least as much time on housework, and probably more, so a factory with sophisticated plant expends more rather than less real time. Much of this time is taken up outside actual production in such activities as the basic research needed for new processes, the design and development of new machinery, the sales effort required to sell more expensive products, and the considerable effort required to install, adjust, commission, and maintain equipment. Because the plant is more expensive there will generally be more effort expended in raising finance, arranging insurance, transport, and so on. More time will also be required to train operators and in administration. The advantages derived from scale are considerable, but this should not hide the fact that they are usually paid for in time elsewhere. Man-hours on the factory floor, where they are noticed by accountants, may be reduced, but the amount of time spent in other sections of the economy increases. For this reason improved productive techniques rarely result in widespread unemployment. Sophisticated plant represents no more than items with which a greater amount of time and effort can be involved, even if this involvement is indirect. In other words, as productivity increases, a larger and larger proportion of time is being brought within the ambit of economics.

This is one reason why the growth of the developed economies appears so spectacular. More and more activities which previously had no economic significance have been brought within the measurement of gross national product. A pioneer or a hermit making his own living in the wilderness contributes virtually nothing to the economy. He grows his own vegetables, hunts game, constructs his own dwelling and furniture, makes his own clothes and even cuts his own hair. Such a Waldenesque existence adds nothing to the measured GNP. A city dweller who buys his food, house, furniture, and clothing and pays barbers' bills contributes significantly to the GNP by his consumption. Yet the end result is much the same. Consider another case. If two tailors make suits for themselves in their spare time, there is no addition to the GNP, but if each makes a suit and sells it to the other, GNP is increased. Adam Smith, in his discussion of pin manufacture, demonstrated that specialization is a major contributing factor to a nation's wealth, yet specialization may add nothing to the real wealth of a country. It may simply ensure that an activity is measured in economic terms, rather than going unnoticed.

There is a further reason why the wealth of industrial societies appears greater than it actually is. The speed of circulation of money is higher than in the less developed economies. In consequence people appear to possess far more than they actually do. A monarch owning a palace full of treasure would for instance be regarded as rich, but if he had access to the treasure for only one day of the week, sharing it with six other monarchs, or if he owned only one seventh of the treasure at any particular time, he would be considered less affluent. This is in effect the situation of a consumer in a developed economy. The wealth that he has access to is shared wealth. The family car or cars will be jointly owned by the family and a finance company. The house may have two additional owners, depending on the number of mortgages taken out, the furniture will be jointly owned by a number of finance companies. Because of the limited life engineered into consumer hardware, repairmen will make frequent visits, becoming in effect part owners of the goods, since they can demand a part of their value to maintain them. The council becomes a part owner of the house, demanding a percentage of its value for the right of occupancy.

While people living in a developed country appear to have vastly more wealth than those in underdeveloped areas, this appearance of wealth is largely illusory. In fact they probably own about one half of their nominal possessions. Credit schemes and time-payment and lay-by schemes enable money to circulate very rapidly, giving the impression of far more wealth than actually exists. The same effective wealth registers more frequently in the GNP. Just as a bull-roarer, swung with sufficient speed, gives the impression of a solid circle, so wealth, circulating rapidly, appears far greater than it actually is. And as a corollary, any slowing down in the rate of circulation effectively reduces the wealth of a society.

These objections shed doubt on the validity of equating GNP with the true wealth of a community. Specialization brings formerly non-economic activities and interests within the scope of economics to register as GNP. More liberal credit and the more rapid circulation of money give the impression that the true wealth of a society is greater than is actually the case.

Assuming, however, that economic growth is genuine, and that more goods and services are becoming available, there remain some substantial problems. Expansion of the primary goods section of the economy can take place only slowly, as regards both production and consumption. It takes considerable time to open new mines, or to bring a new crop, for example rubber, to harvest. It also takes time to find new markets for primary produce, as the food consumption of a population is fairly static, and the market for raw materials is limited by the capacity of the manufacturing industry..Secondary industry is capable of more rapid expansion, but again it is limited by the quantity of goods—clothes and durables, etc.—that people can wear out, or be induced to buy. This leaves the service industries as the one area in which rapid expansion can take place. In contrast to primary and secondary goods, there is virtually no limit except time to the amount of services people can make use of. These services currently include teaching, maintenance of equipment, provision of information and entertainment, medical and religious services, cosmetic attention, financial servicing in the form of tax counselling, insurance selling and brokerage advice, as well as transportation and home decorating. Virtually every service that can possibly be of use is now provided on an economic basis.

The result of this specialization is again that a larger and larger proportion of people's time is brought within the scope of economics. The labour made redundant by technical improvements in primary and secondary industry must move into the service industries if wide-scale underemployment is not to result. Since the service industries do not readily lend themselves to mechanization, economic growth must come largely from more and more time being devoted to the provision of services. The limit is reached when a person's waking time is completely involved with activities that provide an economic return. This is clearly a *reductio ad absurdum* of the growth for growth's sake fetish. Yet it is true that improved techniques and machinery can only contribute so much to productivity, and that such plant itself requires a substantial if hidden participation of labour. If further economic growth is required, it can only come about by the production and consumption of services that can be measured in economic terms.

Increased gross national product not only results in more and more time being taken up with production; it also means that more time must be spent in consumption. Engineering a limited life into products and introducing styling changes extend the market to some extent, but there is a physical limit to the amount that can be consumed. Moreover, consumers eventually grow wary of buying clothing, furniture, and durables that date long before they have seen reasonable use.

Two other complications beset a society that desires a continually expanding economy. These are the problems of obtaining the raw materials required to keep production going and of disposing of the wastes resulting from manufacture, problems that have been so well documented as to require no elaboration. Despite extensive prospecting for new sources of minerals and the use of synthetic substitutes, there comes a point at which material shortages throttle an advanced economy. This point has been reached in the case of several metals, and can be expected to grow worse in the next few decades. Pollution of water supplies by chemical wastes and of the atmosphere by smoke and dust are technical problems theoretically amenable to technical solutions. In many cases, however, the technical changes required—the addition of filters, precipitators, settling ponds, and treatment tanks—often make the process uneconomic. Thermal pollution of rivers and lakes by power stations and noise pollution of urban areas by heavy industry or from airports are even more intractable problems and will inevitably grow worse as the level of economic activity rises.

28

BALI TO NEW YORK

The problem of obtaining raw materials and disposing of wastes raises the not unfamiliar question of why economic growth or a continually expanding GNP should be so desirable. This is a question that most economists have refused to admit even exists; where they do recognize it they hold it to lie outside the mandate of economic speculation. Economics provides the techniques and tools to attain certain ends agreed on by the society—ends such as the economic well-being of the individual and the economic stability of the society as a whole. These are so widely accepted as to require no justification.

There are two reasons why economists could concern themselves to a greater extent with the ends of their own discipline. Their specialized knowledge and training places them in a unique position to understand the results of economic decisions and the possible ends open to economic policy-making. To some degree they are in a similar position to nuclear scientists with respect to the debate on nuclear weapons and policy. Initially most scientists took the view that the end of their research was outside their field of reference. Decisions on nuclear applications were left to politicians; scientists simply provided the means. Over the last ten years this attitude has changed radically. Nuclear scientists realized that they were in a unique position to lead the debate on arms policy, simply because they understood far better than politicians the implications of nuclear war. This debate has profoundly affected the climate of opinion, making a partial nuclear test ban possible, and probably reducing the possibility of nuclear war. Economists are now in much the same position as the nuclear scientists ten years ago. A widespread questioning of economic goals is now taking place in the community; the real value of the affluent society, the desirability of increasing economic activity, and the nature of the society that it is giving rise to are all being critically re-examined. Yet with several notable exceptions, economists remain aloof from the question of the ends of economic activity.

A second reason for economists to examine the ends of economic activity is that such examination may well provide new insights within the field of economics itself. Questioning the end of economic behaviour and working back from that point may well provide perspectives that would not otherwise arise. This fresh vision or novelty of approach could bring to light weak points in existing economic theories, besides providing new directions for economic research.

Bali is a classic case of an underdeveloped area. *Per capita* income is in the range of a hundred dollars a year. Roads and communications are poor, electrification does not extend beyond the main towns, and the population is largely engaged in rice-growing and the raising of livestock. Local industry, with the exception of curio manufacture for the tourist trade, is virtually non-existent. Modern metropolises such as New York, Tokyo, or London by contrast have all the economic advantages that Bali lacks. *Per capita* income is high, averaging up to four thousand dollars a year; roads, transport, and communications are extensive, modern services are available, and industry and commerce are well established.

Yet the disparity between underdeveloped areas and the highly developed countries of the West are by no means as great as economic factors indicate. Indeed, if the whole style of life is considered instead of simply its economic aspects, a good case can be made for preferring the underdeveloped countries to more developed regions. While the transport facilities of Bali are poor by Western standards, it is still possible to reach most parts of the island by bus and truck. The buses are antiquated and uncomfortable, the roads in poor repair and in places impassable at times, but transport is still adequate to the island's needs.

Per capita income is low, but this is of less importance than in parts of the West, as the island is largely devoted to agriculture. Most of the population grow their own rice on communally owned fields, and raise sufficient vegetables and livestock for a balanced diet. Food prices are low, so that even those not directly engaged in agriculture eat adequately. Clothing can be had cheaply and, as timber is plentiful, there is no shortage of housing. The buildings may be unelaborate by Western standards, but they are cheap to construct and provide adequate shelter. While electrification is unknown in the villages, it is hardly missed; food is cooked over charcoal or kerosene stoves, and kerosene lamps provide adequate lighting. Lack of entertainment in the form of television, magazines, cinema, and live theatre goes unnoticed. Gamelan and dance performances, temple ceremonies, and village festivals provide entertainment in which the villager is at once onlooker and participant.

Bali is clearly a special case—an underdeveloped area blessed with fertile soil, good rainfall, and most important, a rich and vital culture. But what applies to Bali applies to a lesser extent in other underdeveloped areas. Discrepancies in income are not particularly significant, since a person in a backward area can obtain for fifty dollars a year all the essentials that cost a Westerner four thousand dollars a year—food, shelter, clothing, and transportation. Necessary facilities usually exist, but in a much more primitive form. Instead of having a six-element automatic electric range, housewives make do with a simple wood or kerosene stove. Instead of buying plastic-wrapped processed food at an air-conditioned supermarket, buyers haggle over raw produce in the village square. Instead of relaxing in an elaborate chrome-fitted bathroom, one brings water from a stream or community well, and washes from a bucket. Instead of travelling by a late-model Detroit V8, most people ride in the back of crowded open trucks, in conditions far from comfortable, or more usually, since time is not important, they walk. While such an existence may not appeal greatly to the average Westerner, the differences in mode of living are not as great as they appear. Wealth ensures personal comfort and convenience, but it does little more.

Aware that comparisons of *per capita* income provide no true indication of living standard, economists have developed a number of other indices to measure conditions in underdeveloped societies. Typical of these are infant mortality rate, living space per person, nutrition standards, and the extent of literacy. Countries that are economically backward are usually characterized by high infant mortality rates, crowded living space, and low standards of education. While this is unquestionably important, it is easy to overrate the importance of these factors. No humane person can contemplate a high infant death rate with satisfaction, yet it may be better for a sickly child to die at birth than to linger on in illness, a handicap to the social group and a misery to himself. Additionally, there is the Malthusian consideration that infant deaths are one of the major checks preventing population from exceeding its food supplies.

Ideas and values exist against a background of their social utility. The West has long held, at least nominally, ideals concerning the value of human life and the importance of the individual. These have proved to have utility in a society that is competitive and individualistic, but there is nothing absolute about them. Other societies, particularly in Asia, place a much lower value on the individual, influenced in part by the fact that there are simply so many people. It is hard to believe in the infinite value of any entity, from human beings to synthetic jewellery, if they are as numerous as the sands of the desert.

Placing a lower value on human life does not prove that the society is corrupt or even that it is less developed morally than Western society. It is an indication that, in the circumstances, high estimates of the value of life are maladaptive, whereas low values have social utility. An idealistic Westerner who examined India from a standpoint of the infinite worth of the individual would go mad with anguish. People modify their humanitarian ideals in the light of reality. While high infant mortality rates shock the West, they are accepted in less developed countries in much the same spirit that the West accepts road fatalities. They are an indicator of certain conditions in the society, but little more.

The amount of living space available per individual is an even more suspect criterion of well-being. In tropical countries—which include most of the underdeveloped areas—far less shelter per person is needed than in cold countries, since much of the time is spent in the open air. Sociological factors are also important. Children in unsophisticated societies are used to sharing communal living and sleeping space with brothers, sisters, and parents. If they were suddenly removed to their own separate rooms they would be at a loss. In all probability the household would promptly move into the largest room, and life would go on as before. If not, the same gap between individuals and between generations that characterizes developed cultures would appear in primitive societies. The preoccupation with privacy and independence allows personal development, but it is purchased at a very high price—the loss of a communal sense of belonging.

Discussions of nutrition also tend to assume their conclusion before they begin. While it is true that millions of people are literally dying of malnutrition—they can be seen at any time lying ignored on the footpaths of Calcutta, Madras, or Bombay—the situation is not as black as alarmists picture it. Many people who are undernourished by European standards have adapted to a diet that would be inadequate for Westerners. The Nepalese, for example, survive on a diet that is almost entirely rice. Thai hill tribes not only survive on a diet lacking by European standards, but perform heavy physical work that would leave most Westerners exhausted. Prisoners of war in the Pacific during the Second World War survived on diets which theoretically were not capable of sustaining life. This is not to claim that improved nutrition is not desirable—it most obviously is—but simple counts of calories and protein intake are at best a rough indication of requirements and make no allowance for adjustment to local conditions.

Literacy and education appear to be unassailable conditions for well-being. Yet even these have value only in particular social settings, and can be disruptive outside these settings. V. S. Naipaul has commented that illiterates often seem more sensitive to the nuances and subtleties of social intercourse, an idea that communication theorists may find interesting. And South-East Asia, to note only one example, is oversupplied with young university graduates who cannot find work appropriate to their qualifications. Education has unfitted them for traditional or menial work, but the society has no use for their particular knowledge. Dissatisfaction, often expressed as social disruption, is almost inevitable in such cases, particularly as universities are often associated with radical political ideologies.

The strongest objection to these indices of development, however, is that they simply reflect the conditions in the West. European nations have low infant mortality rates, large areas of living space, higher levels of nutrition, and almost universal literacy. Basically the use of such criteria is as arbitrary as the assumption that an income of four thousand dollars a year in a country with a high cost of living is superior to an income of fifty dollars a year in an underdeveloped country. If instead of mortality rates, living space, nutrition, and education such yardsticks as cost of crime per head of population, suicide rate, rate of alcoholism and drug addiction, area of unpolluted land per head available for recreation, rate of psychotic disorders, and extent of moral education were used this would be immediately apparent. Though such yardsticks are no more valid as indices of general welfare, they are no less so. Infant mortality is regrettable, but it may be preferable to a life wasted in gaol, in a psychiatric clinic, or terminated in misery by suicide, alcoholism, or drug addiction. A large area of living space is desirable, but if there is nowhere else to go, no parks that are free of criminals and rapists, no unsettled countryside unaffected by pollution, the living space becomes a prison.

Nutrition levels are important, but Westerners probably induce a disease rate from poor diet approaching the disease rate resulting from malnutrition. Obesity, heart disease, stomach disease, and tooth decay are the results of consistently overindulging in overprocessed food. Education is important, but more important are the values that determine how the education will be used. Illiteracy rates are high in underdeveloped countries, but the rate of moral illiteracy—the absence of emotive-mechanisms—is even higher in the West. And the inability to act within a social context is far more important than the inability to read and write.

Westerners who visit an underdeveloped country see what they want to see, and avoid seeing what they prefer to avoid seeing. Westerners, particularly those of the middle class, have intensely strong values associated with physical dirt. These values go far beyond the scope of common sense and hygiene; houses are expected to be spotlessly clean and dusted from curtain rail to carpet. This cleanliness fetish has been cultivated by detergent manufacturers and appliance retailers to the extent that most housewives would not be happy in a class 100 cleanroom. Consequently, when such people come to an underdeveloped country they notice the cows in the streets, the beggars defecating in the gutters, the flies on the food stalls, the grubby beggar children, the grimy buildings, and the contaminated water supplies. Unfortunately they notice little else. It is easy to assume that people who lack material goods and live in a less than spotless environment must be miserable, wretched, and in a state of permanent despair. This may be so, but as often as not these people find their lives satisfactory. They cannot imagine any other way of life, and if they could, would hardly find it attractive. An Asian Buddhist monk, travelling to a developed country, would be likely to notice those aspects that go unremarked by Westerners—violence, the level of hostility, the frantic tempo of activity, and the crime rate. Presumably he would indicate Buddhist tenets as a cure for the situation, although Buddhists, unlike Christians, are not given to militant proselytizing.

Economists who recommend economic solutions to the problems of underdeveloped countries are in much the same position as the religious person who seeks religious answers to economic problems. Every age attempts to solve problems by means of its own strengths and interests. Medieval Europe, a basically religious society, attempted to solve the problem of plague—a medical problem—by religious means, by prayer, offerings, and contrition. The United States of America, a technological society, attempted to solve Vietnam—an ideological problem—and the strife in the cities—a sociological problem—by technological means. Improved weaponry, better fighting techniques, chemical agents, electronic devices, and still more improved weapons were brought to bear in both cases but with little result. Technology is largely ineffective when strong motivating relations and ideologies are involved, a central tenet of Maoism.

Advocates of growth as a cure for sociological problems often fail to realize that development is an indivisible package. Development provides a multiplicity of goods and services—the automobiles, the household appliances, the stereo sets, photographic equipment, synthetic fabrics, and the varied entertainments available in developed societies. It also requires rigid work discipline, time spent in unappealing and sometimes unhealthy environments performing work that is often uninteresting, and the loss of freedom to a highly centralized government. Development provides high standards of medical treatment, improved education, community facilities such as museums, art galleries, libraries, and universities. It also results in industrial pollution, crowded and uncomfortable transport facilities, traffic jams, stress diseases such as ulcers and psychoses, a high crime rate, and destruction of the natural environment. For an individual the choice between an economically developed and an underdeveloped society is not the simple choice between affluence and misery, squalor, dirt, and disease. It is a choice between affluence with all its accompanying drawbacks, and relative poverty with all the compensations of poverty. Both tend to be idealized to an unwarranted degree, but in the final analysis there is no rational basis for choice. This will depend on a person's taste, way of life, and upbringing.

This raises again the original issue—why bother with economic growth? What is the justification for high levels of economic activity, of an expanding economy and the accumulation of wealth? A person can be well off or badly off in a highly developed economy, and equally well of or badly off in an underdeveloped setting. Well-being is virtually independent of the level of economic development. From the viewpoint of an individual it makes little difference whether economic development eventuates or fails to eventuate. Both types of society have distinct advantages and equally distinct disadvantages. The justification for, and more significantly, the causes of, economic growth lie beyond individual considerations despite ideological insistence to the contrary. They are to be found in social factors, in particular in population numbers and the interaction of a society's environment, its population, and its ideology.

29

POPULATION AND SOCIETY

Population is the mainspring of history. In its three aspects—population numbers, population density, and rate of population growth—it determines almost every aspect of a society's history, its economic system, and indirectly its ideology and values. This is the obverse side of the Marxist coin. In Marx's view, all characteristics of a society are determined by its economic structure; from this viewpoint the characteristics of a society, including its economy, are influenced by population factors. These do not determine every aspect of a society in detail, but they do form the most important influence.

Every society adapts to a particular physical environment—climate, resources, and land fertility—a political environment determined by adjacent and competing societies, and an intellectual environment characterized by its technologies, knowledge, and ideas. Most societies in almost every age have established an equilibrium with their environment. This results from their evolving value schemes, religious lore, and ideologies that are adaptive to their technological level and particular setting. These values—emotive-mechanisms—are passed on by the spiritual equipment of the society and usually result in an equilibrium of population with environment, as long as the values are socially adaptive. Where they are not, overpopulation may result, or alternatively military expansion or large-scale emigration may take place.

As an example of such values, many of the Pacific Island native societies developed permissive attitudes towards abortion and infanticide, which allowed them to hold population reasonably steady. A more sophisticated society, Japan, has similarly turned to abortion and contraception to hold its population in check. Many of the Arab desert societies developed values involving sexual taboos, homosexuality, female circumcision, and segregation of the sexes to limit population to numbers that a hostile environment could support. The Irish, traumatized by the potato famine of the 1840s, which reduced population by one-third, developed values relating to late marriage as a means to limit population.

Incidental religious and social factors often complicate the development of values which could adapt a society to its environment. The attitude of the Catholic Church prohibiting contraception and abortion has closed off one major route of social adaptation. Consequently, the societies of South America and southern Europe in particular must either adopt European economic values, in the hope that economic expansion can keep ahead of population growth, or find alternative values capable of restricting population. As a similar instance of maladaptive population values, peasant societies of many underdeveloped areas, in particular India, hold values that run counter to population control. Despite intense government propaganda, the average peasant woman realizes that her survival depends on bearing at least six children, for only in this way can she be sure that at least two male children will survive to support her in old age. Otherwise she will starve; the government that is prepared to pay her to limit her family will not feed her in old age and widowhood.

Population growth is the main determinant of social and economic change. Where population is static, owing either to natural checks such as disease, war, and starvation or to the operation of adaptive values, social change is unlikely. Where adaptive values have not been evolved, population growth will not be accompanied by social change, and poverty, misery, and squalor will result. If, however, a society can evolve adaptive values at the same time as population increases, it stands a good chance of constructive social change.

Between 1750 and 1850 Britain went through a social and economic shift since described as the Industrial Revolution. A large-scale movement of population from country to city coincided with the development of new technologies, new economic institutions capable of providing capital in large quantities, and the opening of overseas markets. Simultaneously the population of England and Wales increased from approximately 6 million in 1740 to 17.9 million in 1851, and the ideology of capitalism developed. Population increase was not the sole cause of social change, neither was it the direct effect. Social change and population growth took place side by side, displaying a continuous interaction of cause and effect. Growing population made social change necessary; social change made population growth possible. It now appears that an initial increase in population followed minor changes in the eighteenth century; improved livestock breeding and agricultural techniques, improved sanitation, and the absence of the disastrous plagues of the seventeenth century. Nonetheless, without the development of an ideology around which the society could be reorganized, population would have stabilized at a much lower level than was actually the case. This economic ideology or set of emotive-mechanisms was by no means universally held in the early stages. It required only a minority of inventors, holders of capital, and small businessmen to embrace economic values initially and for these values to prove advantageous for the ideology to spread. Where economic values failed to appear, population growth either ceased entirely or, where it took place, resulted in major hardship. Ireland, being a predominantly Catholic country and inhibited by British rule, was unable to develop the Protestant ethic. Population growth was not accompanied by social reorganization, with the result that starvation and emigration became the effective means to restore equilibrium. Britain just managed to avoid the predictions of Malthus, but Ireland was by no means as fortunate.

Because low levels of economic development and squalor are often associated, economists accept as a matter of faith that the two are directly related. But economic development by itself has little direct bearing on the welfare of a society. Population, environment, and value systems, in particular the latter, determine how well off a society is and how well the quality of life is maintained. The economic systems of Western countries represent the working of only one particular value system, just as the empire of Rome or the feudal system were manifestations of other value systems. A society whose population is low and in equilibrium with its environment has no need of a highly developed economy; should such an economy be imposed from above, it will cause disruption to population, dislocation of values, and social unrest.

The North American Indians, the Pacific Islanders, the Eskimos, and the Australian Aborigines were typical of equilibrium societies. Before contact with European civilization these societies had evolved sets of values and modes of life that were uniquely adapted to their setting. While poor in that they owned few possessions by Western standards, all shared a well-developed social system, highly evolved spiritual equipment, and a body of religious belief, myth, legend, and folklore that made life intelligible. Individuals were well off in the sense that they had a feeling of belonging to the society, had social and economic security, had contact with their environment, and had reasonable health and personal freedom. Many primitive societies, in particular some Australian Aboriginal and American Indian tribes, enjoyed a more genuine democracy than prevails among European societies at present. This is not an attempt to idealize the noble savage; tribal life has very obvious drawbacks and hardships. It is an illustration only that economically underdeveloped societies need not display the ills normally associated with poverty.

Squalor and misery arise in most cases from the breakdown of traditional values. With the coming of Europeans to the Americas, to the Pacific Islands, and to Australasia, the equilibrium of population, environment, and value systems was destroyed. The environment was altered as large tracts of land were taken over for stock and agriculture. Value systems were destroyed by exposure to European ideas and religion, by the breaking up of tribes and their forced migration from tribal areas. With the loss of land and food supplies the tribal structure and associated spiritual equipment collapsed. Individuals became demotivated because tribal emotive-mechanisms could no longer be transmitted, and had in any case become as maladaptive as the Christian value system offered in their stead. Unmotivated and denied their natural resources, the Aborigines, the Indians, and the Eskimos were moved to reservations or shanty towns, or else withdrew to inhospitable areas that civilization found economically useless. In every case there followed a drastic fall in population and growing social disintegration and misery.

Extreme poverty and squalor are always associated with major historical transients. Calcutta is one of the most miserable and poverty-stricken cities in India, and possibly on earth, but Calcutta is historically of recent origin. Founded by the British at the beginning of the eighteenth century as a trading post, it subsequently grew without adequate planning or control into a city of five million. Nehru was ever quick to point out that the most impoverished areas of India are those first brought under British control, and attributed this to systematic plundering by merchants and the British army. In fact, this impoverishment can be traced to the social dislocation involved in foreign conquest. In this regard India is a special case, for although British occupation hastened its fragmentation, the society had been stagnant and divided for several hundred years. Conquest simply hastened its disintegration, so that today India is divided into competing racial groups, language groups, religious groups, and political ideologies. It is less a nation than an uneasy coalition of states, races, and creeds maintained by simple inertia.

Elsewhere, foreign conquest has had much the same effect. The occupation of Indonesia was motivated almost entirely by trade, rather than the pursuit of political power. Consequently, the Dutch restricted themselves largely to the area around Jakarta, and it is here that they have had most social impact. The effect of this is obvious; Indonesia is generally underdeveloped, but the worst conditions are to be found in and around Jakarta—overcrowding, dirt, disease, filthy canals, and a high crime rate. Urbanization by itself destroys traditional value systems. Combined with colonization and the imposition of new economic organizations, it results in a normative vacuum, social disruption, and uncontrolled population increase.

For the past century at least Europeans have visited underdeveloped areas of the world, observed poverty, misery and squalor, low standards of sanitation, poor nutrition, and short life expectancy and concluded that these were the result of economic stagnation. What they were in fact observing was the impact of their own culture on less aggressive, less well organized cultures. Many of these societies were extremely primitive, others—the Indian and Chinese—were highly developed, but lacked the organization and technology to resist European domination. Afghanistan, Japan, and Thailand have been almost alone in the capacity to resist the destructive impact of European culture. The majority of present-day political problems can be traced directly or indirectly to European expansion. By destroying or overruling existing social structures, European influence has eliminated the values that held traditional societies together. The result has been either demotivated apathy, retribalization in the form of militant nationalism, or more usually the two going hand in hand. Most important, by destroying the value systems of other societies, the check on population growth was removed. It is no coincidence the population crisis is developing now rather than a thousand years ago or several thousand years hence.

The importance of values is one thing that Malthus failed to consider in his discussion of population growth. He held that natural checks—war, disease, and starvation—alone were capable of limiting population growth, and that in their absence standards of living would fall. Mill, somewhat more optimistic, believed that working-class people would in time have the sense to limit their birthrate. Both were influenced by the fact that Europe was experiencing a period of population expansion, brought on in part by the emergence of new value systems. Neither realized that population had been relatively stable up to that period because of adaptive value systems. Malthusian factors certainly operated, but they were reinforced by values, attitudes, and beliefs that generally held population short of the Malthusian limit. In all probability these values originated from experience of starvation and poverty, but once developed they made the natural checks largely unnecessary. Populations do not automatically move to subsistence level unless there is a breakdown of population-limiting values.

Factors other than the Malthusian checks and the play of social values operate to restrict population. Overcrowding experiments with rats, admittedly of dubious validity to human society, have shown that biological factors also limit population density. Under conditions of marked overcrowding, stress diseases occur shortening life, females conceive less readily and abort more often, and animals become more susceptible to disease and parasites. There is an increase in neurotic behaviour, a diminished will to live in some cases, and a high degree of hostility. These reactions tend to reduce population density to a level that is psychologically acceptable.

Parallel effects can be seen in human society, resulting from the overcrowding of urban life. Stress diseases, neuroses, and psychoses are the most marked results, but there are others; the emotional bombardment of faces, faces, faces, forces people to isolate themselves emotionally, resulting in anomie, loneliness, and a failure of communal contact. The sheer number of people reduces the psychological value of the individual. Moreover, overcrowding reduces the degree of freedom that individuals share; the greater the population density, the more complex things become, and the more rules become necessary. On a desert road a person can drive how and where he likes; in crowded city traffic it is necessary to observe a host of detailed rules, regulations, and restrictions.

Population considerations provide partial answers to the question previously raised: Why bother with economic development? Economism, the ideology associated with economics, is one of the few ideologies that accept, and even welcome, population growth. The values of primitive society are such as generally to limit population to the capacity of the environment and the prevailing technology. Economism takes the opposite approach, forcing technology and organization to keep pace with whatever growth in population occurs. On the positive side, population growth is seen to represent new markets, increased production, a growing GNP, and the pressure behind new technical developments. From a more negative point of view population growth is inevitable but can be accommodated by technical and scientific improvements. The classic case of this is agriculture, which, as a result of intensive mechanization, crop breeding, and large-scale organization, involves less than 10 per cent of the GNP in developed areas, while still yielding crop surpluses.

Economic organization results in a well-organized and highly disciplined and motivated population. Standards of education and medical care are generally high. These factors do not have great importance for the individual, since there would be compensating advantages and disadvantages in a less developed society, but they are important for the society itself.

The reason that European society has been able to dominate or replace other societies lies in the values of economism. Respect for knowledge and technology as such, a high regard for individual effort, the capacity to develop large-scale self-renewing organizations such as business corporations and government departments, a degree of competitiveness—all are characteristic of European societies.

It was suggested earlier that groups develop emotive-mechanisms that further the survival and well-being of the group as such rather than the interests of members. This is inevitable since all groups, be they religious, social, or cultural, are in competition with other groups for membership. If a group evolves values that simply benefit the individual, it is more than likely to suffer encroachment by more aggressive groups. An example is provided by two hypothetical labour unions, one moderate and one militant, engaged in wage negotiations. The more moderate would in all probability be working in the best interests of its members, for, while the wage rise it negotiates may be small, strikes and dislocation are avoided. The more militant union would ask for excessive wage rises, indulge in heated negotiation, and in all probability go out on strike. On the whole this is in the worst interests of its members but in the best interest of the union, for in a setting of conflict and struggle the allegiance of members to the union is made more certain. Thus the moderate union will slowly lose members through dissatisfaction and indifference, while the militant union, through its aggressiveness, will gain members. A comparable process takes place among societies. Those which evolve values strengthening the society will survive. The effect on individuals is unimportant until a stage of potential revolution is reached. Then values must be modified to benefit the individual, a change that may also benefit the society.

Any group or society will evolve values that benefit the group or society over the interests of its members. Economic values are such as to benefit the societies that hold them; they make for economic strength, a high degree of organization, centralization of power, and the capacity to support military activity. Historically, this complex of values is only the most recent experiment in value schemes, one of a large number of possibilities, if one that has proved extremely successful. There is no reason why later value schemes cannot supplant it, should they make for a stronger or more enduring society. This is essentially the reason that economic development has taken place. It strengthens the state or society with which it is involved and makes it more successful in competition with other states. Since economic factors such as high GNP, extensive industrialization, high rates of investment and capital formation, and a developing technology reflect only one possible set of values, the question of individual well-being still remains. Some of the components of euness, such as physical health and education, are promoted by a developed economy. Others, such as a pleasing environment or affectionate relationships, are either unaffected or damaged by economic growth.

Quite simply, the well-being of individuals and the quality of life that they lead depends on sociological factors rather than on economic considerations. They depend on the emotive-mechanisms transmitted, on the motivational relations that exist between the society and the individual, and on the spiritual equipment evolved. Where the values are such as to benefit the individual and hold the society together, the quality of life will usually be high, no matter what the level of economic development. Where values work against the individuals or do not reinforce the society, the well-being of individuals will suffer. Sociological rather than economic factors determine welfare and the quality of life.

30

THE MISSIONARIES OF AFFLUENCE

Trade follows the flag. Not far behind trade, often even ahead of the flag, go the missionaries spreading the beliefs and the value systems of the cultures they represent. Between the sixteenth and the nineteenth centuries Christian missionaries representing the beliefs of the dominant European culture travelled to all parts of the globe. In some cases their influence was beneficial; in others, where it resulted in the destruction of satisfactory value systems, it was harmful. But no matter what consequences followed, the missionaries believed themselves the repositories of the one true and unquestionable faith, and felt that they held a sacred duty to spread this faith to the less fortunate. It never occurred to them that Christianity was only one possible value system, and that while in places it may prove adaptive, in others it would be decidedly harmful.

The economic faith of economism closely parallels Christianity in its structure. Its doctrine embraces economic growth, the efficacy of technology, and expanding international trade. These it worships as items of an unquestionable faith. The Kingdom of Heaven, or more precisely, the Earthly Paradise, is to be attained by hard work, investment, and controlled growth. Its prophets, stretching in a long tradition from Smith to Marshall to Keynes, with an occasional heretical Marx or Veblen, are the bringers of enlightenment.

And just as Christianity sent its missionaries to all areas of the world to spread the gospel, so the missionaries of economism travel to all quarters to disseminate the economic creed. These are the armies of aid missions, international organizations, United Nations agencies, economic and technical advisers, Peace Corps and IVS volunteers that have converged on underdeveloped countries in recent years, bringing foreign aid, advice and technical assistance. They are the missionaries of affluence.

Over the last twenty years or so foreign aid has become a subject of growing importance, both from the point of view of potential donor nations and of underdeveloped recipient countries. Motives in aid-giving range from pure altruism to political opportunism and cover every part of the spectrum in between. The affluence of the West has made it increasingly sensitive to the plight of the have-not nations, a sensitivity sharpened by travel and improved communications. The faces of starving children peer from advertisements in the *Saturday Review* and *Scientific American*, reminding readers of the other two-thirds of the world's population; Lord Snow in his celebrated "Two Cultures" address laid more emphasis on the gap between rich and poor than between the technologies and the humanities.

The giving of foreign aid raises two fundamental problems, in addition to a host of lesser ones. These are the need to alter social values and the necessity of developing an economic theory applicable to underdeveloped economies. The lesser problems involve the actual mechanics of aid-giving and, while significant, can be solved in principle. This does not appear to be true of the issue of value modification.

It is not possible to develop a nation economically without changing the underlying values, ideals, and attitudes of the population. This has been implicitly recognized by Gunnar Myrdal, as well as by a number of other writers on economic development. Robert McNamara, as head of the International Bank for Reconstruction and Development, also seemed aware of the problem, but in practice it is largely overlooked.

Underdeveloped nations are generally handicapped by values such as low esteem for manual work and manual skills, poor work discipline, unwillingness to accumulate capital, lack of a competitive attitude, and, most important of all, a lack of desire for the material goods that a developed economy provides. To some extent Western-style education and contact with Western experts does instil such values, but this is a slow and uncertain process. Not enough is yet known about how values are evolved and transmitted for development experts systematically to change the values of a recipient country. In any case this involves moral issues of social engineering; to what extent, if at all, is one country justified in trying to alter the basic values and attitudes of another country, even if this is believed to be in the latter's best interest?

The point is that it is not enough simply to pour aid into a country, to construct dams, steelworks, roads, and light industry, and to provide the machinery for economic control. Unless the motivating values are present to make the economy work, breakdown will inevitably result. And indeed, money poured into such an economy will be more likely to have a disruptive effect, through inflation and corruption, than to lead to economic growth. Laos provides a classic example.

The same problem exists in microcosm in the city ghettos and depressed areas of the more developed countries. The marginally impoverished will usually respond to retraining and aid schemes because they have sufficient economic values to be motivated. The extremely poor, however, lack even sufficient motivation—sufficiently developed emotive-mechanisms—to induce them to respond to aid schemes. Indeed, they frequently lack even motivation to riot or express their distress. If aid schemes are to work, whether on an internal or an international scale, some provision for altering, or supplying, values must be made; economic considerations are secondary to sociological factors. Only when social changes have been made can economic improvement be effective, for the problems of the poor reflect an uneven distribution of motivation and, to a lesser extent, of education, rather than simple maldistribution of wealth.

Even assuming that basic values could be changed, there is no evidence that any economic theory of any school has a satisfactory explanation of growth or the development of wealth. Some of the necessary conditions, such as the availability of capital, natural resources, and a supply of high-quality labour, are agreed, but the actual process by which an economy begins operation, the means by which wealth is first established, remain a mystery. Even among the most highly developed economies with sufficient economic data, adequate government institutions, and a highly skilled work-force, the increase in wealth cannot be guaranteed. Britain and France, for example, have been trapped in a cycle of economic stagnation for decades, while the United States and West Germany appear at times unable to contain their rate of growth. If these economies cannot be controlled, and in particular if Western governments cannot increase their own national wealth, it hardly appears appropriate for them to advise less developed nations on measures to spur their economies.

Lack of an economic theory of the origin of wealth has led aid experts to take an incredible diversity of approaches. Soviet experts, influenced by their own experience, favour the installation of heavy industrial plant, while Western influenced nations such as Taiwan and South Korea have installed light industry first, then moved on to heavy industry. Some experts advocate the installation of labour-intensive production to reduce underemployment, while others favour capital-intensive plant for its alleged beneficial effect on work discipline. Some experts believe that government should take the lead in development, as for instance with India's five-year plans, while others hold that an underdeveloped economy will expand most rapidly under *laissez-faire* conditions of non-intervention. Most concede that the economic schools of thought appropriate to developed economies, for example Keynesianism, are inappropriate to underdeveloped countries, but no coherent body of theory has been evolved to deal with the case of backward countries. Most economists rely simply on pragmatism and their own particular bias—classicist, Keynesian, or monetarist—in giving advice.

While the practical problems of aid-giving are not insoluble, they are nonetheless formidable. Invariably, foreign aid is distributed at the top of a society, usually via government agencies, and only slowly percolates down through the economy. This introduces practical problems of corruption, nepotism, misappropriation, and waste. There are obvious temptations for national leaders to either retain some of the wealth themselves, to use it to gain political influence by judicious application, or to favour friends.

Where aid is administered directly, as by UN agencies or departments of donor governments, there are still substantial problems. Aid agencies are generally advised by the ruling section of the society, and hence end up with a potentially one-sided view of national needs. Moreover, the agencies will have at best an incomplete idea of conditions in the recipient country and of real needs. There is a temptation to install large and spectacular projects, steel mills, hydro-electric plant, modern highways, and prestige projects rather than concentrate on more limited undertakings.

More important, most aid schemes are aimed, if implicitly, at buying a country's loyalty. As such they are designed to impress national leaders rather than to improve the lot of a population often surprisingly indifferent and even hostile to foreign aid. Politicians in even the most backward countries have generally absorbed enough economic lore to make the appropriate ritual utterances. Indeed, just as medieval Christian heads of state, on meeting, would invoke the Church's blessing on each other and enquire earnestly of each other's spiritual well-being, so now heads of state on formal occasions affirm their mutual interest in economic development, scientific progress, increased production, and expanding trade. And just as medieval statesmen concerned themselves in fact very little with each other's spiritual welfare, so the ritual economic blessings are uttered as a matter of form, without the need to inquire too deeply into the true possibilities or implications of progress.

The average peasant or labourer, on the other hand, who derives as little significant benefit from progress as his Western counterpart, is often disturbed by changes in his traditional way of life. It is generally assumed that the politicians and experts know better than the uneducated masses what is best for them and for the country. But if democracy is to be more than a mere form, the wishes of the majority, no matter how naive, should be respected. In many areas the unvocal, uninfluential majority appear to prefer their existing way of life, with all its drawbacks, to a superficial national affluence combined with political tutelage.

Where foreign aid fails to influence the political forms or the alignment of the recipient country, a not unnatural resentment tends to result on the part of the donor. This is particularly the case with Western nations, dedicated to exporting democratic free-enterprise ideals, and to the Soviet bloc, equally determined to export socialist organization and having, incidentally, as little success as the West in the enterprise.

Newsweek has commented, in regard to the South American nations, that there is no evidence that economic development leads to political progress. There is no reason why it should. Political organization reflects both the alignments within a country and that country's basic needs. Economic factors have little effect on these. At some stage the Western powers must decide whether they give aid to improve the lot of individuals, to strengthen a country militarily and economically, or to modify its political structure and leaning. On the decision will depend the type of aid given.

If the intention is to aid individuals, this can best be done by volunteer services such as Peace Corps, IVS, medical foundations, and the like. Such aid not only is more readily adaptable to actual conditions but stands a good chance of modifying values by face-to-face contact and individual education. If the aim is to strengthen a country militarily, this must in contrast be done from the top. Unfortunately, no scheme has ever been devised to ensure that weaponry will be used only against specified targets, nor is weaponry any guarantee of the will to use it. This again is a sociological rather than a military or economic problem.

If, however, the desire is to change the political and social organization of a country, this can only be done by sociological means, if at all. Economic activity and organization depend on sociological factors rather than the reverse. Western governments have been overinfluenced by Marxism in their belief that economic aid must produce social change.

None of these problems involved in the distribution of foreign aid is insuperable. Neither is it argued here that foreign aid should or should not be given as a matter of principle. It does seem desirable, however, for donor nations to re-examine their aims, to define exactly what they are trying to do, and to look critically at how best to achieve this. In particular, they should recognize that no lasting change to a country's economic condition can take place without a change in social values and organization, and that economic theory is not sufficiently developed to be used confidently in backward areas. The political entanglements of foreign aid could be resolved by delegating all aid programmes to international authorities, although this is probably too radical a course to satisfy most governments.

31
THE THEORETICAL ASPECTS

So far only the emotive content of economism has been considered. But just as the Christian emotology incorporates a purported factual theology to support it, so economism incorporates its own formal theology—the science of economics. And just as theology lays itself open to criticism in its need to support a particular religious system, so the more sophisticated science of economics is vulnerable because it is associated with an ideology. It is vulnerable because its methods and conceptual schemes are inadequate, and it is vulnerable because it attempts to rationalize a non-rational ideology in the service of that ideology.

A discipline betrays its origins in the methods and techniques it employs. Theoretical economics grew out of academic philosophy, a number of leading economists—Mill, Bentham, Marx, and Keynes—also making major contributions to philosophy. In consequence, economics preserves the inadequacies previously charged against philosophy. Economic arguments generally involve language reasoning; as a consequence the categories that it uses are inevitably vague and ill-defined. Where laws are stated, it is never made clear just how far they are intended to extend, nor are their range and limitations defined. Many classical theories seem, implicitly, to be intended for all times and all places, irrespective of the fact that all laws are subject to boundary conditions. Economics is notorious for using concepts that are little more than metaphysical sounds—concepts such as utility, value, and wants—devoid of operational content. Implicit too in the work of early economists is a static world-view, always a danger when language is used as the modelling medium. Keynes re-introduced the all-important quantity of time into economic theory in his discussion of investment, but much of modern economics still fails to consider time as a fundamental variable.

David Ricardo is credited with being the economist who educated the House of Commons in economics. He is also the theorist who developed the intellectual tools now general in economics, the approach of stating assumptions and then drawing conclusions from them. This is described as setting up a model, but unlike the models used in science and the technologies, economic models are purely verbal in nature. The manipulation of these models involves operations associated with logic, rather than direct simulation. A good example is Ricardo's own argument that, as time goes by, rates of profit will tend to fall, and that consequently the accumulation of capital will cease. In its simplified form this argument states that capital accumulates, offering employment to a growing labour force at a fixed wage rate in terms of corn. To increase output, cultivation must be extended to inferior land, with a resulting drop in product per man and a falling rate of return on capital. Finally, the incentive to invest disappears altogether, and capital accumulation ceases. This classical argument few contemporary economists would accept, if only because the consequences predicted by Ricardo failed to eventuate. The logical character of this argument is obvious: "if A and B then C and if D then ... " and so forth. But there is no indication that the behaviour of the economic world can be simulated by logic. No feedbacks, for example a falling rate of population increase as arable land becomes scarce, or rises in wage rates as capital accumulates and circulates, are considered. Other factors, such as changes in technology and better machines and fertilizers, are also ignored, yet in practice the one thing that can be said with certainty of the future is that it will introduce unforeseen new factors. Moreover, Ricardo's argument is taken from the agricultural section of the economy and extended to the economy as a whole. Arguments from analogy are always fallacious, even when their conclusions may correspond with the facts.

Almost every analysis found in classical economics uses arguments based on logic. The Keynesian discussion of inflation, again simplified, states that an increase in effective demand meets an inelastic supply of goods, raising prices. When food produced in a primitive economy suffers a rise in price, this results in increased money income to the sellers, so increasing expenditure. Higher costs of living raise wage rates, money incomes rise, and an inflationary spiral results. Again, while the description of the phenomenon may be valid, a description of events does not represent understanding. This is true of the Marxist classical analysis of the operation of capitalism, taken over at some remove from Ricardo, true of the *laissez-faire* arguments for free trade, true of the disastrous pre-Keynesian analysis of employment factors. Logic is not necessarily a valid tool for analysing economic processes, and ordinary language is not necessarily the ideal medium for simulating economic conditions. Nevertheless, objections to conventional economic theorizing go deeper than its reliance on verbal models. All economics exhibits the descriptive fallacy. It assumes that to describe a situation fully is to understand it.

It is easy enough to describe what happens when a train, for example, is brought to a sudden halt. People are thrown forward, jerk on hanger straps, and bump into one another, and objects fall from luggage racks. Having experienced this a number of times, a person can predict what will happen in a given situation should the train stop suddenly. The ability to describe an event, however, does not mean that the phenomenon is understood. Understanding involves the laws of inertia and motion and the properties of physical bodies. Given these, it is possible to predict how violently people will be thrown together, how much strain will be imposed on hanger straps, and where loose objects will fall, always assuming that the initial situation can be described. This, rather than the capacity to quantify, is what marks the hard sciences off from the soft sciences. The hard sciences have developed models capable of simulating events. The soft sciences describe without modelling.

Economics has shown in general a surprising lack of insight into just what sort of methods it employs. It has assumed that logical arguments—models using language—are the only way, the appropriate way, of approaching economic phenomena.

But mathematics does not progress by means of syllogistic arguments; engineering problems are not treated by means of logical argument; physics does not analyse phenomena in terms of if A then B and if B and not C then D. Each field develops the modes of modelling that prove most useful: mathematical formulae, statistical correlations, dimensional analysis, block diagrams, chemical formulae. Moreover, not only the methods of modelling but the concepts employed have been painstakingly developed to suit each field. The physical concept of *work* is quite different to the commonly understood use of the term. The engineering terms *stress* and *strain* are precisely defined, while in common usage they are taken as interchangeable. Most of the concepts in physics, chemistry, engineering, and metallurgy have moved some way from the commonly experienced world; indeed, one indication of a discipline's sophistication is the extent to which its concepts are removed from common-day experience.

By contrast, the concepts and categories that economics has taken over remain resolutely those of the normal world. There is no concept in economics that an intelligent shopkeeper cannot understand, no enthalpy, entropy, covalency, vectors, grads, or integrals. Not only are the concepts simplistic, they are also intensely value-loaded and reflect the particular interests that prevailed at the time of their formation. Land, labour, and enterprise are not necessarily the most appropriate categories for understanding the origin of wealth; they reflect particular interest groups rather than represent fundamental differences in the economic properties of these concepts. This retention of common-day categories has introduced distinctions into economic theory that are probably harmful, for they distract economists from recognizing the underlying unity of phenomena. The Eskimos possess a dozen different words for snow in its various forms because that is an aspect of the environment that concerns them most; economic man employs a dozen terms for money flow—dividends, taxation, wages, costs—because they are the aspects of his world that most concern him. All, however, are aspects of the same underlying entity, just as electricity, kinetic energy, heat, and sound are manifestations of one underlying entity, energy. It is more useful to consider the transitivity and transfer function of aspects of money flow than the social interests associated with them.

Such criticism involves the methodology of economics, the intellectual approaches that it brings to its field. Additional difficulties arise because economic theory is expected to support the values of economism. This has involved economics in a dogmatic belief in the rationality of man, at least so far as his economic behaviour is concerned, for economic rationality is a necessary assumption if economic values are to be persuasive. At a certain stage of sophistication every ideology attempts to support itself by appeals to reason; Western philosophy was distorted for three hundred years by its attempt to prove the existence of God and to support Christian morality by rational argument. The economic ideology involves dogmas concerning the need for increasing GNP, higher standards of living, and increasing levels of world trade; yet, as E.J. Mishan has pointed out in *The Costs of Economic Growth*, there is no evidence that increasing trade or increasing productivity or indeed that any other item of economic dogma is essential. It may well be that the level of international trade has already passed its optimum or that increasing productivity, as against the redistribution of wealth, is no longer justifiable. Yet it is these dogmatic tenets of economism that economic theory is believed to support. Any number of editorial writers and political commentators can be found to show, in economic terms, why the rate of economic expansion should be 5 per cent instead of 3 per cent or why a minimal fall in the exchange rate or balance of trade threatens national disaster. The preoccupation with growth rates and industrial expansion verges at times on the hysterical to the extent that national priorities are severely distorted. Everyone knows that growth, productivity, progress, increased industrial capacity, and higher economic standards of living are Good Things, but if support for so obvious a truth is needed it is usually claimed to lie in economics. In fact, economics is little more than a description of how economic systems operate, and most professional economists are aware that theory provides no support for value judgements. Nothing in economics supports the need for national economic growth, productivity, or increased trade; these are political rather than economic issues. Hume's observation is still true: there is no way that a value statement can be derived from statements of fact, not even when the facts are located in economic theory.

Economic theory evolved in association with the rise of the modern nation state. The two were closely connected, for economic values are essential for the accumulation of national wealth, on which prestige, political influence, and military capacity are dependent. This has been recognized since the mercantilist era, and the present need for a vigorous economy is probably the only issue on which all politicians are agreed. So long as nation states rather than tribes or ideologies are in competition, there will be strong pressure for each society to maintain its position by increasing its economic strength. The contribution to individual welfare, usually given as the justification for economic growth, is secondary and incidental. Even the lip-service paid to aiding underdeveloped nations is a rationalization, for the Western powers would scarcely be delighted to see the underdeveloped countries rival them in economic power. If all the impoverished peasants of India could be fed, clothed, and housed to Western standards, it would be good, but for India to supplant the United Kingdom or the United States in the league of economic powers would hardly be a welcome development. The emergence of China, which has succeeded in reconstructing its society around the integrating ideology of Maoism, warms the cockles of few humanitarian hearts in Washington, Moscow, or London; one feels that, in the West at least, the prospect of several million starving Chinese could be faced with equanimity if it resulted in a reduction of China's military potential.

The emphasis on growth, nationalism, and economic power has distorted theoretical economics, not only because the science has been required to find theoretical support for emotional values, but also because its fields of inquiry have been dictated by interest groups and social pressures. Theoretical economics developed originally in reaction to protectionist mercantilist interests. Its concern was to build an economically, and hence militarily, strong Britain, and the central issue was wealth, or as it is now described, economic growth. Once a reasonable level of capital had been accumulated the central question involved the distribution of wealth within the economy, and hence the operation of market forces. Here the work of Alfred Marshall and his followers was significant. After the First World War, levels of employment became the prime issue, and it was to handle these that Keynesian economics developed. At present, with the increasing competition between states, particularly between the two major powers, economic growth is again the central issue of economics. Science does not develop in a vacuum, and the history of the physical sciences also reflects social needs and pressures operating at the time. But it appears that economics has been deflected from examining fundamental issues and from developing a solid theoretical basis by the need to respond to immediate pressures and to find *ad hoc* solutions to political problems.

The attitudes, moreover, that various economic theories display reflect the economic ideologies fashionable at the time of their formation in a way that is not always obvious. Free-trade doctrines appeared in England towards the end of the last century, holding that free-trade programmes would always be to the benefit of any country at any stage of its development. It is now clear that this programme benefited England at that period because of its industrial strength, but was probably detrimental to less developed nations. Keynesian thought developed in an age affected by socialist theories, the Fabian movement, and a growing demand for the government to exercise economic control. Consequently, Keynes, although never certain whether to emphasize his conservative or socialist side, stressed fiscal controls through taxation and subsidies to control the economy. These are the measures that involve the greatest degree of, and the most detailed, government control. By contrast, the Chicago monetarist theorists, conservative and business directed, emphasize the role of the quantity of money in controlling the economy. This is the form of government action that involves least detailed interference and hence is most acceptable to business interests. On recent performance there may be much to be said for reducing government control, although some redistribution of wealth is essential in even the most advanced economy.

Ideologies operate because people rationalize the emotional effect of values. This has forced economics to take a rationalistic view of man and to suppose that, in their economic behaviour at least, human beings are generally rational. Maximizing profit and consumption, minimizing costs, and extending markets may seem the most rational behaviour open to people, but in fact, *homo economicus*—rational economic man—is a myth. Even in economic behaviour, human beings are non-rational and at times utterly irrational. Price mechanism theories and the writings of Marshall maintain that, as the price of a given commodity falls, the demand for it will increase. But allegedly rational considerations play a minor role in patterns of consumption. Luxury goods tend to react negatively to the price mechanism; increases in price encourage the belief that quality has improved while reductions in price are associated with deteriorating quality. The effect of advertising, brand image building, and the whole Madison Avenue marketing approach has been to reduce the influence of the price mechanism. The price of advertised goods, such as cigarettes, liquor, and motor vehicles, does not have the influence on sales that the price of a bulk commodity such as sugar has. Brand loyalty limits the substitution of a known brand by cheaper brands; it also limits the substitution of one commodity by other commodities.

Humanitarian considerations also modify behaviour that would be considered rational in purely economic terms. A company experiencing a contracting market would rationally lay off staff, but often considerations of humanity, loyalty to the staff, or more practically, the problem of re-hiring skilled workers prevent this. Thus the linear assumption of many classical economists, that levels of employment vary directly with output, cannot be maintained. All linear assumptions, whether the direct relationship between price and levels of consumption or between employment and levels of production, imply rationality in human behaviour, for all economic decisions are made by human beings. But human behaviour in any field, not only in economics, is non-rational. The assumption of linear relationships between economic variables is simply not valid.

Arguments against the methodology of economics and against its ideological content do not finally condemn it. What does is the fact that economics in its present state of sophistication cannot do what is claimed for it. Quite simply, it has not been developed to the stage where is can provide a basis for macro-economic decisions. In 1969, President Johnson introduced a 10 per cent surtax as a measure to control excessive inflation in the US economy. A number of economists were polled on the effect this was expected to yield, and gave answers ranging from no effect to effective control of inflation. In the event the monetarist school, who predicted no effect, were proved correct. Subsequent controls on money supply and credit produced a similar divergence of predictions, from uninterrupted inflation to a major recession. Several West European countries, in contrast, have been troubled for decades by a stubborn refusal of their economies to achieve their potential growth rate, yet even the most sophisticated economic controls and manipulation have made little impact. Even where economic measures have been successful, there is no indication that the economic theory itself is valid. Keynes overthrew the accepted nostrums of balanced budgets and reduced wages in order to combat the unemployment that troubled Western Europe between the wars, but the elaborate arguments of the *General Theory* are not necessarily validated by the success of his measures. If a vehicle turns right when the wheel is turned left, it is worth reversing the direction in which the wheel is turned. Unemployment remained chronic for as long as the accepted programmes were applied, so that it was worth reversing the accepted procedures, and, in particular, adopting a programme of deficit budgeting. Roosevelt in fact did just this, undertaking a major public works programme and running a major deficit against the counsel of his economic advisers. Hitler achieved full employment in Germany by adopting similar measures.

Any other discipline that made predictions with the degree of uncertainty of economics would be ridiculed out of existence. If engineers were equally divided as to whether a proposed dam would stand or fail or half fail, or if chemists were equally divided as to whether a particular reaction would occur, they would be rejected out of hand. This is not the case with economists, who can show any diversity in their predictions and still be taken seriously. The large economic systems of developed countries have grown up almost arbitrarily, and it is not yet understood how to control them adequately, no matter what claims successive chancellors of the exchequer and chairmen of the Federal Reserve Board may make. The theory that should encompass the play of economic forces and movements of money has never been developed; the reason it has not is that economic theory is committed to the support of ideology. It is almost as if a country were provided with an elaborate power supply network without the basic AC circuit theory ever having been formulated. Frequent lightning strikes, transformer explosions, generator breakdowns, and vaporized cables are regarded as unpreventable acts of God, while the men in control have no idea if too little or too much power is being generated, and are in any case ignorant of which switches control the system. Economics is the aspect of life that has most influence on the majority of people, determining whether or not they are employed, the goods they can afford, and the style of life they can maintain. Yet it is just this influence that is not subject to control. Governments cannot ensure that there will not be runaway inflation or a severe recession, although they have learnt from experience that certain courses generally give certain results. There are, when all is said and done, only a limited number of ways in which a government can act to control an economy. All appear to be used in the developed countries under the influence of statistical methods which often, as in the case of Holland and Japan, yield excellent results. However, statistical methods and correlations are little more than the wisdom of past experience. In its earlier stages meteorology was capable only of correlating atmospheric conditions with weather; low pressure centres tend to produce rain; high pressure centres result in fine weather; cold fronts are accompanied by storms. But as thermodynamics grew more sophisticated, and the power of computers increased, it became possible to simulate weather patterns on computers, projecting them several days ahead, and modifying the model's behaviour by constantly feeding in the actual weather changes. This is a far more sophisticated technique than the correlation procedure and it is one that economics will eventually be forced to use.

John Maynard Keynes is generally considered the most influential economist of the twentieth century. Shortly after the First World War he predicted a future war in Europe if the Allies persisted in their punitive reparation demands against Germany; his major work, the *General Theory*, has influenced every Western government, whether or not they are formally Keynesian in their approach; his influence on international trade has been considerable. Yet for all this, Keynes's contribution to economic theory does not appear to be appreciated. His practical contribution was to provide tools apparently capable of controlling levels of employment, although the consequences of controlling employment levels are only now becoming apparent. Certainly the economic performance of Great Britain, where his ideas have had most influence, has not been outstanding. Keynes's intellectual contributions by contrast were quite different from the practical measures he advocated. Keynes destroyed rationality and he destroyed linearity.

Classical economic theory has generally been linear in its arguments, assuming simply causation and direct correlations. In the classical argument, productive capacity at a particular stage is accepted as a datum, yielding production which is in turn equivalent to national income. The national income is partly saved, giving rise to investment, and so generating greater productive capacity. This straight-line interaction thinking is not unrelated to Hume's billiard ball example and betrays its origin in classical logic. The Keynesian scheme, as it is usually represented, displays a quite different pattern. Investment, via the multiplier and in conjunction with the propensity to save, gives rise to national income which in turn is associated with levels of production, employment, and saving. This is the first instance in received economic theory of a non-linear model. Unfortunately, Keynes and the majority of Keynesians succeeding him then reverted to simplistic models by assuming a direct relationship between national income and employment, a relationship which was at the time tenuous, which does not hold in primitive economies because of disguised unemployment, and which may not hold again when increased automation has had its effect.

Most intellectual advances over the past two hundred years have involved shifts from linear to non-linear conceptualization. The technologies were among the first to introduce ideas of feedback, multiple causation, and cause-effect interaction. Phenomena were no longer to be interpreted in a single chain of cause and effect, but as a field of interacting variables. This type of shift to non-linear thinking has also appeared in media analysis where linear media such as typography are contrasted with non-linear or holistic media such as television. It has appeared even in theories about thinking, where Edward de Bono's flexible notions of lateral thinking are contrasted with straight-line logic. This shift is less a matter of taste than a recognition, however belated, that the world is far more complex and interdependent than at first seems the case. Most disciplines have emerged from the causal chain stage to the more complex field approach in which a large number of interdependent factors interact and where simple cause and effect can no longer be distinguished. It is this type of non-linear thinking that Keynes introduced into economics.

The second implication of the Keynesian model is that it introduces a psychological property into an economic argument —in this case the propensity to save. Keynes emphasized elsewhere that ideas, particularly the ideas of past economists, held a pre-eminent role in economic behaviour and indeed that the world was ruled by little else. But while he recognized that the power of ideas had little relationship to their validity, he failed to see that ideas were the rationalizations of emotional values. Other psychological factors turn up in Keynesian and particularly in neo-Keynesian thought: propensity to import, to export, and to invest, as well as liquidity preference. These impressive terms, with or without the prefixed *marginal*, verge on the meaningless. People save at a certain rate because of a particular propensity to save which is manifested by a particular rate of saving. If these terms have any content at all, it is descriptive rather than explanatory. An event takes place; people save and they do so for psychological reasons and in response to human anticipations. Classical economics often gives the impression of a completely mechanistic system, of an engine that will go on working in its ordained way almost independently of human beings. But saving, spending, investment, trading, and consumption take place because individual people make individual choices about what they want to do. Most of the economic elements could be quite easily done away with if people simply decided that they were irrelevant; primitive societies do not trade internationally and hence avoid the blessing of balance of payment difficulties. There is nothing inevitable about the performance of an economy; it represents the interaction of human choices and needs at a particular time, given particular institutions. Economic systems, like religious systems, are basically motivational systems, but motivational systems of a particular type in that they are circumscribed by financial conditions.

Keynes recognized the importance of psychological factors not only in his "propensities" but also in his well-known discussion of investment. A person invests on the basis of expected returns over the life of plant, but investment is more a matter of "animal spirit"—the desire to try one's luck—rather than a completely unemotional economic activity. Capital is capable of commanding interest not because of any inherent property of capital itself but because it is scarce; interest rates reflect human desires for capital. Indeed, Keynes hypothesized a time when capital would become so plentiful that it would be unable to command interest. Inflation, according to the theory now held by both Keynesians and monetarists, is influenced by the expectation that individuals have about price trends. Past inflation rates set habits of mind and become incorporated into economic planning, contracts, and investment decisions. This perpetuates the past rate of price increase, despite government measures to dampen it down. South American countries, where inflation of currency is expected, operate reasonably well so long as the rate of inflation does not change markedly.

The fact is that all economic determinants exercise their influence through individual expectation and choice, and that no amount of tinkering with delicate economic controls, bank rate, money supply, taxation rates, can be effective if they do not influence individual attitudes. Chancellors of the exchequer have attempted to spur the British economy by the use of economic measures alone, ignoring the motivational effect that these economic controls have. The British economy is not expanding at its potential rate because a generation of British decided after 1945 that the game was simply not worth the candle. Protected by an over-elaborate yet curiously inadequate welfare system, and penalized by high taxation, the average person decided to sit back and take it easy rather than make efforts for which he could see no return. This has made for civilized living at the expense of social dynamism and economic growth. If motivation is to be restored, it will be through the disparaged Conservative approaches of reduced taxation and increased economic incentive, although it seems unlikely now that the British population would tolerate the return of motivation. Other countries, confronted with the choice between hard work with possible rewards and a casual life with little economic growth, have also chosen the latter. Spain, Portugal, and to some extent France are instances, while Scandinavia, Germany, North America, and Japan have quite definitely settled for progress with its attendant problems.

Values are far more important than the detailed organization of an economic system in determining growth. West Germany, with a modified capitalist system, has displayed the highest growth rate among West European countries, while socialist East Germany has led most of Eastern Europe in its expansion. The economic systems are quite different, yet both societies share the Germanic values of hard work, respect for authority, thoroughness, and efficiency, and it is these that have made high rates of economic growth possible.

Economic interactions are non-linear, and economic motivation is non-rational. The consequences of these two ideas are disturbing to economic theory, for simple causal chains are replaced by a cobweb of interrelations between variables in which any variable can affect any other. Nor is this all; the actual effect that any variable has on any other is mediated through human beings with human values and aspirations. It can no longer be accepted that demand will automatically change with price changes, or that employment levels will automatically change with changes in the level of output. Economic laws work largely because people expect them to work, so there can be no generalized theory, in the accepted sense of economic theory, applicable to every economic system at all stages of development. Different national values and ideologies, different interest groups, and different institutions ensure that even comparable economies will respond differently to similar measures. There can only be observations that a particular economy at a particular stage reacted in a certain way to certain measures. In some economies it is probable that Keynesian measures of control will be most successful, while in others Marxist or monetarist measures may be most practical. In all cases the particular theory has its effect through the expectations of individuals. It is an over-simplification to claim that Keynesian methods will only work where they are expected to work, but it is unlikely that they will work where they are not expected to work, or where they do not modify individual values and behaviour.

Each economy at its particular stage of development is unique. Measures that are effective in advanced European economies are useless in underdeveloped societies. What was true of the production-directed society of Britain in the late nineteenth century is not true of the United States consumer society of today. Economic systems cannot be modelled as mechanistic interactions; hence they must be analysed with regard to the values, motivational relations, and social psychology of the particular society. That is to say, economics must be subsumed under sociology as a particular case: the sociology of a society in its economic as against its cultural or religious aspects. This is a programme vastly more complex than classical economists ever anticipated.

Economics becomes sociology; but it is sociology encompassed by monetary constraints. No matter what motivation is available, if people have no money they cannot spend, and if a corporation cannot raise loans it cannot invest in new plant. The consequence is that economics must be split into two sub-disciplines, one dealing with economic motivation and closely involved with sociology, the other dealing with monetary flow, the sources and behaviour of wealth, and the financial constraints that exist in an economy. The first would comprise economic dynamics, the second structural economics. Both must be developed free of ideology if they are to be at all useful as economic tools. Dynamics would bring together information concerning the effect certain measures had under particular conditions in a particular economy, and the type of response that can be expected of particular populations. There is a wealth of comparative information available contrasting the responses of different economic societies that has never been brought together and co-ordinated. Dynamics, as economic sociology, would exist as a social science in its own right, using material and methods drawn from sociology, history, and anthropology while concentrating on the central area of sociology—the interaction between society and the individual. Most of the categories, and certainly many of the value-loaded terms of classical economics, could be quite usefully dispensed with.

Dynamics can be built up on the foundation provided by the social sciences, inadequate as these are at present. The development of structural economics is vastly more difficult, for despite the advances of business techniques and the algebraic and statistical methods of modern economics, almost nothing is understood of the properties of money in movement. We are aware of the properties, or at least of the potential effects, of solid bodies in motion, of fluids in motion, and of electrons in motion. The theory of these, and of the effects they produce, could never be discovered by examining the objects themselves. No amount of observation and description of a solid weight would convince a person that it can possess kinetic energy; no examination of a bucket of water indicates that water in motion can give rise to venturi effects; no examination of electrons reveals that in movement they generate magnetic fields. In the same way, an examination of money itself reveals nothing of the effects that money in movement will produce. These examples all involve energy theory, and it seems that finally energy theory, or something analogous to it, will be required to understand the properties of money. Not money but money in motion is a neo-energy phenomenon. It is certain that something quite definite does happen when money moves and also that the effects produced are quite different from those produced by money in its "store-of-value" aspects, whatever value is taken to mean. The phenomenon is a flow phenomenon, so the obvious approach is one involving resistance-capacitance-potential models, with or without inductance. Once this is accepted exponential growth and decay are immediately introduced, an irritation that most economists could well do without. No matter what sort of modelling is eventually introduced, there are certain general conditions that must be met. Models will need to be dynamic and related to time instead of reflecting a static world-view. They must also be functional rather than existential; that is, they will involve questions of how concepts act and interact rather than what they are. In addition it will be necessary to develop new concepts, often far removed from the conventional concepts and categories of present economics.

Finally, there is the problem of wealth itself, of what wealth is, or more accurately how to conceptualize it, what it does and how it operates. The factors that generate wealth—land, labour, capital, and motivation—may be known, but the question of how wealth actually begins has never been satisfactorily answered. Movements of wealth appear to have properties over and above the simple transfer of something; there appear to be venturi effects that sometimes impoverish the recipient and benefit the payer. Money going to the poor sometimes appears to increase wealth less than money going to the well-to-do, possibly because of capacitance effects. And if monetarists are right, and pouring money into an isolated economy actually reduces its wealth, then new conceptual models are required to account for this. Countries with high GNP invariably exhibit a high cost of living, but there is no plausible explanation for this. Clearly, there are interactions taking place between money, supply of goods, price levels, and existing plant which cannot be explained by psychological factors alone. Just how these interactions are to be conceived is not clear, yet they must be understood if the economies of the world are to be operated for the benefit of individuals.

32

POST-ECONOMIC SOCIETY

Every society has its particular shortcomings. In earlier European communities and in most underdeveloped countries at present, these have been associated with poverty—a shortage of material goods, inadequate medical care, poor sanitation, and natural hazards. Sickness, high infant mortality rates, hunger, and accidents were and remain the major causes of death and suffering in primitive societies. As recently as the mid-seventeenth century, poverty and disease, in particular plague, caused more widespread hardship in Europe than either war or social upheaval. Indeed, in all wars up to the end of the nineteenth century, deaths due to illness, cold, exposure, and inadequate medical care far exceeded actual battle deaths.

The growth of the industrial economy with its sophisticated technology has done much to change this. Industrial organization has reduced, but by no means eliminated, material poverty; improved sanitation techniques and advances in medicine have deferred but not eliminated illness as a major cause of suffering and death. Partly as a result of this, and partly because of changes brought on by industrialization itself, the problems facing modern society are largely associated with social organization rather than with poverty or disease. These fall into three main categories: psychological anxieties reflecting the dislocation between individuals and the society; tensions between sub-groups and the major society; and conflicts between the major societies themselves.

From the individual's point of view, the frustrations of life in industrial society are all too apparent. The more obvious signs are an increase in mental illness and stress disease, juvenile delinquency and adolescent violence, a rising crime rate, civil disorder, and the alienation of minority groups. Psychologically, the defects of industrial society find expression as individual loneliness, a sense of the futility of life, ennui, apathy, boredom, and at times an incapacitating despair. Physically we are healthy enough, but emotionally the major cities of the West resemble a Crimean infirmary of the walking wounded: people unable to establish personal relationships with others; people tired of the boring futility of pointless work and meaningless existence; the haunted unapproachable faces on commuter trains and buses concealed behind newspapers; middle-aged single women living alone, returning to empty flatettes from dull routine shop work; the alcoholics and drug users who can make life tolerable only by destroying all capacity to feel; the homosexuals seeking contact through chance pick-ups in public toilets or gay bars; the self-conscious socially inept young in singles' bars and discotheques; the lonely people who place matrimonial or friendship ads in local newspapers; the elderly widows who every winter die alone of cold and malnutrition in antiquated bed-sitters; the suicides and potential suicides of Chelsea, Greenwich Village, and Kings Cross. The poverty that afflicts modern life is emotional poverty—loneliness, alienation, and boredom—a poverty far more destructive than material poverty. People lacking material possessions can live fruitfully, can function and engage in personal relationships. Emotional poverty destroys the capacity to act, the capacity to love, and finally the capacity to respond to the world with any pleasure or enjoyment.

Alienated individuals present little danger to the society except when alienation leads to mental illness. The case is different with alienated groups and sub-societies; racial extremists, black power supporters, student groups, labour interests, political and religious extremists, criminal and homosexual sub-cultures, and even feminist power groups. These retribalized groups have aims, ideals, and ends at variance with the purported ends of the society at large, and quite often incompatible with the major society. One significant group is represented by the young, notably school and university students and what has become known as the counter-culture. The West is probably the first society which, because of the speed of social change and the resulting deficiencies of its values, finds itself effectively at war with its own children. It has been remarked that only the young who feel themselves lost, alienated, and bereft of any frame of reference are not lost, while those unaware of their disorientation are truly lost. It is significant that the most educated, gifted, and intelligent among the young are often most prone to reject society's values, either by violently attacking the social system or by resigning in disgust from the whole contemporary order and everything it represents.

Conflicts between major societies are more readily understood as sociological rather than as economic or territorial competition. The Cold War, pursued with greater or lesser enthusiasm from Berlin to Saigon, represents the competition between classical capitalistic economism and its heretical offspring, Marxism; the Middle East war represents an ideological clash between Judaism and its Islamic offshoot; the friction between India and Pakistan is the product of a clash between Hindu and Islamic emotologies. War is clearly more than value competition and the operation of bigotry-mechanism, but without these elements it would be an infrequent aspect of human affairs rather than, as made to appear in older school texts, the predominant aspect of human history. A species with different emotional equipment would view war as a bizarre aberration rather than as the enduring component of international affairs.

The mentality that sees the world as problems-to-be-solved—rather than as inconveniences-to-be-borne, as the East does, or as irritations-to-be-avoided, as the counter-culture tends to do—is a purely Western innovation. While no more, and certainly no less, valid than alternative interpretations, it does have unique social utility. So long as aspects of the world are seen as problems, there is likely to be an attempt to interact with them and possibly to make some improvement. The dissatisfaction that many people feel in their emotionally desiccated existence is a fact of life; considering it as a problem assumes that something can be done about it. The same is true of friction between groups and the major societies, and of belligerence between nation states. Before such problems can be solved, or at least mitigated, it is essential to recognize the type of problem.

Most emotional problems are psychological and sociological; sociological in source and psychological in manifestation. They reflect the break-up of community life, and with it the loss of motivational relations between the society and the individual, the consequent lack of internalized emotive-mechanisms that could lead to activity and give life a sense of purpose, and the lack of a coherent social structure capable of providing emotional support. Patrick Moynihan, one-time adviser on urban affairs to the United States president, has pointed out that the major domestic problems facing that country spring from an erosion of the authority of institutions, and that the sense of institutions being legitimate is the glue that holds societies together. This is tantamount to saying that alienated groups are no longer motivated to pursue the ends that the society as a whole pursues. Earlier societies had clearly defined spiritual equipment, generally taking the form of ritual, ceremony, and display, for transmitting the values that provided motivation. With the exception of desultory flag-saluting ceremonies, Western societies have been singularly inept at developing institutions for transmitting values. The schism between state and religion has made any such transmission doubly difficult, so it is hardly surprising that many people are rejecting nineteenth-century nationalistic values. This decay of centralized state power is a problem only to those with a vested interest in preserving the power of government; the more radical groups accept the dilution of the state's authority with undisguised delight. Conversely, those in authority do not view warfare as a problem, except where a war proves intractable, while dissenting groups, particularly those liable to be drafted and the economically underprivileged, tend to view war as the major problem in human affairs.

Societies tend to see their inadequacies as inevitable, as being somehow in the ordained nature of things. The Middle Ages held that poverty was the inevitable lot of much of mankind, that "the poor are always with us". This comfortable assumption allowed the rich to accumulate spiritual credit through acts of charity, while benefiting from the *status quo* with a clear conscience. By Victorian times it had become obvious that poverty, or at least widespread poverty, need not be the inevitable lot of man. Material living standards improved, but this improvement was accompanied by problems of rapid urbanization, water and atmospheric pollution, epidemics brought on by poor sanitation and overcrowded dwellings, and the beginning of social alienation. Improvements in engineering techniques and legislation such as the British Clean Air Act have proved that pollution is not an inevitable consequence of industrialization, although pollution and the destruction of the environment still remain one of the major menaces facing mankind.

The conditions now assumed to be inherent in the nature of things are psychological and sociological problems: individual loneliness, spiritual emptiness, and the catalogue of human despair that the existentialists in particular treat so effectively. One dies alone, and personal isolation is the inevitable human condition. Camus describes emotionally isolated people more or less resigned to their isolation. Sartre portrays people incapable of committed action simply because they are unwilling to risk emotional involvement. Beckett describes the ultimate futility, emptiness, and anguish of life devoid of meaning, sense, or value; spiritual sickness and emotional death find their analogy in physical sickness and an interminable dying. The validity of these writings is not in question; they reflect the condition of the age, just as *The Deserted Village* and the novels of Dickens reflect the impact of industrialization. But alienation is not *the* human condition. There is no enduring human condition, but only a human condition for each society and each age. The alienation of European society is no more inevitable than widespread poverty, plague, or industrial pollution, except that emotional problems resulting from social dislocation are, like pollution, a new development. Stable primitive societies in which the tribal group provides emotional support and motivational relationships are rarely characterized by loneliness and ennui.

Medical problems require medical solutions; economic problems require economic solutions. To recognize the type of problem, assuming it is legitimate to interpret it as a problem, is to go a long way towards a solution. The difficulties facing urban Western society, whether individual emotional problems or fragmentation of the larger society, are fundamentally sociological problems and require sociological solutions. This means developing a far more sophisticated sociology than is yet available if society is to develop in directions favourable to individual welfare, if only because of the extraordinary complexity of industrial society. Simple systems can be allowed to develop by trial and error. A farmer's earth dam or a home lighting set require a minimum of theoretical knowledge for their construction; an extensive hydro-electrical scheme, such as the TVA project or the Snowy Mountains scheme, require not only elaborate planning but an extensive theoretical knowledge of hydraulic theory, electrical theory, and system interactions. Tribal societies, though by no means simple in their organization, have had thousands of years to evolve and accommodate themselves to their particular environment. Contemporary societies are changing at an unprecedented rate, necessitating complex interactions of political, economic, military, sociological, religious, and technological factors. They cannot be allowed to develop by chance or by haphazard *ad hoc* solutions to problems, any more than a hydro-electric scheme can be allowed simply to happen. Contemporary society, rather than the computer or the telephone system, is the most complex creation ever developed by the human race.

Every utopian planner has proposed an ideal and ultimate society without ever attempting to understand the dynamics that underlie social systems in general. This is true of Plato, true of the early humanists and rationalists, and especially true of the Marxists. To plan a society without any understanding of social interactions and sociology is like attempting to plan a bridge without any knowledge of the properties of materials. A concrete bridge reflects in its physical form the properties of concrete, strong in compression, weak in tension; a wooden bridge, a stone bridge, a pre-stressed concrete bridge all reflect in their geometry the properties of the structural materials. Similarly, the form and structure of a society reflect the psychological and sociological properties of its components—individual human beings.

Utopian programmes tend to reflect the values of their advocates: the authoritarianism of Plato, Marx's idealization of the working class, the liberal ideology of the humanists. All assume that the only necessary condition for a society to function is for people to live and work in proximity, but societies no more happen than a biological entity or a machine happens. They are the product of interactions of considerable complexity, and a knowledge of how individuals interact with the society is essential for understanding them. Moreover, there cannot be one ideal society or final condition towards which societies are moving, and in this both Marx and Plato betray an inherently static world-view approach. The future lies in pluralism and in the greatest possible diversity of cultures. Sociology can no more be expected to determine the final ideal society than statics and properties of materials can determine the ultimate bridge. All it can do is specify the general conditions that must be satisfied for a society to function: that motivational relations must exist; that there must be provision for transmitting values to the young; that values must be capable of evolving; and that an ideology of some kind must exist around which the social system can cohere.

Suggestions about planning, particularly social planning, are apt to evoke nightmares of immense bureaucracies, government surveillance, and an extensive sacrifice of personal freedom. But the choice, whether in economic planning or in social planning, is no longer between planned and unplanned development, but between good planning and bad planning. Planning need not result in centralization of power, and the more efficient governments and business organizations have found ways to decentralize power and authority. Heavily centralized control, as exemplified by the Soviet Union and many overorganized business ventures, has proved inefficient owing to the difficulty of acquiring accurate information and of ensuring that the instructions of the central authorities are followed. There is, too, a tremendous psychological advantage in including people affected by decisions in the process of making those decisions. A high degree of planning is not incompatible with democratic organization, as illustrated by the Scandinavian countries, Holland, Great Britain, and West Germany. Effective planning, so long as it is answerable to all sections of the society, is more likely to promote individual freedom than is a lack of planning. A persistent challenge facing the nominal democracies is to find methods of decentralized planning which neither stifle independence nor result in failure to make policies effective.

If it is agreed that contemporary deficiencies are largely sociological, we are committed to social change of a planned type, in contrast to the drunkard's walk development that has proceeded since the Renaissance. A sophisticated body of sociological knowledge can in theory provide the means to direct change, but it cannot provide the motivation required to do so, nor can it make the final decisions as to social ends or the type of society that should eventuate. Social change requires a powerful emotology, and, if the social change is to be directed towards an intelligent restructuring of society, this ideology must be sociological in nature.

Before the Renaissance, ideologies were religious in content, the value transmission equipment was associated with religious institutions, and the prime object of consciousness was religious belief. Subsequently, the prime ideology, the transmission equipment, and the main object of consciousness became involved with economic ends. Both types of emotology were adequate for the societies at the time, but have now been superseded as social change made their limitations obvious. Religious ideology, apart from providing a bond for the society, results largely in religious-directed behaviour; economic ideology results largely in economic activity—buying, selling, producing, consuming, and expanding the economy. But once a certain level of wealth has been accumulated there is less justification for intense economic activity. Economism saturates. Traditional religious ideologies are at the same time rendered irrelevant by social change. Additionally, religious and economic activities represent only a very small proportion of the activities open to human beings. In the past such activities as philosophical inquiry, artistic creation, personal relationships, and academic scientific enquiry have been little more than tolerated by the primary emotology. They represent the triumph of sub-group values or individual curiosity over social norms. If a new ideology can be evolved, adaptive to the present, it must overcome the limitations of previous ideologies. It must be far more widely based in the activities that it promotes than were previous ideologies. It must be associated with the factual information of the society. And it must be concerned with the aspects of life that are of most general interest to the society.

This new emotology which has already begun to coalesce is sociological rather than economic or religious in nature. It stands in much the same relationship to sociological knowledge as Christianity stands to theology, or economism to economic theory. Marxism was the first ideology to be based on a purported sociological as well as economic theory, but the sociology of Marx lacked scientific precision and largely reflected the class divisions of Europe in the mid-nineteenth century. The irony of Marx's work is that, while the first to recognize the importance of ideology, it gave rise to one of the most powerful current ideologies. Despite the immature and fragmentary state of present sociological theory, sociology has become one of the main interests of present society. Political parties are coming to realize that sociological issues are at least as important as the traditional political and economic issues; the British Labour and Liberal parties are typical of this in their concern with the quality of life, while many other political parties are displaying a similar understanding. Even right-wing news magazines, such as *Time* and *Newsweek*, now have a distinctly sociological, rather than political or economical, point of view.

Most people in Western society hold, or at least held until recently, a picture of the future as little more than a glorious technological extension of the present. This future, delineated by numerous magazine articles and science fiction journals, is one of increasing technological sophistication, automatic factories, unlimited gadgetry, the conquest of space, the colonization of near planets, new plastics and materials, high-speed transport, and vastly more powerful computers. Over two thousand books and articles have been published in the last decade indicating ways in which current technology will be extended to make life richer and more pleasant. But what is rarely realized, outside the best science fiction, is that the future will be both qualitatively and quantitatively different from the present. It will not lie in simply more of the same. Changes come when least expected and lead in directions that could never have been foreseen. The dinosaurs could reasonably have expected the future to lie with even bigger, heavier, and more heavily armoured saurians; they could never have anticipated that the insignificant mammals would one day supersede them.

The imperial Romans no doubt anticipated a future of extended empire and military conquest; they could not have foreseen that a despised religious sect would one day appropriate the future. It does not make sense to go beyond a certain stage in any direction, whether in size, power, or technical knowledge. Technology will continue to develop, if only because of the inertia possessed by all human activities and because of the huge vested interest in its development. But economic and technical developments are causing changes in social organization that are even more spectacular than the technological changes. The future lies with sociological rather than with technical development.

A culture's social organization is closely related to its emotology. Tribal organization is associated with particular religious-magical emotologies. Feudal social organization was bound up with the Christian ideology. Contemporary state and business organizations are closely linked with the economic ideology. The present change to a sociological ideology can be expected to be associated with corresponding changes in the forms of social organization; changes compatible with and associated with the new information and values. The role of groups in providing both motivation and emotional support has already been mentioned, and it is in these emotional areas that Western society has proved itself so lamentably deficient. A number of special and general-purpose groups are now emerging, usually within the main social framework, but providing facilities that the larger society either cannot or will not provide. These groups grew out of the use of psychotherapy groups and many exist for therapeutic purposes; Alcoholics Anonymous, Synanon, Daytop, Neurotics Anonymous, the Alpha Drug Treatment Unit of St James psychiatric hospital, Portsmouth.

Some groups are relatively open and informal, others are closed and authoritarian. The Marriage Guidance Council in Britain uses group situations of limited duration to train counsellors in human relationships. Esalen in California uses group situations, among other methods, to explore aspects of human personality and relationships. American corporations are experimenting with the use of T-groups to improve personal relations within organizations and to achieve higher levels of motivation. The much publicized Scandinavian experiments in group living, the misnamed group marriages, are experiments in the use of informal group structures to provide emotional support for members. Various sections of the youth counter-culture—the Hell's Angels with their chapters, the hippies with their communes—are more or less deliberate experiments in group living. This pattern of group reorganization hints at the future shape of Western society; a loose collection of continually changing groups, rather than the tightly organized business and administrative structures of the present. Group dynamics will replace hierarchy. The use of open groups for social ends can be expected to spread, if only because the social milieu of middle-class affluent society represents a wilderness that few people would willingly tolerate once alternatives are available.

Many of the advantages of a sociologically based culture are obvious. Because it is not restricted to economic or religious emotive-mechanisms, it opens up a far greater variety of activities. There has already been a considerable shift away from the view of man as a possessing being to that of man as a doing being. Aristocrats were previously distinguished by having more and a greater variety of goods than common people, but with growing affluence this distinction is becoming less relevant. The new aristocracy are those having the more interesting and satisfying occupations: scientists, architects, engineers, businessmen, writers, artists, and academics. Financial reward in these occupations is generally less important than the challenge or interest found in the particular occupation. The justification of a developed economy is not so much that it makes a variety of goods and services available, but that it opens up a far wider range of activities. Goods have relatively little effect on personality, whereas activities have a fundamental influence on how a person develops.

The impetus of economic growth has, in addition, equipped the West with far more material plant than it genuinely needs, even though this overabundance is often badly distributed. Having discovered that poverty and the lack of material comforts are not the inevitable lot of man, society has overreacted by setting up values and institutions to increase production to the utmost. The slightest drop in a developed country's GNP, rate of growth, or trade figures leads to reactions verging on hysteria on the part of economic analysts, financial journalists, and politicians of every conviction. To this extent, they are trapped within their economic ideology, just as previous generations were trapped within a religious ideology. The problem now is not so much to increase the quantity of goods available, but to make greater use of the plant that exists. Unmodified economism has no incentive to use consumer goods, as contrasted with capital plant, more fully, for this would tend to reduce the magical GNP figures. A sociological ideology by contrast is capable of developing values and institutions that make fuller use of consumer goods. Buckminster Fuller has predicted that leasing and renting of equipment will in time replace the present tendency for every person to own as much plant as possible, most of which goes unused much of the time. There is no sense in every person having a car, television, motor mower, and vacuum cleaner when they are only occasionally used. Co-operating social groups, with values directed towards activity—and hence sharing rather than simply owning—could make far more use of communal facilities. In the same way, much of society's institutional plant, such as asylums and prisons, could be done away with by changing social institutions and by social reorganization. Dr Alex Baker, director of the British Hospital Advisory Service, has commented that most of the seventy-eight thousand patients who have been in mental hospitals for two years or more could have been better cared for in a day hospital, where they would have experienced aspects of a normal community life. The same is true of minor criminal offenders who, as is shown in Sweden, can be effectively reformed—"cured" of criminal emotive-mechanisms—without removing them completely from the community. Isolation of any group leads to intensification of values, or, in the case of the emotionally disturbed, of their lack of values. Such changes in the treatment of mentally ill and criminals require new social institutions and changes in values, not least on the part of the public, medical profession, and judiciary. That is, a substitution of social organization for physical plant is required.

Much of this society's equipment can be put to far better use either by more intensive employment or by using one piece of equipment in a variety of roles. The centres of most European cities, the shops and offices, are deserted empty shells at night while suburban houses are hardly occupied during the day. In South-East Asia, by contrast, small shops and offices become at night the living-room, bedroom and kitchen for the family. In Thailand, religious buildings—wats—double as schools, while in India temples of many denominations are also used to house pilgrims, travellers, and the homeless. This contrasts with the Western situation where churches are used for a few hours a week, schools for only a limited number of hours five days a week, and literally thousands of families lack acceptable accommodation. No economic change, but only a change in values and attitudes, is needed to make more socially desirable use of equipment. There is virtually no item of Western plant, whether accommodation, office, place of worship, school, or factory, that cannot be put to more satisfactory use if only social values can be modified.

By transcending the limits of economic society and ideology, a sociological society can open up more activities and make more flexible use of equipment possible. The emotional support provided by new social organizations, in particular group sub-societies, will make possible greater exploration of personal relationships and the development of a wider emotional repertoire. Relationships with others are at least as important to people as political and economic aspects of life, and a society disregards this at its peril. Most important, the change to a sociological ideology will encourage the move towards a wider-based and more acceptive society. For centuries this society insisted on very strict religious, sexual, class, and behavioural conditions for those it was prepared to accept as members. Religious nonconformists were reluctantly accepted in the eighteenth and nineteenth century; somewhat later, the working class were admitted, at first into political then into social respectability. The same process of acceptance is now going on in the sexual field; *de facto* sexual relationships are widely accepted, and even homosexual relationships, now legal in most West European countries, are increasingly tolerated. R. D. Laing has indicated that the narrowness of the West's definition of social roles causes much of the difficulty for the mentally ill and psychotic. Society is still extremely narrow in the patterns of behaviour and conceptualization that it is prepared to tolerate, just as it was narrow in the religious, class, or sexual groups it was prepared to accept. Indian society, which is far less strict in its role-defining in many ways, allows those who would elsewhere be considered mentally abnormal to live as *sadhus*, religious mendicants and monks. They remain, if imperfectly, within the motivating milieu of the society. A sociological society would eliminate some of the problems of outsiders by extending its base and enlarging its definition of the acceptable.

The task of evolving emotive-mechanisms more appropriate to new conditions has fallen to the young, particularly to students and to members of the counter-culture. These new values are selectively liberal, anti-militaristic, anti-nationalistic, and anti-authoritarian; in short, they comprise a radical reaction against most that is implicit in nineteenth-century values. The importance of the conflict in Vietnam was not primarily in its political or economic consequences, but in the fact that it was a nexus around which anti-war, anti-militaristic values accumulated. Militarism as a successful value scheme reached its peak during the Second World War, a conflict still glorified in books, films, and television when most other conflicts have been effectively discredited. But the advent of nuclear technology has rendered major wars effectively self-defeating as matters of national policy, while minor wars stubbornly refuse to conform to old notions. For the intellectual realization that war is self-defeating to be transformed into an emotional value-complex required an intensely emotional political experience, provided by Vietnam. Anti-war attitudes have been in existence for a long time, particularly among minority groups such as the Quakers and in the novels of Tolstoy and Remarque, but it is only now, when they have unquestioned social utility, that they are becoming widespread.

Concern with freedom, a preoccupation of nineteenth-century liberalism, has also acquired new importance owing to changed social conditions. The concept of freedom has become a major issue, just as concepts of honour, duty, salvation, and nationalism were the prime objects of consciousness of the nineteenth century. There is no way to judge whether people are more free or less free at present than in other ages and societies. Freedom may indicate the absence of physical restrictions or it may refer to the totality of possibilities open to a person. A hermit on a desert island is completely free in the legal sense, but utterly restricted in the possibilities open to him. Moreover, the use of freedom as an emotive counter has changed; freedom in the past has been the rallying cry of minority religious, ethnic, or geographical groups, linguistic groups, and tribal minorities. The freedom sought has been the freedom to observe the particular practices of minority groups or to preserve societies under attack. It has acted for the benefit of groups rather than individuals.

The freedom now sought is a complete independence of the individual, rather than freedom that serves the ends of groups. This value complex has grown up in reaction to the demands made by government bureaucracy, the authoritarianism of large business organizations, the paternalism of schools and universities, the depersonalization of urban life, and every influence now reducing individuality to computer ciphers, administrative files, and statistics. As such, the ideal is laudable but is in the final analysis unworkable. Absolute freedom, even if it were attainable, can never be to any group's advantage. A sub-society that sincerely believed in complete independence of its members would soon fragment, or at best lose its adherents to more highly motivated and demanding groups. This is quite apart from the fact that the more highly organized and interdependent a society grows, the less independence is possible. The nineteenth-century liberal ideal of a pluralistic society in which each person is free to pursue his own ends is both practically and sociologically unattainable. Bigotry-mechanism can be expected to limit the variety and liberalism of any society; moreover, as long as the world consists of competing nation states, a nation lacking in consensus and unifying ideology is a potential prey to other societies.

The awareness that it is pioneering new and possibly more socially useful emotive-mechanisms has given the counter-culture a certain arrogance. Each radically new ideological group imagines that it will inherit the future and be finally justified by history; the early Christians share this sense of certainty with the more radical Marxists. But while hippies and the counter-culture as a whole are an indication that major value changes are taking place, they are symptoms of change rather than the future itself. Their anti-intellectual, anti-economic, and anti-scientific attitudes relegate them to a cul-de-sac. It is not conceivable that the race will discard the knowledge so painstakingly acquired over two millennia; evolution has never once reversed itself. The uncomplicated Waldenesque Elysium that many young seek existed only in the trees of a central African jungle. In addition, a continuing society requires strong internalization of values, something the counter-culture go to any extreme to avoid. But while the future may not lie with any particular section of the new dissent culture, it most certainly does not lie with the mainstream middle-class, economically directed, conservative interests. That society is so involved with the *status quo* and with limited economic values that it is trapped in a social impasse. The increasingly frantic oppression of dissent in any form and what is often referred to as the reactionary backlash, whether against students, coloureds, or political radicals, indicates how deeply the value conflict is running already and how threatened the conservatives feel.

Fascism is a pejorative used so readily against more extreme forms of conservatism and authoritarianism as to be almost meaningless. But the more extreme reaction now being shown by many governments can only be described as Fascist and, moreover, as a Fascism comparable in degree to Nazi fascism in 1933.

Early in 1970, the United States House of Representatives passed a bill which effectively repealed the fourth, fifth, sixth, and eighth amendments to the Constitution. It granted unrestrained authority for the police to enter private homes without announcing themselves, and provided for night searches and unlimited seizure of property. In addition, it gave the police broad authority for wire-tapping, provided for pre-trial detention of up to sixty days for suspects previously charged with violent crime, and introduced savage mandatory minimum sentences for felony of up to twenty years with no parole, suspension, or probation.

The violence of the police and National Guard at the 1968 Democratic Convention and the murder of students and militant blacks, while outraging liberals, have been greeted with tacit approval by the conservative middle class. In South America, where Marxism and Catholicism are merging into a new ideology around which those troubled societies can integrate themselves, military regimes are resorting to violence, torture, and murder to halt change. In France, the beating and gaoling without trial of dissidents has become commonplace, and restrictive laws have been introduced effectively preventing any gathering opposed to authority. This type of reaction against liberalism and change is world-wide, proving that governments, like radicals, are capable of acquiring behaviour patterns by imitation. It has appeared in the United States, France, the South American republics, Greece, South Africa, and even Australia, all countries nominally pledged to democratic organization. Law and order has emerged as the universal rallying cry of conservatism, as though these were in some way absolutes; it is never made explicit just whose law or which particular order it is that must be maintained. The situation is paradoxical in that most conservatives are emotionally committed to the ideal of progress, but technical progress and economic expansion inevitably produce social and value changes which are violently resisted.

Authoritarianism, compulsive law-making, and bureaucracy tend to go hand in hand. In their extreme form they are a symptom of social stagnation. Western societies now attempt to regulate by law what goods may be sold at what times and by whom; what forms of sexual intercourse may be indulged in and with whom; what forms of intoxicant may be used by whom and under what conditions; and what type of literature may be read. This could be no more than an encumbrance except that many of these laws discriminate against and penalize unjustly the poor, the young, and those whose behaviour, while not dangerous, does not conform to the norms of society. The controversy as to whether law should attempt to protect the attitudes, moral sensibilities, and beliefs of the majority, or whether, as liberals contend, its role is simply to prevent socially disruptive behaviour, is an old one. The indications are that, in many developed societies at least, the first view is prevailing.

Authoritarian governments in general and dictatorships in particular are curiously incapable of seeing dissent as anything other than an aberration or a disease to be cured. This cure is almost always held to be in the interests of social dissidents themselves. The Spanish Inquisition, the Greek colonels, Stalin's bureaucracy, and the Comstocks, Anslingers, and Eichmanns of the world genuinely believe in the righteousness of their measures, no matter how repressive, even when these measures involve violence, torture, and imprisonment without trial. Appeals to reason, common sense, or humanism achieve nothing, for authoritarians are trapped within their rigidly internalized emotive-mechanisms. Bigotry-mechanism, the identifying with others of similar values, has both positive and negative aspects. On the positive side it generates a bond between people with similar ideologies and behavioural responses, making society possible. On the negative side it generates hostility between groups with conflicting ideologies. Authoritarian personalities, particularly those formed by military or lower middle-class backgrounds, tend to hold rigidly internalized values, as a result of the severe discipline involved in their socializing. Hence their bigotry-mechanism reactions tend to be more violent; they are more prone to moral dogmatism and far less tolerant of students, intellectuals, long-hairs, blacks, homosexuals, and foreigners than are the less rigidly conditioned professional classes. Polemics against authoritarian governments and organizations are in consequence pointless, and in any case simply represent the emotional values and the bigotry-mechanisms of radicals and liberals. It is only by understanding why authoritarian and repressive laws and governments exist, and the sociological forces determining them, that positive changes can be made.

Unfortunately, as the interests of government and industry have become more unsure of themselves, they have reacted with increasing violence. This has engendered an equally violent reaction, and hence counter-reaction, both from the simple need to survive and from the imitative transmission of violence values. Few people can live in a society where violence is taken for granted without internalizing violence emotive-mechanisms. The tendency towards official violence—or responding with violence—has generated radical revolutionary values, just as it did in pre-revolutionary France and Russia. Quite serious appeals for revolution, whether violent or non-violent, are now being made by most sections of the underground, by black militants, and by student radicals. The implications of this have hardly been understood, least of all by revolutionaries whose professed Marxism goes hand in hand with an abysmal ignorance of history. Revolutions are more than changes in political institutions; revolutions effectively destroy through emotional hysteria the values that hold a society together. They are analogous to the extreme emotions that precede brainwashing and religious conversion, and which expel old emotive-mechanisms to make way for new. The temporary result is the value vacuum that characterized revolutionary France and Russia, in which every excess resulted in a greater excess because there were no values to act as restraints. Such a value vacuum is psychologically and sociologically unendurable. The consequence is usually a dictatorship temporarily worse than anything that went before—the brutal militarism of Napoleon, the bloody purges of Stalin. A new post-revolutionary emotology emerges in time, around which the society can integrate itself, but this emotology and its associated institutions will often be extremely repressive. Social order will finally be bought at almost any price. Even when the revolutions have been comparatively mild, as in England, a Cromwell has emerged to restore an authoritarian order. When the original society has lacked cohesion, revolt against an external power may destroy the bonds holding the society together: the American Civil War had its sociological roots in the War of Independence.

Revolutions have almost always been followed by authoritarian regimes, and there is no reason to believe that the counter-culture's revolution would be any different. Quite apart from this, fatalities among revolutionaries have invariably exceeded deaths among those supporting the established order. The Establishment is the Establishment simply because it controls the military, political, legal, and economic levers of power. It is rarely as monolithic or coherent as revolutionaries tend to imagine, but when threatened seriously it has usually been capable of response at the appropriate level. Non-violence is not simply a Gandhian eccentricity but finally the most effective way of achieving change. Evolutionary as against revolutionary change modifies values selectively, thus ensuring that there is a sufficient reservoir of values to hold the society together. It is a process that has been going on since the beginning of civilization and breaks down only when authoritarian governments prevent change for a sufficient period.

The consequence of value evolution is that ideologies can only emerge and diffuse at a finite rate and that this rate may not be sufficient to accommodate economic, technical, or social changes. Even the United States and Britain preserve pockets of earlier and generally less adaptive values, as for example in the Deep South and the more isolated districts of Britain. There is a limit to the speed with which people, conditioned into one set of values and strongly attached to these values, can be expected to change. At a certain rate of value change, the younger generation will be perpetually alienated from the older generation, as new values are evolved to handle social change. The term *future shock*, comparable to culture shock, has come into vogue to describe the alienation that rapid technical and social change produces. Arnold Toynbee has suggested that change in Western society may already be exceeding people's capacity to cope adequately. Certainly, excessive rates of change are undermining the certainties of the old and leaving the young with no certainties whatsoever. A continually renewing society requires the rejection by each generation of values that have lost utility, but this rejection must take place without driving a wedge between age groups or generating intense reactions into conservatism. Progress is regarded as being inherent in a technological culture, as to some extent it is, but progress itself is the product of the values of economism. An ideological change, if it were marked enough, could substantially reduce the speed of change, and lead to a flattening out of the S growth curve. A period of consolidation might not be a bad thing so long as it did not result in stagnation, and would at least allow comprehension to catch up with social realities for a time.

Western society, the twenty-first civilization on Toynbee's well-known reckoning, is unique in a number of ways. Not only does it possess a more sophisticated technology than did previous civilizations, but it is also self-aware in a sense that others were not. It sees itself as one civilization among others, going through stages comparable to those encountered by other cultures. Possibly for the first time a whole society is now aware that it is entering a transition phase as the phase begins.

The shortcomings of the economic ideology are now apparent; "private affluence, public squalor" in Galbraith's celebrated words, and a desiccation of the emotional life of those engaged in economic pursuits, a desiccation that Lawrence, Dickens, and Henry Miller have constantly stressed. These shortcomings are an indication that a new and more flexible ideology is needed. The friction between generations, between interest groups, between intellectuals of every conviction, and between radicals and conservatives marks the birth pangs of the new ideology or ideologies. Since most of the present problems of society are sociological, it is reasonable to assume that the new ideology will be linked to sociological science. It is inconceivable in any event that a knowledge of how societies work will emerge without affecting the emotive-mechanism structure of the society. Indeed, it is not certain that a fully aware society, comprehending its own dynamics, can continue to function at all. Once people understand how they are motivated or "manipulated" they tend to react against their conditioning and against the motivating milieu that constrains them. For people to refuse to play the games that hold society together is finally more destructive than any amount of radical violence. Assaults on the society produce equally violent efforts to preserve it; utter rejection of social values baffles those who still believe in these values and subtly subverts their beliefs.

Changes in ideology interact with changes in social organization in a cause-effect relationship. Some of the emerging social patterns are already evident in embryonic form—for example, sub-societies, special purpose groups, and institutions such as consumer organizations linked neither to government nor to business organizations. Others will only appear decades hence by a process of experimentation, trial and error, and response to new situations. It seems likely that these new forms of organization will be as diverse and pluralistic as the society can accept, for a growing organism tends to radiate out in every direction and explore every possibility. New institutions may supplant the nation state as the repository of power and arbitrator of values. There is no inherent reason why the state, the Church, or the tribe should have final power over the individual.

Western society is also the first to be widely aware that it faces the danger of breakdown, or at least of serious fragmentation. The sombre ghost of Gibbon has never ceased to stalk the Western imagination, while the wreckage and histories of ancient empires, of Babylon, Tyre, Akkad, Sumer, and Mohenjo Daro, of the Incas, the Aztecs, the Khmers, the Minoans, and the Hittites, continue to excite curiosity. It is easy to point out the parallels between contemporary society and Rome, or any other civilization in its declining stage. But the fact that the West is qualitatively different from other civilizations invalidates the obvious conclusion. Unlike earlier civilizations, the West has never had an enduring centre of power. Its political and cultural axis has shifted from southern Europe—Italy, Spain, and Portugal—to northern Europe—France, Germany, and Great Britain—and thence to the ideological competitors, Soviet Russia and the United States of America. Each country has made unique artistic, political, and technological contributions to what has been, in the last analysis, a single continuing culture. Professor C. E. Ayres has suggested that new civilizations develop on the frontiers of the old by adopting the technology and knowledge of their predecessors while remaining unencumbered by old values and institutions. Europe represents the frontier area of Greco-Roman civilization, while the United States and Russia represent the frontier areas of European civilization.

The new frontier areas of Japan, China, and Africa are already absorbing Western technology and culture while developing new institutions and ideologies to use them. Western society can thus be seen as a completely new phenomenon from Roman, Chinese, or Central American civilization—a culture that is transitive rather than terminative. It is continually branching out in new geographical areas rather than stagnating, as did Chinese society, or fragmenting, as did Roman society. The laws that appear to apply to earlier civilizations do not necessarily apply to a world culture with highly developed communications and an almost compulsive urge to borrow from every source. Western civilization is in short the first meta-civilization, differing from past civilizations as much as they differ from tribal cultures.

Nonetheless, sections of Western culture do appear to be either in a state of stagnation, as are areas of southern Europe, or else entering a period of disintegration. Civilizations, or sections of civilizations, deteriorate from a number of causes: by exhausting resources of fertile soil and water, by foreign conquest, or by economic failure. But the factors that bring an end to a culture, like the factors that bring it into being, are fundamentally sociological. Civilizations fail from within, and it is only when they are weakened internally, when there is a loss of will and vitality, that the barbarian at the gate, the depletion of resources, or economic mismanagement bring about complete failure.

The determinants of any society are sociological—value systems, motivating relationships, ideologies, and spiritual equipment—and if a society is to be understood and prevented from embarking on catastrophic experiments a developed theory of sociology is essential. The present pre-eminent position of the United States and Europe is largely the result of investment in the physical sciences, particularly the energy sciences, in the nineteenth century. Societies that are now investing in the social sciences will enjoy a similar advantage in the twenty-first century, for they will be in a position to influence their own development, to reduce adverse influences, and to promote an integrated social structure. Societies that cannot develop or at least import sociological knowledge will go the way of Calcutta—disintegration, anarchy, fragmentation, poverty, and squalor.

The capacity to control the direction that societies take is essential, but once achieved raises again the question of ends. There is no reason why the nightmares of *1984* or of *Brave New World* will not eventuate, or why a future Hitler will not succeed where the last failed. Early gas turbines, sound in thermodynamic theory, failed because the necessary metallurgical knowledge was not available. Hitler failed because the techniques of manipulation and control of conquered peoples had not been sufficiently developed. Advances in electronic surveillance, drug mood control, and particularly in sociological theory will in time make Hitler's dream practicable, just as developments in the metallurgy of nickel-chrome-iron alloys made the gas turbine possible. Such a perversion of knowledge can be prevented only if the majority of people have an understanding of social dynamics and some idea of the type of society and the way of life that they desire. There is no guarantee that the future will turn out to be favourable, just as there is no guarantee that it will turn out to be unfavourable. Sociological knowledge can provide the means to achieve specific social ends; emotions in general and ideology in particular can provide the will to attain those ends; but a developed philosophy of ends is required to enable people to choose between ends and to provide direction for societies.

EPILOGUE: UNDERSTANDING ENDS

This book is a commentary on ends. It is concerned with the general problem of determining the right or good course of action in any situation, of choosing between alternative ends in a non-moral context, and of the point, meaning, and purpose of human life.

Questions of ends, by their very nature, admit no permanent solution. There can only be systems of ends, evaluative techniques and means of attaining ends appropriate to each age and culture. In consequence there is nothing here that could not be revised at some later stage, nothing claimed to be ultimately or finally true. As new information and modes of conceptualization become available, and new social needs arise, new approaches to ends will prove necessary. The process is a continuing one. Every society must solve the questions of ends for its own time in a manner appropriate to its particular needs.

Rather than attempt to define enduring solutions, the aim here has been to raise the questions of ends that appear relevant to the present, to define the problems, and to indicate the directions in which solutions could be sought. The aim is to show that the problems of ends are real problems, rather than simply the abstractions of philosophy, and moreover that they are important. They are important because whatever answers are established will influence the quality of individual life, and they are important because these answers will influence the nature of future societies.

There can be no way of knowing beforehand what questions are raised in understanding ends. The approach taken has been to surround the issue with whatever questions appear capable of being raised—What ends are pursued? Why are they pursued? How are they to be achieved? How to choose between competing ends?—and to see where these questions lead.

The question of what ends are actually pursued leads, in this society, to a consideration of human happiness, welfare, and economic goals. The question of why these or any other particular set of goals are actually pursued leads to an examination of motivational relationships, of the ways in which values and dispositions are evolved and instilled, and of their social utility.

The question of how to achieve particular ends takes in the nature of knowledge, of what it means to know and understand something, and of how knowledge in the abstract is to be conceptualized. Knowledge not only provides the means to attain ends previously decided on, but, by extending the range of ends, makes evaluative methods more independent of means.

As emphasized, the viewpoints and ideas advanced are all tentative, to be taken as possible starting points for discussion rather than as dogmatic assertions of value systems. A coherent theory of how social interactions take place is essential, and such a theory seems likely to be concerned with emotional factors. The emotivist approach described is a theory amenable to empirical test, both experimentally and by way of material drawn from sociology and history. The development of theories of social interaction requires far more knowledge of the emotional nature of individuals, of the manner in which values and attitudes are internalized, and of the ways in which people respond to the emotional patterns of their society. If the emotivist approach is rejected, it must be replaced with something more satisfactory. A theory of social motivation, and of the ways in which values emerge, is essential if more rational or adaptive schemes of ends are to be developed.

The idea of knowledge as a system of analogue models is not, by contrast, an empirical hypothesis, but a method of conceptualization that appears useful for the present time. Other approaches to knowledge are obviously possible and can be expected to emerge as new modes of conceptualization develop. But again, if this approach is not accepted, it must be replaced by something more satisfactory. Knowledge is so fundamental to human life that some method of conceptualizing it is essential.

In the same way, nothing absolute or final is claimed for the possibilities criterion as a means of evaluating ends. It is a technique to be used when it proves appropriate, and rejected once better criteria become available. It has advantages in that it is more comprehensive than existing ethics and capable of continually refining the criteria on which judgements are made, so making dogmatic value systems superfluous. New evaluative techniques can be expected to emerge in time as social change makes the shortcomings of the possibilities criterion evident.

New approaches to understanding ends, new evaluative techniques, and new conceptual schemes are essential, particularly now that Western society is experiencing a period of accelerating change. But it is also essential to recognize the limits of what rationality can achieve and how far intellectual approaches are applicable to the question of what to do.

Programmes are useful over only a limited range, and analytical approaches to knowledge can go only so far. An understanding of ends is important, but there is a point at which understanding itself ends. Here new and non-intellectual approaches to values, ends, and the meaning of life must be sought.

London, 1970

BIBLIOGRAPHY

NOTE: While this book was completed in 1970 it was not accepted by the publisher in its final form until 1976. Accordingly, a number of books published after 1970, and which are relevant to its themes, are included in this bibliography.

Abraham, J.H. *Origins and Growth of Sociology* Harmondsworth, Mddx.: Penguin, 1973.

Aron, Raymond. *Main Currents in Sociological Thought*, 1 & 2. Harmondsworth, Mddx.: Penguin, 1970.

Ayer, A.J. *The Problem of Knowledge*. Harmondsworth, Mddx.: Penguin, 1956.

———*Language, Truth and Logic*. London: Gollancz, 1958.

Burnet, Macfarlane. *Dominant Mammal*. Harmondsworth, Mddx.: Penguin, 1971.

Camus, Albert. *Carnets 1942–1951*. London: Hamish Hamilton, 1966.

Childe, Gordon. *The Prehistory of European Society*. Harmondsworth, Mddx.: Penguin, 1958.

Cooper, David. *The Death of the Family*. Harmondsworth, Mddx.: Penguin, 1972.

de Bono, Edward. *Po: Beyond Yes and No*. Harmondsworth, Mddx.: Penguin, 1973.

Einzig, Paul. *Monetary Policy: Ends and Means*. Harmondsworth, Mddx.: Penguin, 1964.

Emery, F.E., ed. *Systems Thinking*. Harmondsworth, Mddx.: Penguin, 1969.

Frankfort, H. and H.A.; Wilson, John A; and Jacobsen, Thorkild. *Before Philosophy*. Harmondsworth, Mddx.: Penguin, 1961.

Frankl, Viktor E. *Psychotherapy and Existentialism*. Harmondsworth, Mddx.: Penguin, 1973.

Hayter, Teresa. *Aid as Imperialism*. Harmondsworth, Mddx.: Penguin, 1971.

Huxley, Sir Julian. *Essays of a Humanist*. Harmondsworth, Mddx.: Penguin, 1966.

Illich, Ivan. *De Schooling Society*. London: Calder and Boyars, 1971.
Kant, Immanual. *Fundamental Principles of the Metaphysics of Ethics*. London: Longmans Green, 1959.
Koestler, Arthur. *The Roots of Coincidence*. London: Hutchinson, 1972.
———*The Ghost in the Machine*. London: Hutchinson, 1967.
Laing, R.D. *The Divided Self*. Harmondsworth, Mddx.: Penguin, 1966.
———*The Politics of Experience and The Bird of Paradise*. Harmondsworth, Mddx.: Penguin, 1967.
Lausch, Erwin. *Manipulation*. London: Aidan Ellis, 1974.
Lorenz, Konrad. *On Aggression*. Translated by Marjorie Latzke. London: Methuen, 1967.
McLuhan, Marshall. *Understanding Media*. London: Routledge and Kegan Paul, 1964.
———*War and Peace in the Global Village*. New York: Bantam, 1968.
Marcuse, Herbert. *One Dimensional Man*. London: Routledge and Kegan Paul, 1964.
Mead, Margaret. *Growing Up in New Guinea*. Harmondsworth, Mddx.: Penguin, 1963.
———*Male and Female*. Harmondsworth, Mddx.: Penguin, 1962.
Mishan, E.J. *The Costs of Economic Growth*. Harmondsworth, Mddx.: Penguin, 1969.
Nowell-Smith, P.H. *Ethics*. Harmondsworth, Mddx.: Penguin, 1954.
Pareto, Vilfredo. *The Mind and Society: A Treatise on General Sociology*. Translated by A Bongiorno and A. Livingston. New York: Dover, 1963.
Pirsig, Robert M. *Zen and the Art of Motorcycle Maintenance*. London: Corgi, 1976.
Reich, Charles A. *The Greening of America*. Harmondsworth, Mddx.: Penguin, 1971.
Riesman, David. *The Lonely Crowd*. Rev. ed. (Studies in National Policy No. 3) New Haven, Conn.: Yale University Press, 1969.
Robinson, Joan. *Economic Philosophy*. Harmondsworth, Mddx.: Penguin, 1964.
Ross, Sir David. *The Right and the Good*. London: Oxford University Press, 1930.
Ryle, Gilbert. *The Concept of Mind*. London: Hutchinson, 1949.
Sargant, William. *Battle for the Mind*. London: Heinemann, 1957.
Sartre, Jean-Paul. *Existentialism and Humanism* Translated by Philip Mairet. London: Eyre Methuen, 1973.
Schweitzer, Albert. *Civilisation and Ethics*. London: Unwin, 1961.
Skinner, B.F. *Beyond Freedom and Dignity*. New York: Bantam, 1976.
Sprott, W.J.H. *Human Groups*. Harmondsworth, Mddx.: Penguin, 1969.

Stevenson, Charles L. *Ethics and Language*. New Haven, Conn.: Yale University Press, 1943.

Taylor, G.R. *Rethink*. Harmondsworth, Mddx.: Penguin, 1974.

Teilhard de Chardin, Pierre. *The Future of Man*. London: Collins, 1964.

———*Man's Place in Nature*. New York: Harper and Row, 1966.

Toulmin, Stephen, and Goodfield, June. *The Discovery of Time*. London: Hutchinson, 1965.

———*The Architecture of Matter*. Harmondsworth, Mddx.: Penguin, 1965.

Toynbee, Arnold J. *A Study of History*. Abridged by D.C. Sommervell. London: Oxford University Press, 1960.

Tribe, David. *Nucleoethics: Ethics in Modern Society*. London: MacGibbon and Kee, 1972.

Ward, Barbara. *Only One Earth*. Harmondsworth, Mddx.: Penguin, 1972.

Wittgenstein, Ludwig. *Philosophical Investigations*. Translated by G.E.M. Anscombe. Oxford: Blackwell, 1974.

INDEX